## The Michael Newton Institute

# FINDING PURPOSE

## Stories of the

## *Afterlife*

## that Inspire

MNI
**Publishing**

First Edition 2024
Published by *MNI Publishing* – a division on the Michael Newton Institute a 501c Not for Profit organization based in the USA.
This book contains the term 'Life Between Lives ®' a registered trademark of the Michael Newton Institute.

ISBN: 978-1-7636840-0-3

More about the work of the Michael Newton Institute can be found at www. newtoninstitute.org and via social media and tech platforms including but not limited to Facebook, Instagram, and YouTube.
Postal Address of the Publisher:
MNI Publishing
1121 Military Cutoff Road,
Suite C337, Wilmington,
NC, USA 28405

# Books by
## Dr. Michael Newton

*Journey of Souls*
*Destiny of Souls*
*Life Between Lives*

## Other Books by The Michael Newton Institute

*Memories of the Afterlife*
*Llewellyn's Little Book of Life Between Lives*
*Wisdom of Souls*

## Quarterly Journal

*Stories of the Afterlife*

# DEDICATION

To all those who seek deeper purpose and understanding in their lives.

This book is dedicated to you—the dreamers, the seekers, the souls who strive to uncover the mysteries of existence and find meaning in every moment. May these stories inspire you, guide you, and provide solace on your journey of self-discovery.

To the 26 authors and Life Between Lives Facilitators who poured their hearts and wisdom into these pages, thank you for your courage, insights, and unwavering commitment to service and explorations of the depths and expansiveness of the human spirit.

Special appreciation goes to Dr. Michael Newton, Founder of the Michael Newton Institute, whose pioneering work has paved the way for profound exploration into the realms of consciousness and the afterlife, who has helped thousands of people discover their true selves, and to Patricia Fares O'Malley, Ph.D., a distinguished psychotherapist and hypnotherapist with over 30 years of experience, specializing in meditation, guided imagery, and holistic healing approaches, and who served as the Director of Research at the Michael Newton Institute, embodying a profound dedication and passion for her work.

And to the editors, Sanela Čović and Elizabeth Lockhart, whose dedication and expertise shaped these stories into your cohesive collection, thank you for your invaluable time, energy, and devotion contributions.

Finally, to our family and friends whose love and support make everything possible, this is for you.

With deepest gratitude,
The Michael Newton Institute

# MEET THE EDITORS

## Sanela Čović

Sanela Čović is a deeply empathetic and intuitive hypnotherapist, regression therapist, Life Between Lives® Facilitator, Certified Master Trainer, and holistic coach, among other pursuits. She is the founder of The Inner Arts Academy, where her mission is to provide high-level transformative education for individuals seeking to become competent practitioners in hypnotherapy, regression therapy, holistic coaching, and related therapies.

As the founder of the *Oneness Initiative*, Sanela's mission is to guide people toward personal transformation and global unity.

The *Oneness Initiative* is a global research project aimed at fostering peace and unity by transcending cultural, linguistic, and religious barriers. By engaging with diverse minority and native communities, the project gathers spiritual insights, emphasizing the interconnectedness of all humans. Through spiritual regression, storytelling, and meditation, it seeks to promote compassion, respect, and understanding, highlighting universal themes of love, oneness, and shared humanity.

Sanela's therapeutic approach integrates a range of modalities, including clinical hypnosis, NLP, and Reiki, offering unique healing sessions designed to address emotional wounds and guide clients toward personal and spiritual growth.

Sanela's journey into healing is rooted in her early life experiences during the Yugoslav Wars. This exposure to trauma gave her an intimate understanding of the human condition and fueled her passion for helping others transform pain into growth. Her deep desire to assist others in finding balance, happiness, and fulfillment drives her work. She believes in the power of healing to connect individuals with their true selves, allowing them to realize their full potential.

Her impressive certifications reflect her dedication to the field of healing and personal transformation. She holds a master's degree in Croatian and German Philology and is highly credentialed across multiple fields. Her qualifications include certifications as a Myers-Briggs® Personality Type Indicator Facilitator, a Life Between Lives® and Quantum Consciousness Facilitator, and a Board-Certified Hypnotherapist. She is also an IACT Certified Regression Therapy Therapist and Master Trainer, Clinical Hypnosis Therapist, Executive, Life, and Teams Coach, Master Practitioner of Neurolinguistic Programming (NLP), and Usui Reiki Master Teacher.

Sanela has held leadership positions within the Michael Newton Institute, where she contributed to strategic development and European outreach. Her work is internationally recognized, and she offers sessions in English, Spanish, Bosnian, Croatian, and Serbian, both online and in person. Her retreats in Spain, Bosnia and Herzegovina, and other countries offer immersive opportunities for individuals to explore their inner selves and discover their soul's purpose.

Sanela's mission is simple yet profound: to help individuals transcend their past, heal deeply, and find their path toward a fulfilling and purpose-driven life. Whether through one-on-one therapy, workshops, or retreats, she is committed to guiding others on their journeys of self-discovery, healing, and empowerment.

## Elizabeth Lockhart

A near-death experience when Elizabeth drowned at five years old inspired a spiritual openness within her that has persisted throughout her lifetime. Although she holds a BS in medical technology and has worked as a medical technologist in clinical laboratories specializing in microbiology for over 30 years, she yearned to work with people more directly and deeply in a healing capacity throughout her career. With this in mind, she studied Reiki I and went on to learn Reiki Level II. Thirteen years later, she completed a yearlong apprenticeship with Patricia Keene, Reiki Master/Teacher, to become a certified Traditional Usui Reiki Master/Teacher.

After reading Dr. Michael Newton's *Journey of Souls* and *Destiny of Souls* many years ago, Elizabeth knew she had to learn how to facilitate Life Between Lives® spiritual regression sessions - this was a calling! She trained to learn transpersonal and past life regression hypnotherapy with Paul Aurand, MHt. Elizabeth is an IACT-certified hypnotherapist and certified past-life regression hypnotherapist. Seeking a strong foundation for this work, she earned an MS in clinical mental health counseling from the University of Southern Maine and is a National Certified Counselor. Many clients who come to her are seeking guidance and understanding regarding their life's purpose, support with grief, healing from trauma, overcoming "stuckness," persevering through life transitions, finding meaning, and more. Fulfilling her heart's dream, she trained with the Michael Newton Institute in 2016 and became certified as a Life Between Lives (LBL)® facilitator the following year. Being an LBL facilitator has become her life's work.

Elizabeth apprenticed as a sound healing practitioner with Kalee Coombs of Vibrations of Joy and offers Reiki and sound healing elements in sessions, aromatherapy using doTerra pure essential oils, and crystal/mineral therapy as guided. She trained to become a Level I Integrated Energy Therapist. Her serving as the chief editor of The Newton Institute's *Stories of the Afterlife* quarterly journal from 2018 to 2020 was highly meaningful to her.

Elizabeth established her practice, Mariposa Hypnotherapy, in 2014. She offers in-person and virtual sessions in West Baldwin, Maine, in the summer and Tucson, Arizona, in the winter. She is a highly intuitive practitioner who is passionately devoted to empowering clients to connect with their deeper Selves in a safe and nurturing environment, thereby facilitating healing, well-being, and wholeness.

Her work is intended to heighten awareness and increase understanding of oneself and to harmonize mind, body, heart, and soul. Ultimately, she intends to help raise and expand humanity's consciousness, a ripple at a time. She believes that once clients experience themselves and others as fellow souls on a path, primarily through LBL® work, unconditional love, acceptance, compassion, peace, belonging, and unity are achievable on Earth.

# Editor's note

## Dear Reader

Welcome to a unique tapestry of voices, a collection of stories woven together by The Michael Newton Institute's Life Between Lives Facilitators. Each author brings their distinctive style and cultural background to the table, yet a common theme unites all: exploring the afterlife, referred to here as the Life Between Lives.

As you journey through these pages, you will encounter a rich variety of perspectives and experiences. Topics range from Freedom and Free Will, Learning Through Relationships, Understanding Loss and Grief, Healing, Connection (community and oneness), Guides and Advanced Beings, Divine Guidance, to Healing the Earth.

Some stories may challenge you, while others may comfort and reassure you, but all are intended to inspire and provoke deep thought. The diversity of the authors' voices reflects the multifaceted nature of spirituality—how it transcends boundaries and resonates within us in unique ways.

Each author has poured their heart and soul into their writing, offering insights and reflections based on their practices and experiences. Their stories remind us that, despite our differences, we are all connected by the universal quest for purpose, understanding, higher perspectives, and expanded consciousness.

Through the storyteller's words, you will discover new ways of viewing the world and perhaps new ways of seeing yourself. We hope this collection serves as a mirror, reflecting your quest for meaning and the many paths that can lead to a life filled with purpose, self-actualization, and soul growth.

May these stories ignite your spirit, encourage your heart, and guide you toward richer understanding and heightened awareness, thus embracing your soul's journey.

Thank you for joining us on this transformative and purposeful adventure.

With heartfelt appreciation,
Sanela Čović and Elizabeth Lockhart
Editors

# FOREWORD

*Tell me a fact and I'll learn. Tell me the truth and I'll believe.*
*But tell me a story and it will live in my heart forever.[1]*

In the May 2018 issue of *Stories of the Afterlife*, marking the 50th anniversary of LBL – Life Between Lives™, a 2013 letter from Dr. Michael Newton was published emphasizing our mission as an organization and including the following statements:

> *We want to bring a new form of personal spiritual awakening to an ever-expanding range of people around the globe. I see our mission as twofold. First, through training and supporting our practitioners and secondly, to foster public awareness of the benefits we are able to offer people seeking to uncover spiritual knowledge within their own minds. Our movement is designed to*

---

1    Schank, Roger C. & Abelson, Robert P. (1995) *Knowledge and Memory: The Real Story.* In: Robert S. Wyer, Jr (ed) *Knowledge and Memory: The Real Story.* Lawrence Erlbaum Associates. 1-85.

*help human beings mentally become whole by connecting with the essence of Oneness in the life between lives, and while in this life experiencing a transformational discovery of the true nature of their eternal soul within the matrix of a physical brain.*

*For spiritual unity to take place, we cannot depend on the methods of current religious practices on the one hand, or science on the other to bring answers to the great mystery of life. Our organization is pledged to offer a new way with enlightenment springing from the mind of each individual, regardless of their prior institutional belief system or lack of it. In the complex world of the 21st century, people need the conviction more than ever that a divine universal consciousness exists within a pure spiritual order. They must discover this principle within their own minds for real conviction to take place. Eventually, if enough people come to this realization through our efforts, there will hopefully be a lessening of external conflict in our struggle for survival. The ethical compass of humanity would have a stronger meaning since it would come from personal enlightenment.* [2]

In the early 1990s, Dr. Michael Newton published his first book, *Journey of Souls*. The format of this book was stories organized around themes that had emerged during his work with the many clients with whom he had worked. He was a dedicated researcher interested in uncovering information valuable to his clients and sharing his findings with others for their more significant benefit. As the format for this book evolved from the thousands of case studies he

---

2    Newton, Michael (1994) *Journey of souls: case studies of life between lives*. Llewellyn.

had accumulated, the greater intention of engaging a broad audience with his findings also emerged. Sharing client stories also appeared as an efficient and engaging way to present complex concepts concerning human life and experiences of the afterlife.

So why use stories to support this goal of enlightenment? According to Schank and Abelson (1995), "stories about one's experiences, and the experiences of others, are the fundamental constituents of human memory, knowledge, and social communication." They argue that

"1) virtually all human knowledge is based on stories constructed around past experiences;

2) new experiences are interpreted in terms of old stories;

3) the content of story memories depends on whether and how they are told to others, and these reconstituted memories form the basis of the individuals 'remembered' self."

Storytelling has been and continues to be a very traditional way of human communication. It was a means of communicating culture, tradition, information, and news. Stories included not only the data of what was being offered but also intuitive opportunities for learning through feeling and emotion. As one listens to a story, one hears the words and engages with them in an internal dialogue that processes them within the framework of the individual's understanding. Thus, a story can elicit various responses depending on the listener's internal screening framework. You might pick up something completely different than I do simply because you and I have different emotional contexts, cultural backgrounds and norms, and different understandings of the meanings of words.

Storytelling engages the listener or reader in the facts of the story, the functional knowledge, the creation of meaning, the feeling and emotion elicited in the individual, and the potential impact and action that might occur.

> *Human memory is a collection of thousands of stories we remember through experience, stories we remember by having heard them, and stories we remember by having composed them.* [3]

We apply old stories to new information we receive as they help us quickly understand and use what we are learning, giving us a known context and meaning to support the new information that we are gaining. So, as we read a new story, we think about what it means to us based on what we already know, feel, or interpret.

When one often works with a client in therapy, the work revolves around supporting the client in reframing their stories, releasing old beliefs, and developing new meanings that can facilitate the changes the client seeks to accomplish. Introducing new stories into the mix of the client's own stories may expand their awareness of the potential for more significant meaning or options, thus creating hope for a wider variety of outcomes.

In his introduction to *Journey of Souls*, Michael explained his rationale for using stories and case studies to present the findings of his research.

He stated: "I found thoughts about the spirit world involve universal truths among the souls of people living on Earth. It was these perceptions by so many different types of people which convinced me their statements were believable. I am not a religious person, but I found the place where we go

---

3    Schank, Roger C. & Abelson, Robert P. (1995) *Knowledge and Memory: The Real Story*

after death to be one of order and direction, and I have come to appreciate that there is a grand design to life and afterlife.

When I considered how to best present my findings, I determined the case study method would provide the most descriptive way in which the reader could evaluate client recall about the afterlife."

Following in Michael's footsteps, the Michael Newton Institute (MNI) has continued to publish case studies and stories in our books and our quarterly journal *Stories of the Afterlife* (SOTA), published quarterly since 2017. We recognized a continuing hunger for stories and connection beyond what was being published in books. While our journal reaches a wide range of readers, most have learned about the journal through contact with our facilitators, our website, or through engagement with others who have serendipitously uncovered our quarterly offerings. All the stories in SOTA and in this current volume, *Finding Purpose*, follow Michael's principle of storytelling: they provide insight into one's exploration of life and the afterlife, uncovering meaning from outside our human incarnations.

As you browse the chapters, you will see that these are familiar themes, challenges, and topics that most of us are likely to encounter at some point in our lives. As with Michael's stories, these are case studies that do not follow the entirety of a client's experience through one or more sessions; rather, they capture the flow of the client's experience and the learning and healing that results from undertaking this work.

These stories also do not speak to the variations in the client's experience of going into altered states to reach the connection with the Universe. Each of us has our way of processing, experiencing, and understanding what emerges in a session, so sessions unfold differently and have many variations of experience and outcomes. I encourage you to feel these stories and engage with the learning that emerges.

Diana Paque, DPA, CCHt
Executive Director, the Michael Newton Institute,
2019 – Present
Editor, Stories of the Afterlife (SOTA), 2020 - Present

# CONTENTS

# CHAPTER ONE
## ON FREEDOM & FREE WILL

# INTRODUCTION
## on Freedom & Free Will

*Between stimulus and response, there is a space. In that space is our power to choose a response. In our response lies our growth and our freedom.* [4]

At times, the terms freedom and free will may seem as though they are unattainable ideals on Earth's plane. From the soul's perspective, these ideals are attainable and necessary for our growth and the evolution of our consciousness. The concepts of freedom and free will indicate the ability to make choices. While on Earth, there can be many barriers to our ability to make choices; these can range from environmental, cultural, physical, psychological, and psychospiritual imprints. As human beings, we may not be free to choose certain physical realities we desire or find ourselves in. Yet, we are free to choose how we respond and

---

4    Viktor E. Frankl *Man's Search for Meaning*

to harvest the lessons and growth we are experiencing from a higher perspective.

A desire for evolution and expansion often serves as the soul's impetus for embarking on a sojourn here on Earth. Experiencing LBL as a human being on Earth can be a beautiful way to connect with one's soul and other loving energies and beings within the soul realm, including Source. One can experience the truth of one's soul's lineage as it follows our choices, whether discarnate or incarnated. Through insights gained in an LBL experience, we can develop more "fruits of the Spirit," such as love, joy, peace, forbearance, kindness, goodness, faithfulness, gentleness, and self-control (Galatians 5:22-23, Bible New International Version). I would add that we can garner courage, acceptance, truth-seeking, compassion, understanding, forgiveness, generosity, and more to this list.

Life in this physical realm affords us opportunities for soul growth we might never encounter without incarnating. For example, through experiencing and participating in various dynamics of duality and contrast, we can feel what it is like to be both victim and perpetrator. Various lifetimes offer experiences of a seemingly opposite nature: pain and joy, loss and gain, poverty and wealth, isolation and intimacy, ostracism and belonging, receiving and giving, bondage and freedom, torture and pleasure; grotesqueness and beauty, illness and wellness, and more. While in human form, many of these experiential lessons may go relatively unexamined or leave us stuck in an emotional state such as anger and resentment. Life Between Lives® therapy offers us insights, higher perspectives, and deeper understandings; these can lead to the working through and releasing of denseness, "stuckness," and negativity and lighten our spirits toward their natural states of freedom and joy. This often occurs when forgiveness takes place, for example – forgiveness of self, others, and even the Cosmos!

Although this growth often involves living many lifetimes, undergoing varied experiences of self and otherness, and serving as mirrors for one another, ultimately, we learn and grow. Some lessons may take longer than others, and some may engage different facets of the same truths. We begin to love and recognize ourselves in one another as fellow souls on a journey. Compassion and appreciation, rather than judgment and criticism, develop for the unique aspects and characteristics of each being and their uniquely guided quest, including the choices they make.

The wisdom we gain and the sense of "Oneness with All That Is" diffuse into our higher awareness when we open to it. LBL therapy is what I refer to as "The Great Opener." Through our travels to the soul realm and encounters with spirit guides, soul groups, our Council, and others, we are more quickly aware of these truths as the veil between worlds is lovingly lifted. Through our examination of and expansion into lessons that lay before us, freely chosen by our souls for our highest healing and evolution, we find ourselves in awe of the courageous and creative expressions of our soul's Divinity.

In the following case stories submitted by the Michael Newton Institute certified facilitators of Life Between Lives® spiritual regression therapy, the themes of freedom and free will are explored in a plethora of ways, not only related to the soul's choices but to choices made by the incarnated version of a soul. Free will is a beautiful gift from the Creator, imbuing all souls with the ability to create in measureless and meaningful ways, whether as a soul or in a physical state.

The following case stories involve free will choices

around embracing our power to choose, finding and living one's spiritual purpose on Earth, and clearing any baggage or blocks that interfere with fully living one's soul purpose.

Using one's unique spiritual gifts to help others, being a catalyst for positive change, speaking authentically and thus becoming empowered, caring for oneself while learning to set boundaries, completing a soul's mission in a lifetime, and sharing esoteric knowledge attained from the soul realm are all important and highly intentional tasks.

Whatever circumstances souls find themselves in, the freedom and free will used to make choices, including the option not to choose, are divine spiritual gifts.

Elizabeth Lockhart
Editor

# A Freedom Loving Spiritual Healer

## Ann J. Clark, PhD

During an age regression recall of childhood memories, my client Judy found herself at home with her parents.

> Client (C): My Mom is making me laugh. My Dad is there too.

Later, she relayed that this scene surprised her because she had a complicated relationship with her mother, which was such a happy time. We then regressed to just before her birth.

> C: I'm not sure if I like my body. My leg hurts because it's cramped. My body is not a good match. I had difficulty integrating with it. (After a pause) I can't tell the difference between this body and my mother's body.

Facilitator (F): When did you join the fetus?

C: At one-month gestation.

F: Did you just stay there after that?

C: No, I come and go.

F: Can you tell me about your brain?

C: It's purple, it's different. It makes me feel like smiling. It's pretty.

We then entered the tunnel to visit Judy's immediate past life. Judy found herself in the body of a teenage boy in a diner.

C: It's daytime, and I am in a diner.

F: Are you a male or female, and how old are you?

C: I'm male and in the 10th grade.

F: What's your name?

C: Billy. Billy Franklin.

F: Do you know what city you are in?

C: Cincinnati, Ohio.

F: Do you know what year it is?

C: 1950's.

F: What's happening in the diner?

C: I'm buying drugs from a dude.

F: Is this your first time?

C: No, my 2nd or 3rd time.

F: How did you get started with drugs?

C: A girl broke my heart. She loved me and kissed me, and then she found someone else. F: I want you to look deeply into that girl's eyes, Billy, and tell me if you recognize her as anyone from Judy's life.

C: Ah, she's my mother's best friend, Dee.

F: Let's move to the last day of your life, Billy.

C: Pills killed me. I took too many and died. I knew I was dying, and I was all alone.

F: How long after you bought the pills did this happen?

C: Just a few days.

F: Who discovered you after you had died?

C: My mother and she was shocked. It was so sad. I could see my body lying there. It was an accident. I didn't mean for it to happen. I was shocked that I died. It was stupid.

I needed to be more protective and take better care of myself.

Billy's mother was not recognized as someone in Judy's life.

F: What's happening now?

C: I'm moving away from my body. Very high above the Earth. I no longer have any interest in what's below.

While some individuals stay around for a short period, comforting loved ones and attending their funerals, others move quickly away. It is common for interest in Earthly matters to dissolve as the soul heads rapidly home.

C: I'm moving up quickly. Everything is a blur. There are trails behind me like shooting stars make.

F: What do you see around you?

C: It looks darker, but it feels lighter. Oh, now it is really light. I am just encompassed in light. The movement is slowing down.

F: Are you aware of any other beings around you?

C: It feels like there is the presence of two spirits on my right side. Now, the light is super bright and pure white. It's all around me, like a TV screen. It's like someone in a white room.

F: What are you experiencing now?

C: Oh, they have a sense of humor. They ask how water feels when you're in the water. I say it feels really good!

F: Do you recognize the presence?

C: I don't recognize them, and I can't really see them well. I just feel them. Now they're circling around me. I'm feeling some slight discomfort. They're working with me.

F: Let's ask your Guide to come forward and help you with that discomfort.

C: My Guide has come. They're telling me that it takes me a little longer to completely disengage.

Judy has started taking rapid, shallow breaths and moving irritably on the table.

F: Ask your Guide how I can be of help.

C: They're clearing the energy from around my head to help me disengage. Everything is clear now except for some pressure on the top of my head that feels like a metal plate.

They're asking you to remove it.

F: I'm doing that now.

I placed my hands about 4 inches from Judy's head to clear the energy.

C: It's gone. (Heaves a big sigh of relief.)

This is a report of an unusual experience in the return to the spirit realm. As Billy described, difficulty in disengaging sounds as if it might be unique to Judy's soul, given what the spirits were telling her. Or perhaps it was related to Billy's sudden and unexpected departure from Earth. Most likely, Billy and his guide and spirit helpers were handling his disengagement just fine on their own, but they allowed me to play a role since I asked if I could be of help. Spirits find numerous ways to let us know they are working with and assisting us during LBLs. This situation requires further investigation.

> F: What is your Guide's name?
> C: Gabby. She's such bright light, and I can see her long, flowing hair.
> F: Is she communicating with you?
> C: I'm told I'm doing good work. We're passing through the Gate, moving very slowly.
> (Judy sighs heavily.) Everything is FINE! Very quiet. We're just floating along together.
> F: What is your soul's name?
> C: (Loudly) No, that's not possible! Andromeda.
> F: Help me understand why you don't think that is possible.
> C: (Long pause and then mumbles) I don't know.

Andromeda is a Goddess in Greek mythology, and there is a constellation by that name, but it was not made clear why Judy/Billy did not think that that could be her soul's name.

F: Andromeda, is this a good time to ask your guide some questions?

C: Yes, please.

F: Why does Judy feel so alone?

C: It's because no one else meets her where she's at. She knew this was how it would be before she came here. This was not unexpected.

F: Tell me more about that.

C: She's so fast-moving and ever-changing.

F: What goals did Judy set before coming into this incarnation?

C: To be a catalyst, to bring more love and light to the world, to open consciousness.

She's making fantastic progress.

F: Judy would like to know what actions she can take to make more progress on these goals.

C: She needs to have more drive and to do more planning. She needs to keep to a schedule.

F: Judy wants to know if she is carrying some negative attitudes or some misconceptions.

C: She still has a few walls around her, and that keeps her lackluster.

F: Tell me what you mean by that.

C: She's keeping herself from shining as brightly as she could. Also, she has difficulty keeping balance in her life. She has too much energy at times and not enough at other times.

F: What actions can she take to improve this situation?

C: She just needs to practice. Also, she still has a need for approval.

F: How can she address that?

C: She's already doing that right now. Her walls are coming down.

F: Are there some talents or skills Judy has that she has not yet discovered?

C: She's using almost all her talents and skills now, but she also has the ability to jump in and out of timelines more easily.

F: What do you mean by that?

C: When she is working with people, she can jump through their timelines to clear blockages. She can go back to the core issue and help them clear it.

F: How can she cultivate this ability?

C: Just being aware that she can do it and practicing will strengthen it. By doing more meditations, she will bring more modalities to her as needed.

F: Judy is uncertain about how to proceed with her practice. Should she stick to her physical practice, go online, or do both?

C: She needs help with YouTube. We've been telling her to tell everyone she knows who she needs: a young person with social media skills. They are here in town. There's a young man and a young woman. She has resistance to males, but the best one is the male.

F: Tell me more about this resistance.

C: She has the idea that she should focus on working with women because they are more pliable. But she will learn to work with men. She will be attracting an assistant in the future. It will happen organically (naturally), as everything does.

F: Judy is wondering if she should start a membership site online.

C: Yes, she should start one. She can finish her six-week class and then work on a monthly program online. She'll need a few weeks in between. She has the framework; it's just the doubt. It's the hesitancy to start that creates the stagnation in her energy. Some doubt is necessary, but don't sit there too long. Keep moving forward.

F: Judy wonders if this is the best place for her to live.

C: Yes, she's right where she needs to be, here in the South. She has the space she needs. She'll be in this area for about nine years, and she'll be able to use her gifts. Her son needs to be here.

F: Help me understand why her son needs to be here.

C: It's the best place for him to grow, and it's good for her too.

Judy had several questions about practical matters, and her answers were rather mundane, but when I asked her about her husband, she received some straightforward answers. Often, questions about relationships are less direct and focus on individual choices. Judy, however, received some very informative answers.

F: Judy wants to know more about her marriage to Bob.

C: She won't be staying with him for the long haul, but for now, needs to set things up to be on her own. This will take some time, about 12 to 18 months or so. The amount of time she is investing in him, and his business is just right for now. She thinks Bob always gets his way, but he needs to think that for her to get the best from him. (Then Judy is addressed) You won't be short-changed. You don't need to do anything more than you are doing right now.

F: Judy is worried about Bob's health. Do you have any information for her?

C: Bob's physical health is not good right now. It's up to him what happens next. He'll either die or choose to change. Judy has little influence over this. (Judy starts to cry.)

C: Judy asks: Will our bodies connect in a positive way? (Gabby answers) No.

F: Judy wants to know if Bob is capable of love as she wants it to be.

C: No.

F: Is that kind of love possible?

C: Yes, it is, but I will not be with him. She feels exhausted in the relationship. She should give only as much as she can comfortably. It won't go on much longer. She'll have several relationships to choose from in the future. Her idea of a relationship is one that is not needy but mature and enhancing, with a feeling of freedom, ease, and ability to make own choices, as opposed to fast, hard, and with limitations. It would include intimacy, physical love, and openness.

F: Is Judy blocking this?

C: No, it's not time yet.

Next, Andromeda moves on to visit her soul family.

C: They're all sitting around a table, sort of a

casual party atmosphere. There are 20 or so, and it is so joyous and open. I see my mom and also Karen (a close friend who shares spiritual interests), Don (deceased brother-in-law with whom she could communicate telepathically), and Helen (another close friend she works with). I'm surprised to see my mom there, and Kevin is standing just outside the group (new male friend).

F: Why is Kevin standing outside of the group?

C: He's not ready to join the soul group yet. My mom is not ready either, but she is sitting there. There are souls at different levels of advancement in the group. Mine is an advanced soul. They'll be adding more. They have different levels of advancement on Earth. Some incarnate more than others.

F: Tell me more about your soul group.

C: The soul group works with freedom. We're a collection of souls above group guiding (those who serve as guides). Gabby is here with me. The guides work together to make things happen.

Next, Judy visits her Council of Elders.

C: I don't really like meeting with the Council because it is the antithesis of freedom. In my life as Billy, there were too many moving parts, and there were too many changes. Billy couldn't meet his goals, and so we extracted him. (We mean Andromeda with assistance from other spiritual entities.) Billy's mother in that life is very, very old and still living.

F: Does the Council have any message for you?

C: No messages. They leave me alone. They know

15

that I am making very good progress.

F: What's behind their leaving you alone?

C: It's my attitude about freedom. They understand the battle with not feeling you have free will. So, they don't get involved too much. Judy feels that when she is used as a pawn, it creates too much resistance in the great big chess match. She feels that she is not in control of her actions or what's coming out of her mouth when we use her to help others. She agreed to it, but after it happened, she didn't like it. But she will still allow us to use her in that way in important cases.

Andromeda explains that her current Council is comprised of 12 members and a male-appearing leader. She explains that her Council changes after each life. She is a floater, which means she takes classes to work with different groups.

F: Do you expect your Council to be easy with you or more severe?

C: Why would they be severe? As a light being with the highest intention, you don't need a Council to treat you with severity. They're helpful. They help you make progress. (After a pause) I'm feeling some discomfort in my physical body on the right side. (Then continues) There's intention for freedom. It feels not so free with Council—time to go.

Andromeda next moves to a classroom area.

F: What are you working on now?

C: Structure, physical make-up, actual evolution of the human body. I really don't need to come here (to classrooms in the spiritual realm). Knowledge is brought to me. Now, I am studying the lengthening of telomeres so people can live longer and use their bodies better. As humans are born, their DNA will be changed. Judy is working now with those who weren't born this way to improve their quality of life. The human body is getting lighter and less dense. Soon, there will be more telepathy and spirituality. Energy can do the same. Humans will not be able to use energy to create matter for some time, but many on Earth are very talented in the use of energy and are advanced. They can create healing in the body, dissolve tumors, and move bones. Psychic surgery is very useful. (Pausing) If you can imagine it, it can happen. Intention is very important and must be held by you and the person you work with.

Andromeda now moves briefly to a recreation area where she likes to do acrobatics and dance. She says she also likes to travel to other dimensions for pleasure.

She says she can travel in only 15 dimensions but knows there are more.

F: Do you ever visit places you've lived on Earth?

C: Yes, I can make my energy lighter and visit other places. Sometimes, I take a body and can communicate telepathically.

F: When you take a body, are you ever seen by humans?

C: Yes, sometimes I am. Sometimes, I take over

a body, and then that person can speak to one who needs to hear. This most likely involves the insertion of thoughts in an incarnated entity's mind rather than a total energetic takeover of the entity's body. It does imply, though, that we may receive spiritual advice out of the mouth of someone speaking to us here on Earth when we are not expecting it.

Next, Andromeda moves on to the life selection area.

F: How do you know when to prepare for another incarnation?

C: I volunteer. I like the pleasures of being in a body. There were only 15 to 18 years between this life and the last incarnation. When I'm ready, I go to the selection area.

F: Describe the selection area to me.

C: It's a white room. There are guides there, and there is machinery. They're sort of like computers with a screen that I can look into. I can choose my body from an endless selection of bodies. I like small bodies best because they are easier to control and to hide if you need to. My favorite and first body was a small Egyptian female one. It was springy and athletic. But I have been all sizes.

F: Do you prefer to be male or female?

C: Definitely female. I have been female about 2/3 of the time. I like the way it feels, and I like to have a big man hold me.

F: What purpose did you set for your upcoming life as Judy, Andromeda?

C: There are many choices for a life. You can do

whatever you want to do. This time, my primary purpose is to educate the next generation of influential energy workers. This is the first time I could handle as much energy. Previously, I was a healer, a medicine woman, but could not use as much energy as I wanted. Now, the Earth has greater capacity and will evolve even more.

F: What proportion of your energy did you bring into this incarnation?

C: About 12 to 20%. I use about 45% for daily life and up to 55% when engaged in spiritual activities. My energy is increasing as I grow spiritually.

This is an unusual answer since Dr. Newton found from his clients that the energy brought into an incarnation remained constant. This could be conscious interference, a different view of the question, or a reflection of Andromeda's status as an advanced soul or, possibly, the increased capacity for energy on Earth, as she reported.

C: I can see people on the screen with whom I will be working to help me with my purpose. I have not met most of them yet, but I will in the next several years.

F: Can you tell me more about this?

C: It will unfold.

F: Tell me about the selection of your mother and father.

C: I chose my mother so I could learn to open to freedom when restricted. My father brought family into my life. His brother was the biggest influence. He was my molester. That was a planned experience to be in the absence of light. It was a chance to choose light and healing.

F: Is there still a need for healing?

C: Most of the healing has been done. There is still a little integration going on. That is happening now. There are three little pricks, but they are lightening up now.

F: Did you set up any way to recognize planned events or people in your upcoming incarnation?

C: Yes, there are triggers. It's the energy signature. I recognize them through their energy.

F: How did you feel about this upcoming incarnation?

C: Very joyous and full of anticipation.

F: How about the selection of your son?

C: He chose me as he wanted to learn about my way of life. He will also be a light worker but is different from me. I will not have any more children.

After a brief look around, Judy was ready to leave the spirit realm.

Judy reported that she felt light as air after her session. However, that was followed by a very rough week with her husband. There was a lot of indecision about whether they would move again or whether he would move, and she and her son would stay here. She was concerned about how she could support herself and her son if that happened since she is not yet making enough money from her practice. But then things calmed down again. Judy had a chance to reassess her situation, concluding that it was not time yet. Judy's husband now has a new job and the three of them will be moving soon to a new location. She anticipates an easier move this time.

There were several unique aspects to this case. Judy reportedly is an advanced soul and values freedom and free will highly. Her resistance to her Council was unusual, as was her physical difficulty in re-entry into the spiritual realm. Additionally, while she was not told what choices to make, responses to her questions concerning her marriage and her practice were very specific. This reflects her rapid progress on her spiritual path.

# Follow the Thread
## of Choice

### Gayle Barklie

Sometimes, working with other therapists can prove to be an interesting challenge.

Dolores, a 60-something veteran psychotherapist, was visiting Maui. She only had time for two sessions, one to address past lives and the other for Life Between Lives. I requested her Cast of Characters to assist with understanding linkage connections between present and past relationships. She presented an extensive family tree going back several generations. I wasn't too surprised, knowing her detail-oriented profession.

She acknowledged several areas she wanted to address: a trust issue resulting from something happening with her father, always feeling like an intruder, and illumination about her work since she was uncertain about her next step.

In her past life regression, she described a lifetime as

a woman traveling with her husband. I asked about her husband.

C: His name was Albert, and he was a blacksmith. He was cold and indifferent; it doesn't feel like there's any love between us.

She explains this with some sadness.

C: I think we got married at nineteen in upstate New York and then started this journey. The marriage was one of convenience in the 1840s. We became some of the young settlers in Utah and then converted to Mormonism.

She sat quietly, putting some pieces together.

C: I had a daughter in that past life, Samantha, and she recreated the same kind of indifferent marriage. When I saw it happening to her, I realized that I no longer need to tolerate that in my own marriage. I deserved to be treated better. I knew I could take care of myself. I didn't need to tolerate this!

She repeated this last statement emphatically. Interestingly, these feelings of indifference and not being important appear in her current work situation.

C: I focus my attention on Samantha. I'm acknowledging her feelings, letting her know they were valid. I'm trying to counterbalance her loss of love by aiming to empower her, show her how competent she is. It looks like I succeeded because she ended up leaving her husband, even though they had a child, a boy named Jack. I was so proud of her for stepping into her true self.

F: Tell me about Jack.

C: I see him playing in the dirt near a vegetable garden. Oh… no! He died at the age of six; a terrible epidemic got him. Samantha and I are both grief-stricken over this loss.

She wiped spontaneous tears from her face.

C: Wow, this is so bizarre. I'm getting that Jack is my father in my current life!

This realization somewhat takes her aback.

C: He had a short lifetime as a slave in Greece, but he was forced to come back: required to be my father.

She paused.

C: I see that he feels really resentful. That makes sense since my dad was a rage-acholic in this life. But the timing of all this needed to occur so I would be born in Berkeley in 1951. I needed to be around in the '60s so I could be part of the anti-war movement. I needed to be a voice that chipped away at the power of injustice. No matter how scary it was, I needed to be speaking up for others. But why?

She continued to follow the threads of connection between their relationship, present and past.

C: My dad was able to connect with me in this life since he had been so lonely in his family of origin. His mother, in the Mormon life, eventually remarried and lived in a cozy house out in the country. She felt obligated to take me with her since I was her mother, but she resented my being there. I was left alone more and more until I died at 97, old, tired, and disappointed.

F: Go to the moment of your death. What do you notice?

C: I'm looking forward to being at peace. I see myself left in bed to die. I'm feeling glad to stop being so responsible. Duty. Survival. Respect for and dependence on others.

F: Tell me more.

C: I see that a pretty young girl found me, though I'm not sure who she is. She patted my hand. She pulled the blanket up to cover me and said goodbye. She was very tender.

She feels like Elizabeth, my daughter, now in this life.

F: Describe what's happening around you.

C: I'm floating away from Earth. There's a light coming toward me. It's yellow-golden. It envelops me in feminine energy. I'm feeling all is well and that I shouldn't worry. I'm feeling, not hearing: "Trust: You have the answers."

F: I'm wondering what some of your life lessons were.

Asking clients to focus on the lessons they are meant to bring back from each lifetime helps them understand why they're in their current life. This can clarify their progress through those lessons.

> C: Just learning about trust. It's my biggest challenge in this life, and now I understand why that is.

Out of hypnosis, I acknowledged her work and assured her that the Life Between Lives session would allow even more to unfold.

Two days later, Dolores arrived, ready to dive in. After explaining the LBL process, I asked if she had identified any other issues to address.

> C: Actually, the more I've been thinking about feeling like an intruder, the more important it seems. I really hope something comes up that explains that. It pretty much runs my life, even at work where I'm the boss.
>
> F: Well, we can't control where a session goes or what your subconscious needs to have you focus on; however, we can certainly put it out there as important and see what happens.
>
> C: Oh, and I'd also like to understand why I've lost my sense of joy.

Regressing to various key ages, Dolores landed at eighteen months.

> F: What are you sensing there?

C: I'm in a crib, sharing a room with my sister. There's a blanket that separates the room. I have a sunburned shoulder, and I'm crying. It hurts so bad! My mom comes in to take care of me, and I feel my sister's irritation at the disruption of her bedtime. I always feel like an intruder in my sister's life.

F: Let's go back further to when you were in your mother's womb. Just trust whatever comes to you.

C: I'm seeing myself as the woman in Utah, reincarnating into my current body. The constriction of space makes me anxious to be born. I'm feeling my mother's nervous system. It's prickly; she's uncomfortable and very emotional.

F: What else about being in the womb?

C: Not sure why, but I'm feeling disgusted with sex. It's so invasive. Intrusive is a better word.

F: Let's ask why that feeling is there.

She immediately described a past life in Roman times.

C: I'm a man, and I'm raping someone. One of our ranch hands. I carried that feeling of intrusion with me. She is my sister in this life, and I feel so guilty about doing that.

She saw more about her relationship with her father.

C: My father is excited to get to know me. He feels familiar. It's like we're getting a second chance to connect. He's not close to my sister. She's almost eight when I arrive. She thinks I'm hers, but I'm already pushing back energetically. The spiritual contract was to be here with my mom and dad, not her.

F: Tell me a little bit more ...

C: My sister was the one who intruded. She and my grandmother had a spiritual agreement about her being here. That got in the way of me bonding with the two of them no matter what I tried. When I arrived, I upstaged her!

F: So, let's check in on your parental and family choices.

C: I see myself in a bassinet at the hospital. My dad was hovering about, watching me. Suddenly he left, and I'm all alone. I realized right then that I need to step into this body to make sure to keep it safe.

F: Tell me what you realized was important right then.

C: I needed to learn about my own power, depending on myself and no one else. Just like in the Utah lifetime. How sad I had to set it up like that to learn, though.

Dolores wept quietly for a few minutes.

C: I just flashed on a previous life in Nazi Germany as a young man.

F: What's that about?

C: Well, it's all about misuse of power, not speaking up for what's right. I sure understand why I was so involved in the resistance movement in the '60s. My spirit needed to stand up to injustice, which I didn't do in Germany!

F: Is there anything you're supposed to receive about your connection with your mother in that life?

C: Yes, actually. It was pure love. Nurturing. Total trust. Quite a gift in such an ugly lifetime. That love is imprinted on me, like the Divine Feminine. I think my mother was reincarnated as Bethany in this life.

F: Who is Bethany?

C: Oh, she's my guide, a guardian angel to me. We've been together in several lifetimes, and in this one she's in the spirit realm, guiding me, loving me, giving me messages not to get discouraged and not be so anxious. She teaches me that love never dies. Right now, she's saying that I can give myself pure, unconditional love.

Dolores started crying as she heard that message of self-compassion.

She then began describing a group of people she sensed was her Soul Group. She termed them a "Barn Family," and they were singing old gospel music. She mentioned Mr. Thomas, her primary Soul Group member.

F: What is Mr. Thomas trying to communicate?

C: He says nobody expects you to do it alone. He encourages me to bring joy, laughter, and lightness to my life. He wants me to expand my horse business and share horses with others. He promises to be patient and that it will unfold later down the road. He says, 'You can't push the river; this project will take time.'

F: Anything else about that?

C: Yes, he says the flow is open. That expressing joy will bring the reward of pure love and fun. And, to not waste my time comparing myself to others because it's useless.

F: Is there anything else he's telling you?

C: Well, he's telling me that my selection of this body was about letting go of negative body beliefs brought with me from the Nazi lifetime. It's time to be loving and kind to my body. Be grateful for it! Forgive myself for its limitations and know it's serving me beautifully!

F: That's great! You had asked about what's next in your career. Can you ask him if he has anything to share about that?

C: Yes, he's telling me that I'm to work with children. I'll be doing for children what Bethany, my guardian angel, does for me! I am here to see and encourage the spirit in all.

She then stated the following message with pure joy.

C: Always make sure I am working with love and kindness. That's the key.

After the session, Dolores reported the following shifts in her life. Seeing past life events helped dematerialize the negative energy between her and her sister, allowing a new sense of love and peace. The sense of being an intruder was dissolving as their new connections emerged. She added Equine Assisted Psychotherapy with children to her practice. There was also a new sense of lightness that filled her after these powerful sessions.

# Honoring
# Authenticity

## Veronika Elias

Andrea first came to me for a session that included past life regression and Higher Self-communication. This happened at a time when she was contemplating leaving her jealous and controlling husband, Armand. During that session, we uncovered a significant past life that exposed the dynamics of their relationship. In this Egyptian life, Armand, the Pharaoh, had selected her from among many female commoners to become one of his concubines. While this bestowed great honor upon her and quickly elevated her to a status that afforded her many privileges, it was a relationship fundamentally imbalanced in power, devoid of genuine love or understanding. Andrea's Higher Self revealed that Armand's current behavior had to be severe; otherwise, she might be inclined to repeat this past pattern and remain trapped in a loveless relationship. It was also revealed that if she decided to break free from this cycle, their contract would be completed together.

A year later, Andrea returned for another session focused on Life Between Lives (LBL). By this time, she had separated from her husband and was amid a turbulent divorce. The court proceedings consumed much of her energy as Armand fought relentlessly to prevent her from securing what she considered a fair settlement. Stripped of shared assets, Andrea had to swiftly find a job to support herself and her young son and move out to an apartment since Armand refused to leave their family home. Her primary concern was the outcome of the court proceedings and what the future held as she painstakingly tried to rebuild her life.

Andrea entered an altered state of consciousness effortlessly and conveyed her experiences with ease and great depth. Her childhood memories revolved around instances of her shouldering responsibilities beyond her years. Being the eldest child of immigrants, she was tasked with translating for her parents from a young age, managing household chores, and looking after her siblings when her parents were away. While she took pride in helping her family and being helpful, a part of her felt unseen and as though she had been robbed of the carefree innocence of her childhood. Her earliest memory was that of being gently rocked in a hammock by her grandfather, the one person who truly saw her and shared a deep, loving connection with her.

In utero, Andrea discovered that her purpose in this life was "to be free... To learn to be free while wearing a human costume. To wear this human costume with grace."

Her current incarnation was pivotal, representing the culmination of many past lives and a point where all her learning would finally come together. True happiness can only be found in this life by consciously choosing to break free from situations that bring her suffering. Andrea realized that leaving her marriage was the final lesson that would solidify this learning.

When we delved deeper into her purpose, she stated, "My spirit incarnated here to bring a lot of awareness and joy to the lives of others at a time where it feels like a pivotal moment on the Earth plane," suggesting that humanity now has a choice between "destroying planet Earth or entering a different consciousness." Andrea recognized the significance of her responsibility to hold her awareness high during this time and spread love to others. This explained her attraction to her current job in sales, allowing her to meet many people and transmit energy to them. As it was explained, this facilitates small shifts in their energy field, enabling them to make the necessary changes in their lives. The energy continues to ripple through these transformations, affecting those connected to them, like throwing a pebble in a pond.

She recalled the past life of a powerful female druid practitioner named Fiona, who lived in 16th or 17th century Scotland. We joined her in a scene where she learned that English soldiers were coming to kill her son, who was one of the organizers of an uprising. Even as she was running to warn him, she knew deep down that she would be too late, that this fate could not be altered. Following her son's death, Fiona gave in to the hatred that consumed her heart and turned to dark rituals for revenge against the English. Eventually, she fell ill and chose not to heal herself. Reflecting on that life, she recognized that she had been governed by deep intuition and shared a profound connection with nature and the planet, but in the end, her sorrow clouded her mind and heart.

From there, Andrea transitioned smoothly into the Spirit World. At the gates, she was greeted by a great entourage of loved ones. In a heartwarming scene, her mother showed her that she would have two more children. Initially hesitant due to the trauma of her first delivery, Andrea was assured that the previous difficulties were due to the energetic circumstances surrounding her marriage and that the subsequent deliveries would be smoother as she would be more aligned then with her authentic self. She also understood that the first labor helped her, in a sense, to birth her inner strength.

Next, we met her main guide, Reiner, who projected a robust male energy described as having "the strength of an iron rod in the middle of a lightning storm."

He emphasized that in her past life as Fiona, she couldn't prevent her son's loss, but where she made her choice was when she began to draw forth the dark side.

He stressed, "Absolutely never sell out ... It is important just to do the work in every lifetime, no matter what happens ... The power is always in the reaction that we choose." Regarding her current life, his guidance was clear: "Keep going, don't quit! "

She needed to navigate this challenging phase without stopping. He emphasized that "Everything else will dissipate by just rinsing and repeating, rinsing and repeating."

The rhythm of action was crucial, "like a steady gallop."

Andrea was shown an image of herself riding a horse through a dark, dense forest, and the guide explained that it was important to keep pushing forward without stopping. If she stopped, it would not be easy to regain the momentum.

When probed for further information and practical tools, Reiner shared that although the next three months of her life would be difficult, this process was essential for her development. During moments of self-pity, anxiety, uncertainty, or low energy, she was to pause, connect with Spirit, and ask for guidance. The advice was to "ask and then trust" and take inspired action, as this could "change the energy of (her) day in a split of a second."

Asked about a vision of her potential future life, Andrea saw an image of a comfortable house in the countryside, surrounded by her children and a loving husband who felt like her equal in every way and with whom she shared a deep, loving bond. Her daily life was rooted in an awareness of her inner self, stemming from her strong connection to her sense of worth, self-love, and understanding of the true abundance within. She realized that she was the conduit for her experiences and that she takes steps toward the future she is creating every day.

The Elders of her Council appeared tall and radiant, "as if sunshine were hitting a diamond." They encouraged her to embrace her authentic self and always to speak her truth. Using her voice authentically, they said, was a tool that helped her honor herself, and the more she honored herself, the brighter her inner light would shine.

Regarding the court proceedings, the Elders projected an image of viewing the process as sweeping the floor and discarding garbage. They emphasized the importance of acting with neutrality and trust, even when it seemed things weren't going her way. A surprising realization emerged: the court process was an essential lesson that Armand's soul had agreed to participate in for her benefit. It allowed Andrea to assert herself and demand what she deserved without shying away from the challenge. The council advised her to be firm during the proceedings and act with loving kindness toward Armand outside of the court, recognizing in him the wounded little boy who had never truly experienced love.

Following the Council, we explored several other places in the Spirit Realm, including the Place of Life Selection. When asked about alternative life paths, Andrea described the life of a Russian male engineer in Saint Petersburg who was now 40 years old, more than ten years her senior. His main challenge was his immense intellect and living in a stifling country. Ultimately, Andrea's soul chose her current life because immigration was predestined for her, whereas the male engineer never left Russia. His high IQ also makes it difficult for him to embrace spiritual growth. In contrast, Andrea is open, flexible, and more willing to accept and embrace the intuitive aspects of her existence.

Andrea's journey to and through the LBL experience was profoundly empowering and transformative. She had initially come to the first session on the brink of making a defining decision in this lifetime: leaving her marriage's security and material luxury to someone who could not provide the love, understanding, and deep soul alignment that her spirit yearned to experience. We discovered that the themes of not being seen or loved unconditionally had emerged early in Andrea's childhood, so to see her make the decision to break away from these patterns and to watch her follow through with this commitment as our work together unfolded had been truly remarkable.

The LBL session provided crucial context, enabling us to understand her life's narrative, the lessons she was learning, the meaning and significance of her experiences, and why certain things in her life had to happen the way they did. Furthermore, it offered immediate guidance and practical tools from her spirit for navigating her current distressing situation, which had been draining her energy and resources.

Lastly, she gained a glimpse of the future, not merely in material terms but also in terms of the internal unfoldment that was underway and the energetic space she would come to inhabit. This empowerment was immeasurable.

In our latest update, the court proceedings have yet to be concluded. However, Andrea managed to go through the legal process with a newfound sense of acceptance and determination. She better understands what to expect as she navigates this challenging phase, which gives her the strength to persevere. Additionally, she's grown to appreciate her job more, recognizing the significance of her interactions with people and their positive impact by allowing them to experience her energetic field. She also experiences a greater sense of lightness because she knows she manifests her life as she had always dreamed.

To summarize, some of the most profound truths brought forward during this session that can almost be universally applied to any life were:

One of the things that we strive for is "to learn to be free while wearing a human costume. To wear our human costume with grace."

"It is important just to do the work in every lifetime, no matter what happens… the power is always in the reaction we choose." Regardless of the circumstances, the choice of what meaning we assign to them and how we choose to react is always ours. And in doing so, we must "absolutely never sell out."

When going through a difficult phase, keep putting one foot in front of the other. "Everything else will dissipate by just rinsing and repeating, rinsing and repeating." The rhythm of the action is essential to avoid losing momentum.

When feeling stuck, lost, anxious, depleted, or

discouraged, quiet your mind and ask your inner being for guidance. Then, follow with an inspired action. This can change the entire day's energy, even if things aren't going well.

Our voice is a tool for honoring ourselves. Always use it to communicate your truth authentically. The more we do that, the more our inner light can shine through.

Every situation contains lessons that are essential to our further development. Always ask yourself: What does this situation ask of me? Who could I become if I address this with courage and integrity?

# CLEAN UP YOUR STUFF!
## Don't let past life imprints make life & love miserable.

### Sophia Kramer

Hae Kyung is a 33-year-old Korean woman working as a corporate director in the IT department. She flew in from Chicago and now sits in front of me in New York. She is slender and fashionable, lively and yet a bit reserved.

Multiple fears and anxiety stop her from being the leader she wishes to be. Her marriage is falling apart, which brings her great sadness and conflict. Both she and her husband, Frank, feel that they are soul mates. They struggle to get their love back for their own sakes and the sake of their little five-year-old daughter, Marion. Following Hae Kyung through her sessions helps us understand how the soul's lessons influence every aspect of our existence.

In our introductory conversation Hae Kyung tells me,

"Being Korean and growing up in a culture in which yelling and hitting is a usual thing with Asian parents, I am not surprised that I am not able to express myself. I want to break through areas of disempowerment in my career and with my finances. I want more financial security."

Hae Kyung stops and then takes a deep breath before continuing, "And I have to understand what is going on with our marriage. What happened? Frank and I had such a strong attraction, and we still love each other. We are best friends, and yet we argue over seemingly nothing. It always ends with our blaming each other and with me feeling guilty. Our little daughter suffers from this, and our romantic love is nonexistent."

She pauses and looks a bit embarrassed. Then she goes on, "As a matter of fact, I moved out. I have my own small apartment, and I have a lover, Tom. Tom is not my great love, but he is more masculine." She sighs deeply, appearing conflicted and sad. She continues, "I feel so trapped! I love Frank, no doubt, and, oh, I miss my daughter! I wish Frank and I could somehow figure out how to heal our marriage and re-spark our sex life. He was such a romantic man. He is good looking, but now he is passive and feminine."

I always like to spend a significant amount of time in talking with a new client. It is important for me to get information behind the "story." In other words, I listen with my therapeutic ear for hints. Also, it is important for the client and me to feel a good energy flow and a sense of trust with each other. I always address this in the email exchanges or phone conversations prior to our first meetings.

Hae Kyung is worried about not being able to see or feel anything during her hypnosis/ regression session. That is a general concern for a person beginning with this work. I had to explain to her how, when you do this for the first time, you have to really trust what you receive. Everyone has a different way of receiving deeper memories. Instructing her extremely active and assertive conscious mind to assist her by stepping back and just watching and listening is a helpful approach.

In our first session we worked with Family Constellations using hypnosis. Hae Kyung first wished to explore hidden dynamics and unseen forces from her current family system related to healing her failing marriage. Additionally, she searched for underlying issues that contribute to her fears that may be holding her back from being the leader she feels she could be. She would like to quit the corporate job and build her own healing career with a focus on helping women.

Then she says, "But I run away from it. I easily give up and am so afraid of making a mistake. And as much as I know deep within that I have leadership qualities, I am feeling insecure and afraid."

In this first session we especially worked on the emotional and physical abuse she received from her father. She understood the root of her father's behavior and the related circumstances. We uncovered some information regarding unknown family dynamics influencing her, which was later confirmed by her mother. Astonished by this, following this session Hae Kyung emailed me and was ready to continue exploring Past Life and Life Between Lives Regression.

One week later, on the day I facilitated a Past Life Regression for her, Hae Kyung had no doubt about being able to be hypnotized or receiving information. She easily went back to her special place, a nice warm rock by the waterfall where she went quickly into a deep and peaceful relaxation. Suddenly I saw a shift in her expression, and I asked a probing question.

F: How is your mind feeling about you having a regression session?

C: My mind feels tired and fatigued and is used to trouble focusing, so it is trying to figure out which bus to take later to get home and rest.

F: Your mind can go into the background and rest right here. As a matter of fact, the mind cannot do the journey to the soul state, so you can tell it to just take all the rest it needs right now.

That shifted everything, and within less than a minute Hae Kyung was in a deep trance state. We continue our moving backward in her present life as a prelude to moving further backward into a previous life.

C: I am crawling … I feel uneasy… I don't know, but I am afraid…

It becomes clear to me that here in her childhood we already sense some fear. It does not surprise me after knowing her childhood history with an abusive father. We do a brief interaction, and then I redirect her to a neutral or happy experience for the sake of the regression. In PLR and LBL we do not work on childhood trauma but use happy or neutral memories as a warmup exercise. Having said that, there are, of course, sessions in which we first must address trauma. There are occasions where we will first have to do inner child work. But as I mentioned earlier, we already did a session with family systems work, and we were able to continue without interruption.

C: (at her earliest memory) I see my crib in my

parent's bedroom, and I see my brother. I feel so loved. Hahaha, everything I do is CUTE, so cute! (she laughs out loud again and then continues) Good. (she sighs) I forgot about this and what it feels like! Oh, and CLEVER! Everything I do is clever!"

Hae Kyung giggles and snuggles in the therapy chair. The expression on her face is adorable. I give her some time to enjoy the feeling.

C: My parents look so loving and happy when they look at me.

This was a good verification for Hae Kyung to remember something in trance that her conscious mind did not remember. She knew that she was not just making this up in her mind. I instructed her to now go back to the time in her mother's womb.

C: (cringing) I feel fear. I feel fear and am worried if I will make it.

Wondering if it is her mother's fear she is feeling, I direct her back to around the seventh month.

C: I still feel fear, but this time I realize it is my mother's fear. (she stops breathing and then shouts) But I am also wondering if I will make it!

Now Hae Kyung tells me that her mother had three miscarriages and lost a daughter before her pregnancy with her. I have no doubt that these experiences have a strong influence on her mother's feelings about this pregnancy. I direct her back to an even younger time in the womb.

> C: (looking very distressed and holding onto my chair) Here it is even worse. My mother's feelings of fear are huge.
> F: And how are you feeling at this time?
> C: (with amazement in her voice) I feel fine! Actually, I feel curious and excited about life!
> F: Hae Kyung, how has this impacted your life?
> C: I can feel the feelings of others very easily.

I then suggest she move back to an even younger moment in the developing fetus, and I ask what she is experiencing.

> C: It's very early, and I feel even more hopeful. But also, more fearful now. I feel exactly what my mother feels.

In this moment Hae Kyung understands how she became an empath. She has been feeling the feelings of others since her time in her mother's belly. But she told me in our introductory conversations that the feelings of others often agitate her, because she feels invaded by them.

> F: Now leave your current mother and your developing body. Allow your soul to float through time and space. You drift and float safely. (I see a peaceful look come over her face) Go to a lifetime that will help you to explore your fear of standing out as a leader.
> C: (speaking rather slowly) I am a woman. I'm

still fairly young. I'm outside standing in the mud. I am wearing a dress. (pausing) There's a man tied to a pole, a wooden pole. It is Jesus!

Her face is puzzled, and she clearly is confused. Catching that critical moment, I tell her to go deeper and trust the memories to unfold.

C: No, it is not Jesus. It is a man who gets punished, like they would do with Jesus! (slowly she retrieves her memory, speaking one word at a time with a shaky voice) I have to be careful.

F: Why do you have to be careful?

C: We have to cover all of our hair. We are wearing long dresses…And we have to stay silent! (then with a strong voice) Here we have rules! I don't want to get in trouble!

F: What would happen if you did not obey the rules?

C: (shrieking) Everyone would turn against me and see me for being improper! (becoming very still) My name is Amrata. I have two children. I'm stressed and fearful, and my body is anxious all the time! I don't have a strong bond with my children. As women we are supposed to behave, or else we get punished. We get punished by all men, by the father, by the brother, by the husband. My husband has a brown beard and brown hair. He's hitting me, he is very angry! … Actually, he was the man on the pole! People turned on him, and he was punished, which made him even more angry and bitter, and he felt disempowered. Now he is hitting me even more often!

She pauses, and I give her time.

C: I have to be careful, I have to be very, very careful! (holding her breath) I feel so alone, I'm not allowed to say anything. I feel suffocated and unsafe. I am distant. It is not safe to trust anyone! I should help other women, but I am too afraid!

I suggest that she go to the end of her life as Amrata. I ask what she is experiencing.

C: I am in a room by myself. I am tired. I'm exhausted. (after a moment) I am alone, quite young, maybe 30, and I am done. Now I am moving towards something.

It becomes evident to me that she has left her body very quickly and is going towards the Spirit realm. I ask her to go back a bit in order to review her life and hover above the body she just left.

C: My life was miserable! Just miserable. My thoughts are that I survived. I just wanted to stay safe enough. I didn't do anything I wanted to do, and I didn't help other women in need.

There seemed to be a heavy silence in the room. I waited for her to continue.

C: I am realizing that I have to forgive my

husband in that life and find compassion for him. He was shamed by the other people, and that broke him. He never recovered.

(then with insight) I realize now that it is nothing that anyone else does, it is because of you, yourself. (with an astounded face) Oh, my husband then, is my father in this lifetime!

In her Family Constellation session, we worked on family problems, especially with her father. Hae Kyung now understands how her life as Amrata impacted her life as Hae Kyung by making her fearful of standing out as a leader. We discussed how as Amrata she had to stay invisible as a woman and live with constant fear and threat of violence. If she didn't follow the rules, or if she stood out in any way, she would have been beaten or possibly killed.

After her prior life regression, her PLR, Hae Kyung did some research and discovered that she must have lived in Persia. It is interesting that there is a theme of "will I make it" that she re-experienced in the womb prior to her being born in this current lifetime. After further understanding and integration, Hae Kyung is looking forward to starting training for the leadership she wishes to incorporate. She says, "I see myself working with a group of women from all different backgrounds and nationalities, and I feel empowered, happy and great!"

Following her successful PLR, Hae Kyung comes back soon for her LBL session. We discuss her previous session when she was a Persian woman. She had done some more research about that lifetime and came across validating facts. She shares, "I really felt it was helpful that you reassured me, and I am astonished about how quiet my mind was. I know

now that this session will be even easier."

For her LBL session Hae Kyung provides me with detailed background information on the main people in her life and has questions for her guide and Council of Elders.

Understandably, the questions are about her marriage with her husband, Frank, and their daughter, Marion, who now lives with him since Hae Kyung moved out of their household. She carries great guilt, describes Frank as her very best friend and yet does not see any future for them as a couple. She also expresses feeling conflicted about being with her boyfriend, Tom. Pervasive fear has been a big theme throughout her life in many ways. Hae Kyung experienced fear of abuse; fear of authority; fear of not knowing what to do; fear of feeling unsafe; fear of not being able to figure things out; fear of failing to fulfill her soul mission; fear of making the right choice with regard to marriage; fear of failing as a mother; fear of falling; fear of water; fear of trusting her intuition; and fear lodged physically in her arms and one shoulder.

In starting another PLR as a prelude to her LBL session, Hae Kyung travels easily back through happy memories in her childhood to a different moment in the womb from when she was regressed during her PLR session. The fear she experienced in her previous womb regression has been cleared. Her experience this time is completely different. She is excited about her life now. To her surprise she notices that she is connecting to an energy that helps her with deciding details about her life.

Suddenly Hae Kyung tells me that it feels as if she is being pulled backwards into what she then recognizes as her most recent past life. At this point I usually direct the client to his/her most recent prior life, but in this case it happens spontaneously.

> C: It is World War II. I am a soldier on a boat, and now we are going to the shore. I see my friend with me. There are so many gunshots. I am so afraid that I don't know what to do.

In contrast to her first PLR, today she is speaking very fast. The words are just shooting out of her.

> C: I am frozen. I feel so much stress. I don't know what to do. It is a constant thought. I don't know what to do! (pausing and breathing heavily she continues) I hide in a trench. I'm frozen with fear. I feel so much stress! I don't know what to do, and the stress is collapsing over me! I don't know what to do. I feel stuck! I have to help my friend, and I can't! I am so afraid. I am too afraid to check on him. (looking sweaty and distressed) Everyone is going to die! I am responsible for them, but I can't find a solution. If I don't do something everyone is going to die! (suddenly) Or I might die!

Hae Kyung is stressed and tense in my chair. Moving her forward in time, she reports that she sees a scene over and over.

> C: This is a repeat scene. Four foreign soldiers are near the trench. They're coming towards me. I have such fear! (shivering in her chair and breathing heavily) I am responsible for my friend, and I don't know what to do! My stress just shoots up even more!

I am paralyzed by fear. I can't act.

F: (suspecting that I already know the answer by noticing her expression) What happens next?

C: I see my body on the ground. I am just hovering above my body. The soldiers shot me in the head, and I die and leave my body immediately.

F: What are you thinking or feeling?

C: I feel relief. Thank God it's over. (A big sigh of relief, but then it is followed by a worried face) I feel such guilt. I cannot believe that I left! I see that my friend is still alive. I let him and other people down. I didn't help. I was a coward and just died instead of being brave enough!

F: What do you conclude from this?

C: I wasn't strong enough to make it. I was not brave enough. I just freaked out, and they really could have used my help.

Hae Kyung starts to cry and believing that Hae Kyung is not someone who cries easily, I wait for a profound statement.

C: My friend is my husband, Frank! (sobbing) He's such a good person. He's my best friend. We were supposed to stay together, and I feel guilty that I left! I failed him! He had wanted to go into the army and be a soldier instead of studying in college. I never wanted him to do that because this terrified me.

Hae Kyung's soul stayed around the battleground for a while. The guilt kept him watching over his beloved friend. He checked in about his friend's wellbeing for a while before moving up.

C: I'm going up. I'm floating up … there's a light right above me. I see many light beings. They are greeting me.

Immediately she recognizes a big bright being who is standing out from the welcoming group. This being is her personal guide.

C: (with a big smile on her face) His name is Azer.

She then connects with her soul group and gets specific insight into her group. Her mother, her best friend, her daughter, and a few others are there.  It is not surprising that her husband, Frank, is in her soul group and comes up immediately, smiling lovingly at her. Hae Kyung realizes that she and Frank are incarnating and connecting over and over for various lessons and reasons.

C: I have so much guilt from the life in WWII. That I was not able to rescue him and help him was horrible. Now I am going to help him to break through and gain strength.
F: Tell me about the other group members.
C: We are not beginners. We are in the middle. I see us as part brownish-green, part gold. Ahhhhh, that's why … we are awakening. My mother is speaking to me. She tells me that in coming into this life I had to experience her fear in the womb. That was no mistake. It was for my soul's learning.

When a soul needs to address a theme such as this one of fear, which is contained or held within the soul, it chooses similar circumstances for continued work on the lesson. Her "will I make it" theme is addressed here.

> F: What is your soul's name?
> C: (slowly sounding out her soul's name letter by letter) L … i … z … a …, my name is Liza.

She and her guide examine the past life that she just re-lived, and she realizes that the fear is something she needs to master. Fear is a theme for Liza's/Hae Kyung's soul. There are life lessons and soul lessons. This is clearly a soul lesson.

Liza sees a symbol of a woman with a dragon. The symbol is switching from woman to dragon and from dragon to woman, and Liza listens to the words of her guide.

> C: Azer tells me that I came into this life with a lot of energy. The dragon means that I have to get the dragon skin, that unburnable skin. I am supposed to be walking through the fire, getting burned, but releasing all fear, releasing all chains of fear. I have to walk into the fire, through the fire, in order to be free. I already AM! That AM means I am thoughtful and free!

Azer and Liza are now on their way to her Council of Elders. She becomes very still and her expression changes.

> C: I'm here. I see this big hall with a semicircle of my high advisors. They are standing there in a kind of royal way. They are three steps up above me, but Azer is here to support me. He is like a coach. He is behind me to my left. I know he will support me. There are

seven council members in front of me. Their color is a shimmering icy blue. They ask me how I feel. I respond with a respectful voice that I feel so honored. So very privileged. And here is so much love. I feel love, so much love!

Liza/Hae Kyung pauses. Her face is radiant. Then she continues.

C: The Council members decide that the Elder on the left is going to be the moderator. My guide continues to stay behind me on the left. The moderator is this glowing icy blue color and is a wise-looking tall, male figure. He starts to speak to me telepathically. I ask about my current state of advancement in comparison to my former lives. He tells me that my fear carries through my past lives. They are telling me that it is not going to get any easier. I have to learn that, and I want to learn that.

F: Why is that so?

C: The only way out is through the fear. (with surprise) It is good for me to have another child!

F: What are you being told?

C: I have to learn more about nurturing, mothering and being caring. With my daughter I didn't embrace her. I didn't like to be pregnant; I didn't like to be a mother. I didn't like to have to stay home and not be able to do what I would like to do. I have to build on my feminine side. The feminine side in me has been beaten down and suppressed. The fear about authority is because of the resentment from the suppression and abuse I experienced in my feminine

53

past lives. Therefore, I am angry at men. The life in Persia we visited together was one of them.

I now remember how resistant she felt about having another child when we talked before the session began.

> C: (continuing) The Council is making me see that one reason I married Frank was out of guilt and obligation stemming from the World War II life. I felt I failed him in that life and had to make up for it this time. I have to let go of this. Now I understand the connection to my feelings of failure from that life. (with clarity in her voice) And we are Soul Mates!
>
> F: What are you learning about being soulmates?
>
> C: We are playing different roles over many lives for each other's learning and healing. It is all about growing, and we support each other in that. (after a pause) The moderator of the Council is telling me about my relationship with my daughter. I have to heal myself and what I passed on to my daughter. I physically can feel that I have to heal my feminine side. The left side, which is the feminine side of my face, feels wilted and atrophied. And the vision in my left eye is not as good as in my right eye. They say that this is all due to my lack of integration of my feminine side. They tell me Marion came to be with me to be my teacher. I have to learn from her. She is the wiser one. She came to support me in our mission. She's so sweet. She is my teammate.

Liza now reports that the Elders are showing her two past lives regarding her chronic pain in her arms and left shoulder.

In the first life they show her she is an African man who has a warrior spirit. He is killed by a spear that seriously wounded his left shoulder.

> C: They are pulling the spear out of my spirit energy body and clearing the injury. (after a pause) In the second life they show me there are ropes tied around my arms. (then loudly) Oh no, there's a fire. I can't get my arms free. There's so much smoke, (choking) I try to free myself.
>
> F: (trying to keep her moving forward) What happens?
>
> C: (gasping for air) I die. (then with a bitter face) And there I go again. Bye! I was burned by my enemies. The Elders look amused by my sarcasm. They say everything will be better once I clean up my past 'stuff'. They are kind of funny about it now.

Often, we experience the wise beings as having wonderful sense of humor.

> C: (continuing) In that life I spoke up for what I knew and believed. I was burned for that. Therefore, I am now afraid of very serious repercussions. But I have to understand that I live in a different time now. In this life I can follow my intuition. They tell me to connect more. I am too afraid. They are telling me that you don't die, your spirit never dies, and you are never NOT fine. The only thing is that fear stays in the body, and you need to find tools like this to clear that. It is unavoidable walking through fire, but if you clear it, you are fine. (after a pause) I ask if there

is anything else of importance for me. I ask whether my family is a soul purpose for me. I am told that I am drawn to it as my bigger purpose. But they are telling me that I already know that. I came to this life out of guilt and obligation, and I need to resolve that. Frank and I are here to help each other. It is not clear if we can make it. I am realizing I have to heal myself first.

C: The Elders say that what I strongly desire IS what my purpose IS! I am getting there.

The energy in the room is changing. I feel the session is coming to an end.

C: (sighing) I feel lighter having received all that. They are telling me that I know how to reach them. They say to stay connected.

After I guide her return to the present, I tell Hae Kyung to check her body to see how it feels. She says that the pain in her shoulder and arms are gone now. I suggest that she check with her mind, and she states, "My mind feels energetic." I respond, "Good. Remember how it was tired and trying to figure out the bus schedule in the beginning?"

She laughs, "Haha! Ya! That's cool, I feel so energized now! "

When we discuss her session afterward, it is most confirming for Hae Kyung that our guide often stays on the left behind the soul during their council meeting. Her response was, "Really? I didn't know that; that is cool! That is so interesting! That is very cool, that makes it feel even more real." She had not read Michael Newton's books beforehand

and didn't know about these kinds of details. That is one of the beautiful aspects of working with a client who has not read the Michael Newton books. Oftentimes, surprising and confirming details emerge.

Hae Kyung had several insights. She stated that multiple sessions made it easier for her to reach the deep hypnotic state required to experience an LBL. The brutal environment during her childhood in her current life and the memories of suppression in her female past lives played out in her marriage with Frank. Additionally, speaking her truth as a woman in her past lives resulted in her being burned to death. This strongly influenced her leadership abilities in this life. Having failed as a leader in her lifetime as a soldier played a huge role in the carryover of strong feelings of guilt. As an atonement she chose Frank as her husband for the experience of the strong commitment a marriage requires. Additionally, she has been reluctant to release her warrior spirit's masculine energy and embrace her feminine energy. It will benefit her to learn about her female power, which is a softer power, but definitely not weaker.

Following Hae Kyung's sessions, Frank decided to work with me and came for Family Constellation work to address his issues. He sought help with his self- suppression and guilt, which were affecting their marriage. He recognized various hidden dynamics that were playing out in their marriage.

Then, approximately two weeks after her LBL session I received an email from Hae Kyung stating that she had broken up with her boyfriend and moved back in with her husband and daughter. Thus, the door opened for them to work together again. They appear committed to healing themselves and their marriage and to taking the next necessary steps. Seeking to change her profession, Hae Kyung enrolled in two different study programs with the goal of becoming a therapist who predominately works with women.

# CULTIVATING PEACE

## Sally Stone, PhD

**W**hen Elle came to me for her Life Between Lives regression (LBL), she felt most concerned about her health. In addition to her self-care, Elle had been accepting frequent and unpredictable caregiving requests from her extended family. These caregiving responsibilities challenged her to establish healthy self-care routines and interfered with her work as a yoga and healing practitioner. Elle had also been exploring herbalism as part of her professional and personal healing path. She yearned for time and guidance to clarify which direction to take her studies.

Over the years, Elle also had fur babies. She referred to them as her "seven angel dogs and one angel cat." These beloved pets had provided love, comfort, and connection for many years, and she still grieved their absence. Her current dogs had some challenging behaviors, so they didn't provide the comfort and peace she longed for, which might have eased her stress.

In the past life portion of Elle's LBL, she found herself as a gangster on his deathbed. She experienced regret and self-loathing for her terrible deeds in that incarnation. She felt she deserved ill health and pain.

C: I'm in a shack, lying on something like a bed, dying of consumption.

F: Who are you?

C: A gunslinger, ma'am. Jesse. I came out West looking for fortune—a better life. But I'm all alone, and I'm dying.

F: Tell me about your life.

C: I could have been a better person.

F: What have you done?

C: Well, lying and cheating at card games. I stole some horses.

F: What have you achieved?

C: Mostly schemes. Breaking the law. Getting away with stuff. Being wild and free. Not answering to anyone but me.

F: What moments of goodness did you experience?

C: Well, I was good to my animals, and I was good to my friends who were loyal. And I was loyal to them in return. I had some good times just having fun. But in the end, I'm just here all by myself, dying in this shack.

F: What's your most important lesson from this life?

C: I'm capable of great harm but also of great things. I just have to choose the good if that's what I want. Or else the bad will creep back in.

F: Choice … that's a lot of power.

C: Yes.

Upon his soul's release from the gangster body at the time of death, Jesse felt free. The first thing he did was release his horse. Considering Elle's affinity to animals and her current life abilities as an energy worker, I wasn't surprised that the horse got untied and set free.

At the Gateway to the Spirit World, the first guides who appeared were Mamí (pronounced "mommy"—Elle's deceased paternal grandmother) and a supportive male guide she called Andrew. They shimmered with golden light.

Mamí and Andrew took Elle to a place of healing: a small garden, which she described as "a plain patch of Earth." The surrounding area was beautiful, but the garden patch was empty. Mamí and Andrew suggested she sow all the seeds of her discontent in the garden and "water it with your tears."

Elle emptied her feelings into the garden, which made the patch of Earth "ugly." She cried about her life as a gangster, her current life of ill health, the caregiving demands, her business, and everything else Elle had been striving to manage. She let her tears water the Earth, and as the tears naturally subsided, she felt at peace. Little shoots came up from the ground and grew into the heather, rue, bluebells, baby's breath, and a few other plants she didn't recognize. Her guides told Elle she could tend this patch anytime, in meetings with them in the Spirit World and at Elle's Earth home.

Her grandmother's guide, Mamí, a "curandera", a Mexican folk healer, told Elle that these plants were "limpia tools", meaning they could be used ritually to spiritually and energetically cleanse the body and atmosphere. She conveyed that Elle could make them into teas, oils, sprays, and dried plants whose healing qualities she could use for herself and share with others. The garden continually "updated" her visions to show her what she needed to grow.

In answer to Elle's question about which direction to take her herbalism studies, Mamí suggested it would be helpful for Elle to seek community from "our people" to learn more about the Curanderismo system of healing.

Elle's healing experience continued with her guides escorting her to a beautiful open space with a vast blue sky, mountains, trees, and land that went on forever. As she relaxed on the cool ground, she felt the cold nose and tongue of her beloved fur baby, Evie, who had transitioned years earlier. Soon, all of Elle's beloved pets who had transitioned arrived. They looked happy, healthy, and active—with boundless energy.

And, she noted, there was no bad breath in the Spirit World!

Elle began to weep with joy as she enjoyed a beautiful reunion with her beloved pets. She felt complete, whole, and at peace in their company once again. She soaked in their love, and they assured her their love was always with her. I offered Elle a future pacing technique where she envisioned herself remembering their spiritual presence whenever she misses them. They also assured her they're helping her current fur babies learn better behaviors.

Now, Elle's guides took her to meet her High Council. They addressed Elle by her spiritual name, Mikkelson. Although Elle is of Indigenous heritage in her current life, Mikkelson felt like a strong Norse energy in her soul's lineage.

Mikkelson's High Council addressed Elle's health concerns right away. They offered her the experience of Mikkelson's soul energy as a strong Viking Warrior. However, that energy wasn't manifesting due to illness. They wanted Elle to fight for herself, to strengthen her body physically. They showed her sword fighting herself and suggested she stop fighting herself and fight for herself. This meant taking care of herself by eating and sleeping properly.

How to do this? They suggested she reinforced boundaries regarding elder care for Elle's grandmother. "Stop taking care of everyone but yourself", they suggested.

Mikkelson responded, "Elle will feel like a jerk saying no to people who need her … Elle is also worried about pushing people away and dying alone."

Her High Council response was that she might die alone but would not be lonely since Elle is perfectly content by herself. Moreover, Elle could die alone, exhausted, and annoyed if she didn't make boundaries.

The bad deeds from her past life as Jesse still weighed her with guilt. In response, her High Council communicated complete forgiveness to Mikkelson: "You've already corrected past life wrongs and learned to understand human suffering. You 'got it.' It's okay to move on."

Her High Council suggested healing remedies that echoed what she'd learned in her rejuvenating herb garden with Mamí: herbs, particularly buckthorn, and more time soaking and swimming in water, especially saltwater.

They recommended she also "drink from the nectar of life" so Elle's life energy could come back. They reinforced this guidance by playing one of Elle's favorite Dave Matthews songs: "Eat, drink, and be merry, for tomorrow we'll die." She saw how her power comes from an inner spark, and the nectar of life keeps that flame alive in Elle's body.

Mikkelson asked her High Council about Elle's soul path as a way of drinking the nectar of life. They answered that experiencing peace and equilibrium would be her greatest achievement on her soul path. Helping others would emerge from her peace, equilibrium, and healing. The best way to attain peace would be Oneness with Nature — working with Nature, connecting to her rhythms, and using her gifts to find her way.

She then had a vision that connected her to the old ways through Earth magic:

An apothecary with jars of herbs, flowers, and potions— her own "nectars".

Feeling into her soul purpose was energizing and inviting and gave her "juice", whereas caregiving with no boundaries felt draining. Experiencing this contrast, Elle thought she could heal and experience peace by drinking the nectar of life and making boundaries she could live with according to her moral compass.

Several weeks after her session, Elle felt a much stronger connection to her guides and angel animals and their support. She recognized her guide, Andrew, as coming from ancestral connections through her maternal grandfather, Charles, who was Scottish and looked to St. Andrew as their patron saint. She could better comfort herself during times of stress by returning to the love she experienced with her angel animals in the Spirit World.

She told me, "Feeling comfort and love from my angel animals helps me cope with the additional stressors I've faced since my session. I also find I'm more connected to the Viking warrior energy of my Soul-Self and much more inclined to speak up and assert my power in situations that feel unbalanced."

Elle enrolled in a self-paced herbalism course to support her health and spent more time in her fledgling herb garden.

She feels more grounded and, like her garden, says, "I'm

blooming where I'm planted."
    This brings her peace.

# CONCLUDING INSIGHTS
## on Freedom & Free Will

Freedom and free will occupy a central position in the tapestry of human experience, embodying the essence of autonomy, choice, and self-determination. As we navigate the complexities of existence, grappling with the interplay between freedom and determinism, we are reminded of the profound significance of these timeless ideals in shaping our lives and societies. Freedom and free will have a profound impact on the human experience.

Freedom is the ability to act and choose without constraint, including external and internal liberties. On the other hand, free will refers to individuals' capacity to make choices independently of deterministic forces, raising philosophical questions about agency and moral accountability.

Choosing detachment opens a path to freedom in a new way. When we are free from attachments, we can experience freedom in the purest sense of the word.

When accessing the soul's wisdom in Life Between Lives

sessions, we encounter many aspects of freedom and free will. When we are in the soul realm, we are not attached. Thus, we can become an objective observer of all our life choices without judgment and with compassion and love.

All the choices we make are a part of our soul´s experience and plan, and the more we experience in the physical world, the more our soul advances.

By accepting the existence of duality, the good and bad, the darkness and the light, we can start to master forgiveness and become detached while attaining peace and ascending as souls.

By choosing our path and making decisions, we are already exercising freedom and free will.

Sanela Čović
Editor

# CHAPTER TWO
## ON LEARNING THROUGH RELATIONSHIPS

# INTRODUCTION
## on Learning through Relationships

It has often been said that relationships are where we "put our show on the road". That is, we can create, perceive and experience all sorts of ideals, beliefs, perspectives, approaches, and responses to life, its challenges, and other people in our lives, and yet putting these into practical action, especially when it comes to relationships, can often be a monumental and complex task. Through relationships, we discover vast opportunities to grow our souls.

LBL therapy can offer support in various ways along one's journey through life, most notably regarding relationships with oneself, other people, Earth, its inhabitants, and Source. While we sometimes find it challenging to ask for support from within Earth's plane or receive the most helpful support from others within our diverse cultures, religions, and societies, the soul realm can provide precisely what we need. Since we are unique as individuals including variables such as our genetic makeup, personalities, circumstances, environments, relationships, and histories, it is on a soul level that we can discover and access the individualized forms of encouragement best suited for our innate desire to persevere, grow, and develop. Relationships in the soul realm are harmonious and full of transparency and unconditional love. On Earth's plane, typically for reasons of survival, we often use our human egos to navigate this realm, along with its desires, fears, and unique perspectives. This can often be at odds with our soul's purposes and introduce many obstacles and challenges to our relationships.

Keeping in mind that we chose to be here in a specific body at a particular time, most of us received much support and coaching in the soul realm before entering an embodied lifetime. The amnesia we are gifted with for our growth and the frequently daunting task of finding our way to our soul selves can sometimes leave us with a sense of being adrift. For many clients, especially during times of struggle, feelings of lostness, aloneness, "stuckness" and generalized existential angst, connecting with their higher soul selves, spirit guides, Council, soul groups, and even Source can be bolstering. Experiencing unconditional love, belonging, acceptance, and deep understanding in the soul realm strengthens and validates. Because existence in this linear physical dimension is replete with flux and change, such a spiritual reconnection can leave one feeling uplifted and upheld, guided and with purpose.

LBL experiences can offer loving support, direction, and ongoing resources to help clients live more meaningful and fulfilling lives. Although there can be times on Earth when we become entangled in physical, psychological, emotional, and spiritual suffering and disconnection, we all benefit from reconnecting spiritually through the sacred opportunity of soul relationships. Perhaps one of the most essential introductions is that of one's human-self meeting one's soul-self. Learning to turn inward, reaching for the soul's presence and energy within, checking in to see if one's human self is in harmony with the soul's desires, develops a priceless relationship overflowing with love, wisdom and guidance.

In *Journey of Souls,* Michael Newton wrote the following:

> *To clearly understand what is behind the spiritual activity of a recognition class, perhaps the word soulmate ought to be defined. For many of us, our nearest and dearest soulmate is our spouse. Yet, as we have seen…, souls of consequence in our lives may also be other family members or a close friend. The time they spend with us on Earth can be long or short. What matters is the impact they have on us while here.*
>
> *At the risk of oversimplifying a complex issue, our relationships can be divided into a few general categories. First, there is the kind of relationship involving love so deep that both partners genuinely don't see how each could live without the other. This mental and physical attraction is so strong that neither partner doubts that they were meant for each other.*
>
> *Second, there are relationships based on companionship, friendship, and mutual respect. Finally, we have associations based largely upon more casual acquaintances offering purposeful ingredients to our lives. Thus, a soulmate can take many forms, and meeting people who fall into one of these categories is no game of Russian roulette.*

*Soulmates are designated companions who help you accomplish mutual goals, which can best be achieved by supporting each other in various situations. Regarding friends and lovers, identity recognition of kindred spirits comes from our highest consciousness. It is a wonderful and mysterious experience, both physically and mentally.*

*Connection with beings we know from the spirit world, in all sorts of physical disguises, can be harmonious or frustrating. The lesson we must learn from human relationships is accepting people for who they are without expecting our happiness to depend on anyone. I have had clients come to me with the assumption that they are probably not with a soulmate because of so much turmoil and heartbreak in their marriages and relationships. They fail to realize that karmic lessons set difficult standards for each of us, and painful experiences involving the heart are deliberate tests in life. They are often the most challenging kind.*

*… I have heard many heartfelt accounts of close spiritual beings who journey across time and space to find each other as physical beings at a particular geographic spot on Earth at a specific time. It is also true that our conscious amnesia can make meeting significant people difficult, and we may take a wrong turn and miss the connection at some point. However, there can be a prearrangement here for back-up conditions.[5]*

Elizabeth Lockhart
Editor

---

5    Michael Newton *Journey of Souls*

# A Path to Transformation

## Gayle Barklie

In a hypnotic state, we began by delving into my client, Louis' childhood, and then further back into his time in his mother's womb. Louis learned that life was a struggle right from conception, and he even had a difficult time connecting with his body in utero. Suddenly, he became aware that his parents had wanted a girl and were unhappy that he was a boy.

From then on, life was a struggle to receive love, and he continued that pattern right into his present-day marriage. He found himself constantly asking: "Why am I still here?"

As we went further back in his regression session, Louis spontaneously connected with past lives and between-lives memories without explaining what to expect. He saw and felt every detail as I asked him questions.

At first, images of people would appear as silhouettes, then become focused. He would also see colors and shapes that eventually morphed into places and things.

A strong memory then emerged...

"I'm in a battle in a jungle... Somehow, I got away... Deep cut on my chest. A woman with cinder-brown hair, olive complexion, and green eyes finds me... She takes me to her village where the houses all have thatched roofs... She is so concerned, so caring. That's her name: ´Green Eyes´ ... It's dark, I sleep... It feels safe... Other women arrive to take care of me... They nurture me back to health... I survive."

As the session continued, more details emerged from that life:

"´Green Eyes´ puts her hand on my chest, her other hand on her heart. She chose me. It feels amazing, like I've come home, but it's not my home. I see us standing together and I'm wearing a sapphire medallion, the same ultramarine blue I saw before. It's our wedding. I don't know how I know this, but it's a Mayan ceremony-- the symbols I saw on the stone are Mayan."

He then fast-forwarded to the end of that life:

"I'm an old man, dying. Everyone was so genuine and kind, taking me in so generously. There were so many lessons I was supposed to learn there, all about the importance of really learning to love. Love and friendship, peace, and innocence are the four most important things. I have to open my heart!"

Those last six words were key for him: "I have to open my heart."

As we returned to a previous time, I asked more questions as we delved deeper.

"It's a gray day. It stinks really, really bad. Burning bodies. Everything, everyone, is gray. There's fighting everywhere, a war... in the Pacific. Everyone's wearing camouflage clothes and eating food out of cans. Dead bodies all around me.

A marine walks towards me. It's Joe! He's emotionally dead. I feel disgusted. I feel guilty. Why did I make it? The minute I have that thought, I get shot in the head. I'm only 20. I will never get older. I lived through the Dust Bowl and the Depression and then died in a no-name spot. This is not fair! Where were the good times?"

After remembering that experience, he immediately started seeing colors—a yellow, white glow that turned into a group of souls. He was in the midst of them.

"I'm at some sort of gateway, and then Vic steps up, leading a group of souls. I'm so happy to see him, and he's just as happy to see me! He's androgynous, old, filled with vitality, and gives me a pat on the back. 'Good job,' he says, in reference to how well I lived that lifetime.

I'm with all these other souls, and they're all glowing. It's like a yellow-and-white glowing cocktail party, welcoming and loving. I can see how all these souls are related. Even though they're in separate groups, some have overlapping concentric circles of energy connecting them."

Between lives is the spiritual realm where the soul goes when transitioning from lifetime to lifetime. It's a 'layover' interval for debriefing, planning, and readying us to move into our next incarnation. This realm is about re-acquainting us with who we really are, helping us gain wisdom, letting go of the tough lessons of previous lifetimes, and reconnecting with other souls we've shared experiences with. It's the time we plan our choice to return with specific intentions for the evolution of our soul.

Louis became aware that this soul group was highly advanced and there to assist him. They had encouraged his return to his current life so he could evolve and build more character, going through many challenging situations.

Then, in this immortal state of being, an insight comes to Louis...

"There's someone there who looks so familiar. Gloria is her name. Oh wow, it's Green Eyes! She's one of my spirit guides!"

As he continued to see details, he realized he has three main guides in his life.

Firstly, Randy, who had mentored him when he was a teenager. Secondly, a dog who taught him open-hearted playfulness and the simple things in life. Finally, Green Eyes/Gloria is his wife from Mayan times.

Although Louis was not as advanced as the others, Gloria had brought him into this soul group because she saw value in him.

Her job was to help him learn three primary lessons: "Love is the motivating factor". Then, "True oneness is the only moderating force", and finally, "Love is all there is".

She chose him in the soul realm and the Mayan life to remind him about who he truly is, using a gentle push on his heart and a sacred whisper to his soul.

Then Louis understood the significance of his relationship with his son, Andrew, in this life. He saw this fourteen-year-old as an advanced leader destined to bring a great spiritual awakening to the world. His role would be to bring more joy, light, and understanding to many.

He realized the importance of maintaining a stable home life for this enlightened soul, nurturing him daily, and teaching him that "Love is all there is". Louis' role is to support him in his spirituality by teaching him about the many aspects of his family's spirituality.

It became clear to Louis that he needed to stay with his

wife for his son's benefit. He accepted that his happiness wasn't important; what was important was raising this special child.

However, by understanding this, Louis was able to stop resisting the lessons he was supposed to learn with his wife. By obtaining this spiritual understanding, he achieved the peace and ease in his relationship that he desperately craved. The healing from this insight alone was deep, powerful, and life changing.

What occurs between lives is held in our deepest subconscious memories. Accessing it can provide a profound understanding of who we are, why we are here, and lessons yet to be learned. Getting in touch with the planning we undertake there—the choices we made, the instructions we were given, the wisdom we obtained—can change this life in countless and beautiful ways.

After letting go of childhood and past life traumas and awakening to his between-life memories, issues started gently falling away for Louis. He had been diagnosed with pre-diabetes, and following our session together, without changing his diet or lifestyle, his body spontaneously lost 35 pounds. He no longer needed extra weight to protect him. His blood sugar also normalized, much to the amazement of his doctor.

My client was thrilled to discover the treasure trove of information to be learned from accessing this between-lives state. Things he'd sensed about his true purpose started to manifest. The lessons he was supposed to learn became a joyous adventure rather than something to avoid. Things that occurred in this life made sense because of seeing the bigger picture. His consciousness awakened as to why he had chosen this existence.

By accessing his authentic between-lives memories, Louis

felt relieved, empowered, and in touch with the wisdom of the ages.

This inner journey was even more significant since his traditional religious background didn't support this type of work. Remarkably, however, he found that this exploration only enhanced an already strong commitment to his faith in a deeper, more tangible way.

After these between-life memories appeared, Louis's logical mind needed a bit of validation. I discussed the documented scientific evidence proving what he'd gotten in touch with, which helped him trust it even more. Unlike traditional religious notions about heaven and hell or the "rest period" concept, Louis's spontaneous personal experience allowed him to know and live his truth.

It was an honor for me to help Louis connect with his life lessons and have such a powerful, life-changing experience.

# More Than One Way

## Hila Kedem-Ferguson

This is a story of a soul learning about the beauty that life has to offer and how there is always more than one way of doing things. As we open to the many opportunities this life has to provide us with, we can see through eyes of compassion that we are all doing the best that we can and remember there is always more than one way for our path to unfold.

Mike is a forty-eight-year-old man born and raised in the U.S. He has been married for twenty-nine years and has three children – two sons and a daughter.

He has been in media and video production for the last ten years and has worked on his spiritual growth through a wonderful online show he created. He is a talented musician and composer, as well. He filled many occupational roles in his lifetime before this career path led him to explore his human journey further. He came from a deeply religious Christian home and had been feeling the call to explore beyond his religious upbringing and find his truth regarding

God and Spirit. As he explored the many avenues of healing this world has to offer, he came across the work of The Newton Institute and contacted me for a past life and a life-between-lives regression.

Mike wanted to gain a deeper understanding of his purpose in this life and how it ties into his work; he felt a calling to expand his knowledge and personal journey further and wanted to become a teacher and a writer to help others on their path. He also wanted clarity about his different relationships with his family members. He wanted to understand why he chose the path of a strict and organized religion and why he chose his parents to facilitate that. He also wanted to understand his present path with his wife as they grow together and the paths that his children have chosen. He told me that his eldest son was struggling with drug addiction and had contemplated suicide. This made the purpose of the session essential for Mike.

Mike experienced a past life regression with me before his LBL. He regressed to lifetimes in a position of power and authority with responsibility for others. His main life lesson was about learning to release the responsibilities that were not genuinely his and to allow others the free will to guide themselves. He also made initial contact with his guide, Ruman, who helped him understand these life choices and how they tie to his current life and relationships. He learned that he is loved and accepted no matter what. Another strong message was that he can help others by showing more compassion and less ego-centered judgment in his everyday life.

We explored further When Mike returned two months later for his LBL session. I set up Mike's safe place before the regression (a therapeutic device used in the LBL process).

Mike's safe place was a beautiful garden set in a meadow with a few benches, a place of peace and tranquility. Later, he will return to this place in spirit form and realize it is the setting chosen for the meeting with his guide.

Mike regressed to a past life where he was a Native American Indian. He connected with his responsibility to hunt as an "Eagle". and as a provider and warrior for the community. He expressed his sadness, knowing that the "white man" would come and take over the land where his community lives.

> C: The white people are in our land; they are trying to cause problems, taking the land that we need to hunt buffalo now. We are riding now (Eagle and the other hunters). I hate them (the white people). I want to kill them, and they want to kill me, so it's war. There is a wagon train … we attack them, and they attack us. There is blood, and I am trying to ride away. I get shot.

Here, Mike begins to rise up and away from his body. Mike is still feeling the anger as he rises, and he is still taking the shape of his physical native body as an "Eagle" and looking down on that life.

> C: I am still angry … why did they come here, take our land … why did they kill me? I was just trying to provide for my family.

His guide, Ruman, intervenes and tries to lighten up the energy. The scene begins to fade away, and he is taken back to the garden from the beginning of our journey. He is joined by his guide on one of the benches. Ruman talks to him about the main lesson of this life as an Eagle. Ruman says there is more than one way to do things.

There were many paths that he could have taken.

F: Ruman said you are holding on to the feeling of injustice when things do not go right.

Is this something that Mike also holds on to?

C: Yes, injustice, taking advantage of … but there is always more than one way to do it. Religion taught me that there is only one way to do things, and he says there is always more than one way.

F: Why was it important for Mike to experience that "one-way" religion?

C: So, you can realize that there are many more ways when you experience the One. There is more than one way to have a relationship; there is more than one way to make money. The universe is abundant, and there are always many ways. Just like a Rubik's cube, there are many ways to solve it.

F: How does this tie to the feeling of injustice that Mike experiences?

C: When I narrow my mind and only see one way, I feel victimized, but there is more than one way. It is the same with Ted, my son. I only see one way, but he can choose a different way to live his life.

Mike is reflecting on his life as an Eagle.

C: There was only one way—the white people had to leave. For me, there was only one way—they wanted me to leave. We could not find any other ways to live. Yet, there were many other ways we could have figured out how to coexist. Creativity is finding other ways. Just like with music, it does not have to be one way; there are other ways to do that.

F: Is that something that Mike can really relate to? Is Mike more open to "other ways"?

C: Sometimes, there is an optimal way to create it musically with a chord pattern, but you can play with that and do different things within the pattern.

F: I want you to take a moment and notice how there are areas in your life, as Mike, where this lesson comes easily to you, even though there are other areas where you find it difficult.

C: That feels so good! There is ultimate creativity; it does not matter where you start, what key you are in, or what chord you are playing; it is unlimited; you can do anything. When I am on the piano, I play the piano; there is joy and peace; I can play sad or I can play happy, I can play angry, or I can play relaxed. I can play everything and create different sounds, rhythms, speeds, and tempos. It is the gift of music that teaches me how to be creative so I can put that into my life. I can feel the music, and I can feel my relationship, my abundance, and the different ways it can be, just like music.

F: Notice you already have some amazing life tools; even though you picked religion to tie you into the one way so you can expand, you also came into the life with music that teaches all the other ways to help you solve problems in your life.

Mike had questions about his marriage and children.

He and his wife have been talking about opening their relationship so they can experience other connections with people. Mike was open to the idea but then struggled with it, and we wanted to get more clarity from his guide.

> C: Ruman tells me I must create it within myself; if he tells me the answer, I will fall into that same trap of believing it is the "one way" (to do it). He says you get to be a creator, and you get to create what you want because there is more than one way. All the answers are within you; you have your intuition, and there is no right answer; whatever you choose is the right answer; anything can work – even if you choose "the wrong way," it still brings you back to your soul's truth. You cannot choose anything wrong because you are always learning and growing from everything.
>
> F: We agree, then; there is no reason to be afraid of making the wrong choice because that does not exist; it's just like making music; there is no reason to be afraid of hitting the wrong notes; we just call that jazz.
>
> C: Yes, there is space where you can mess around and make mistakes, but if you hit the perfect flow, with your notes and music, you will know it, and it will just feel so good.

His guide talked to him about his marriage. How he and his wife make the "band", making beautiful music together, but there are other ways to enjoy others; you can have "guest artists" or private projects, but your core band is always there for you. You can trust that core relationship with your soul mate as you explore other ways together and apart.

I realized that this was such a beautiful way for Mike to understand what he wanted to experience and release the fear that had been present in the past regarding his choices.

When exploring his questions around money and abundance, he received similar messages, where his guide kept showing him the different "breadcrumbs" he had been leaving behind so that he knew the right path to follow, "the trail that leads me to my knowing." Reading books and watching movies that inspire him will lead him down the right path for his book and workshops.

When we opened the rest of the session to other souls that would like to connect with him, he realized that Ash, his son, chose them as parents because they were strong enough to support his hard path, and he had made a conscious choice to deal with addiction in this lifetime. Mike experienced compassion at this point for Ash's difficult path and realized that it takes a strong soul to choose this path of addiction. He would now see his son in a different light.

He then discovered his Soul name, "Na-ion" (like a Lion), and his essence, "I am a courageous and bold soul." The lion symbol will continue to remind him of who he really is.

The main message of his LBL is that there is no wrong way to live his life and that fear is not real. He is here to explore and grow with courage and remember that there is always more than one way to do things.

# RECLAIMING MY COURAGE

## Indrani Sinha Seth

Chandni is a 42-year-old Indian woman who has lived in Dubai for the past 15 years. When she came to see me, she had been in the airline industry for over 20 years and lived alone in Dubai. She was divorced and in a long-distance relationship. Her only child, a daughter, lived with her parents in India.

Chandni wanted to gain a deeper understanding of her volatile relationship with Suraj, her boyfriend. She had been grappling for quite some time with a lack of balance in her relationships— "either too much or too little." She wanted to address this and understand why she tends to "disconnect and detach" from people if she doesn't receive the kind of attention she desires from them. She also wanted to explore her past-life connections with her loved ones in her present life.

She was curious to know about some people in her present life. In addition to her parents, daughter, and first husband, Chandni wanted to know about her soul connection with Suraj. Her daughter, Roshni, was raised by her parents in India, and yet they continue to share a close bond. Chandni wanted to learn more about her special tie with her daughter's soul.

Chandni approached the LBL experience with anticipation but without any preconceived expectations. Although she had heard of LBL and Dr. Newton, she hadn't read his books. She easily relaxed and reached the trance state smoothly and comfortably, able to visualize well and enjoy the imagery of nature in the trance induction.

She experienced a past life as a dancer named Karen who lived in the 1700s. Her life revolved around dancing. She belonged to a close-knit family of her grandparents, mother, and sister, but her grandfather was a strict authoritarian. Karen liked a boy in the dance troupe, but the relationship did not develop. When she was 25, her mother died. Karen then became responsible for the household. After her grandfather's passing and due to her grandmother's advanced age and frail health, she was encouraged to marry at age 40, the same man she had liked from the dance troupe but had stayed away from when her grandfather objected. This was the man she truly loved. From then on, she enjoyed a stable, secure life, happy in her marriage and dance classes. Karen said, "I am now content."

She died aged 70, surrounded by her family. She said, "I have no regrets. I see a lot of flowers around me." Her five children had all grown up. She believed she had followed her heart. She'd never given up dancing; she had married the man she loved and yet fulfilled all her filial duties. She learned from that life, "When something has to happen, it will. Stay strong and stand with family." She died in 1773 in Mount Abbot, with snow all around as she left her body.

The soul exited the body readily and smoothly and moved towards a bright light.

> F: Tell me what is happening now.
>
> C: I feel good floating above the body. My family is sad, understandably, but I am happy! As I move on, it's getting darker. I see multiple points of light spread out. I move straight ahead toward the bright yellowish-white lights. There are a million rays of bright white light and I'm being pulled into a hollow. It's as if I am pulled into something like the sun but it doesn't burn me – I feel happy and secure.

Her guide's name is Hom, an androgynous being who tells her she can stay and doesn't have to leave him. In her debrief with her guide, she learned that her goal from that lifetime was not to let her family down, even though she was reprimanded for her relationship with her future husband in her youth since the family disapproved of him then.

Hom tells her that she should have created her own life and pursued her dreams more, but she did well on most fronts. Her greatest achievements came from her students, whom she trained very well, and the selfless way that she stood by her family. She was disappointed that she subdued her personal desires and prioritized her family over her own.

Satisfied with this meeting and the discussions with Hom, she says it's time to meet her friends. Moving towards a space where her soul group awaits, she sees star-shaped lights in varied colors. Some lights are in pairs, some in bunches, and some scattered. Her face is beaming and glowing. She counts

23 lights in a semicircle with her light in the center.

Chandni's immortal spiritual name is Shooshoo (she describes it as the sound of strong wind). She radiates white light. Shooshoo explains that 10 of the souls are in her life today. She enjoys their familiar presence and is filled with joy at meeting them again. They appear colorful. She says, "They will always fill my life with color." These soul friends will always be there to protect her, Hom says. She recognizes some souls from her present lifetime, all of them close friends and a cousin who strongly influences her. Her group is made up of pleased and creative beings. Creativity is a theme in her soul group. She is intrigued to notice the soul of her boyfriend's estranged wife. Her relationship with Suraj has caused many family rifts and is considered scandalous in their traditional family. The presence of this soul is an acknowledgment that the Earthly relationship challenges are part of her life plan.

Shooshoo now notices another group in their cluster nearby, round beings with a metallic appearance. They seem heavy, solid, and steady in their energies. She sees Suraj, her boyfriend, and her first husband in that group. One light seems brighter and more significant. She recognizes it as Roshni, her daughter.

Following the happy reunion with her soul friends, Shooshoo proceeds to the meeting with her Council of Elders, accompanied by Hom. There's light all around. The Council is composed of seven bright beams of red lights with white centers. Three have a masculine valency, and four have a female valency. They are dressed in white robes and have no hair, but white light emits from their heads. Shooshoo addresses them as "Wise Ones".

They first advise her that this LBL session will yield more clarity so she can carry on with her life and build on the understanding she gained from her previous life session. They ask her to understand the situation with deeper thought rather than analyzing it from a superficial intelligence. Shooshoo observes that her human form as Chandni isn't particularly mature; she should keep going and not lose hope, and she will eventually find her way. She notes that the Council used to be stricter but is now more encouraging and less condescending. Overall, she's told that she's "doing good".

> C: I have to find balance – make it happen and find clarity. I just have to keep going – not give up and I must have patience.
>
> F: Balance between what?
>
> C: The human brain has a greater than average influence over the soul ego. Freedom is the most important individual characteristic. I'm most comfortable living creative lives. Of all past lives, my most productive was of an Indian rice farmer of humble origins. I was happy because I managed and succeeded with limited resources.

When we come to the memory of choosing Chandni's body, Hom is closely linked in this process of body selection, paying close attention to the eyes. Hom chooses the eyes, and Shooshoo chooses the body with eyes that she likes. She is more of an observer in this process of body selection. As Chandni, she gives a lot of attention to her eyes and always enhances them with makeup.

> C: Eyes are very important – they look kind. My lesson is that I should not ignore myself – I must love myself, too. In this body, I'll be able to love myself

more. I'm happy with this body.

Just before incarnating, she recalls being with Hom, talking, laughing, and relaxing.

> C: We are chilling in a forest area, with no people or lights. It's day, and I'm kind of pushed to go!

She tells me that she learned from the last preparation class that this life would be good, that she was reincarnating this time to learn her lessons, and it was her duty to reincarnate. Her attitude towards rebirth is joyful and full of anticipation.

After the LBL session finished, Chandni told me of her surprise about her guide, her life choice, and the past life she visited. All these experiences made her feel "very good". She shared her realizations, her sense of wonder, and her excitement about what she had learned.

Her main observation was that she had gained courage. "Courage made me manage well in my past lives. I learned not to give up, and my spirit is strong." She discussed the importance of family and the need to balance family priorities with her priorities for life. She deduced that she is sometimes judgmental and jumps to conclusions about people. She now acknowledges that she shouldn't judge people on a superficial level. She understands she should not lose focus and deviate from her chosen life path. She accepts her need to think deeper and be more aware of people who may not be essential characters in her life but will still search for their purpose when they are together. She resolves to shift her attitude towards her mother, first husband, and Suraj and resolves to be more patient.

In the year following her LBL, Chandni decided to

reconnect with Suraj and plan a future together. She would leave her life in Dubai and relocate to Kolkata (formerly Calcutta) to live with Suraj. The result of this life change is joy and contentment. Her daughter Roshni now accepts her relationship with Suraj, and so do her parents.

She has started a business in Kolkata and shuttles between Delhi, where her parents live in Hyderabad, where her daughter is studying law, and her home in Kolkata.

Chandni told me, "As your story's heroine, I hope we can inspire and motivate many others to experience the life transformation that follows from an LBL session. I am happy for my story to be written down and made public."

Sometimes, we need to remember how profound the impact of Life Between Lives is.

This makes me reflect on the importance of the healing between the client and their universe ... As a therapist, being a neutral conduit for every client's learning and spiritual development is crucial.

# WORLD OF LIGHT

## Elisabeth Iwona Röpcke (Kupisz)

*"… Until a few years ago, I did not know there was anything like past life regressions. When I read the book by Ursula Demarmels entitled 'Who was I in my Past Life?' in the beginning of 2014, I knew from the first few pages in the descriptions of the afterlife: I want to go there! But also, I was there! I then devoured the books by Michael Newton. For me, it was clear I had to take part in a past life regression! In Iwona Roepcke, I have found a therapist who understands me and leads me well emotionally. She asked her questions, so I am challenged and in the way I 'need' to hear them.*

*I am still fascinated by what I have experienced and am grateful that I was able to experience all of this."*

Karin G. learned from several LBL sessions about her and her past lives. As a result of these sessions, she has become more open and joyful. She created a book (223 pages) from the sessions for herself. Her book contains this story, Takiyomara, with all the transcribed parts from her LBL sessions. Whenever she would like to study parts of the sessions or needs advice, her book is there with her all the time, and she finds this invaluable. Instead of listening to the recordings of her sessions, she can open the book and find guidance and support for whatever happens at that moment in her life.

The remarkable thing is that she gains deeper insights and confidence from reading the book each time she does so. The story Takiyomara has fascinated her because it parallels her current life. She tells me this with great astonishment. This past lifetime as Takiyomara also confirms the authenticity of her LBL experiences. She also finds support from reading about the Council of Elders' advice and insights from other station stops in her LBL.

Takiyomara was a woman who lived in the Mongolian steppe. She was a self-confident, fearless woman, happy, responsible, loving, and mindful of the welfare of others. The entire family group, maybe 15 people, lived in a close community. All of them were very loving and careful towards each other. There was great love towards fellow humans. They lived in a few very spacious, large huts together. The following huts were a bit further away. They never moved; they lived there with their family all their life. They had animals that were housed outside. Amongst other animals, black animals had very short, smooth coats. These animals were robust, strong, and good-natured animals. They were working animals, but they were small. The family also traded with these animals; they were exchanged for goods.

It was a vast, yellow, dusty land without mountains. Due

to the very slow dusk, it cooled down slowly, and before the pitch-black, cold night came in, there was a very long time in the dusk semi-darkness.

The family lived to survive; each one was there for the other. Takiyomara had learned well from her father how to trade and bargain. They often went together to the market and achieved good results. She could have been more domestic. Even though she sometimes cooked the food, she was more interested in other things, like exploring remote areas to search for water.

As Takiyomara dies, she is lying on a plank bed outside the house next to the fireplace in the direction of the wind. She was a little older, but not very old. She was ill and could not move and walk properly. They had put something in the fire, several black roots or pieces of wood from the ground. These things were relatively common in this area. Not too far away, they were "mined" with tools and made into this flat shape. They were used when needed when someone was ready to die. This should remove the pain, daze them, and shorten their suffering.

All family members were there with Takiyomara, standing or sitting around her and taking great care of her. When the wind turned or swirled, and the dense, biting, black smoke seized the others, they flew away as fast as lightning, so they didn't have to inhale the smoke. The smoke was only for the dying, for in addition to the described effect, it otherwise caused irreparable damage to the brain. Takiyomara died in the evening, at the beginning of dusk. After she died, water was thrown on the fire, and all family members sat around her, caressing her, staying for a long time in the dusk and at night beside her.

F: Where are you in relation to the body ...

C: ... (starts to cough heavily) ...

F: ... which you have left now? How does it look? Where is the body lying or sitting?

C: Am I already outside? (Shortness of breath). Smoke is there. In front of the hut ... smoke. The wind has turned, and I smell the smoke .... (she breathes hard) ... I'm lying there. Outside.

F: What clothes do you wear?

C: It's like ... long capes, ... yes, ... wide trousers and a wide cloak. It is dark. Pretty dark already. So ... not night, but dusk.

F: And you are lying there alone?

C: No, no, no! They are all, all, all there too.

F: And you lie there. You see yourself from above?

C: No, I'm still lying there.

F: I understand you are still there. And do you communicate with the others who are around you?

C: Little.

F: Little. Do you know that you will soon leave your life behind?

C: Hmm. Well, that biting smoke, that is what I feel. (shortness of breath)

F: What is it good for, this smoke? What is the purpose of it? Is that a ritual? Is that supposed to help you?

C: (astonished): It smells different; it smells different than usual; there is something else in it!

F: Oh.

C: It irritates. Yes, yes, it irritates. Yes, I believe they have it because of me ... there is more smoke; this is not such a normal fire, but a smoky one, a smoky fire ... there is something in it.

F: Something special?

C: Yes! Something that should fog me, I believe.

F: Are you hurt or ill?

C: No. I am somehow old. Yes, and I can't move properly anymore ... that smoke is, I believe, something that makes you not feel yourself so much anymore.

This should help to take the pain away. Yes, something like that. Exactly! That's why the others are not standing next to me, so that they do not smell, do not inhale. When the wind turns, they come back to me. They are caring towards me.

F: That's so nice.

C: Yes, that feels good, that they are ... Yes, but we've always lived this way, that we are there for each other, and take care of each other and make it enjoyable for the other, that's really good.

I cannot move properly. I'm ... (breathing deeply) ... Can't walk anymore, I have kind of ... fat ... joints ... kind of like that, yes. And long ... I have a long braid, braided. ...

F: You have left the body. What's happening now?

C: Hmm ... I'm above the body and observe it.

F: What are the others doing? Can you say goodbye to them?

C: (astonished) They pour water on ... that ... fire! On the smoke. Then they come to me ... Exactly! When it stops, the smoke ... They caress me. They stand around me, sit, and squat. That means they are around me. Now I'm further up, yes ...

F: Now, I have a question from the perspective

of the soul. What did you experience in this life, did you reach your goals? What connection does this life have with your present life?

C: I felt community ... it was a purpose community, but a happy ... loving community. Because we did everything together and shared everything and ... I experienced a lot of love ... and gave love and ... we all helped each other!

Altogether, Karin found more peace within herself and now feels more loved and supported. She learned this love in the community from the memory of her past life as Takiyomara.

# CONCLUDING INSIGHTS
## on Learning through
## Relationships

Learning through relationships revolves around fostering empathy and understanding.

Engaging with people from various backgrounds and perspectives exposes us to different life experiences that challenge our assumptions and broaden our outlook.

Whether through close friendships, family connections, or interactions with strangers, each encounter offers a chance to empathize and see the world from someone else's viewpoint.

From a soul perspective, our souls choose specific life paths where we'll encounter individuals who aid in our learning, development, and growth.

Sometimes, we'll connect with souls from our soul group, but we may also interact with souls from other groups to fulfill our soul's mission and plan.

From a human standpoint, relationships may be

challenging to maintain due to unresolved issues or opportunities to learn self-love and other aspects of love, such as empathy.

The lesson from human relationships is to accept people for who they are without expecting our happiness to depend entirely on them.

Our physical existence gives us the chance to mend past relationships and traumas, allowing our human selves and souls to evolve.

Recognizing that we possess the answers within ourselves and embarking on the journey of self-understanding leads to happiness and love.

Sanela Čović
Editor

# CHAPTER THREE
## ON UNDERSTANDING LOSS, GRIEF, PAIN & SUFFERING

# INTRODUCTION

## on Understanding Loss, Grief, Pain & Suffering

Loss and grief are among the most painful experiences and states of being in our human experience and generally cause great suffering. While formal stages of grief have been identified, categorized, and explored through the work of Swiss psychiatrist Elisabeth Kübler-Ross, among others, who first introduced her five-stage grief model in her book *On Death and Dying*, these stages are not linear.

Five typical stages of grief include denial, anger, bargaining, depression and acceptance. Feelings of loss, grief, pain, and suffering can backtrack, circle around and pervasively interfere with mood, sleep and appetite. These emotions can be riddled throughout one's dreams and rest heavily on one's chest upon waking. It is common for the bereaved to experience some depression and deep sadness. It can also be discouraging to feel as though one has passed through a few critical stages of grief, only to return to them, often being triggered by events such as the anniversaries of the losses.

The origins of loss and grief can be quite diverse, ranging from the death of a loved one to a job loss to the destruction of one's home or homeland, to natural disasters, war, divorce, trauma, illness, and more. Grief can inspire fear as well, and fear can catalyze grief also known as "anticipatory grief." Anytime we experience a significant loss, grief is there waiting to be acknowledged, felt, processed, healed, transformed, and integrated. These steps can lead to healing; however, sometimes grief can become complicated when other factors have a substantial impact, such as a death occurring before forgiveness has been asked for and given or unresolved trauma.

The human condition requires all of us to experience loss, grief, pain, and suffering on various levels and during different eras throughout our lifetimes. When pondering LBL therapy's impact and what it offers experientially for the embodied soul in easing suffering, I am reminded of a caterpillar's transformation into a butterfly. While in a cocoon, all may initially appear unchanged on the surface, yet many transformations are occurring deep within. The butterfly pupa works diligently to grow and develop, patiently yet arduously seeking to emerge from its chrysalis and spread its wings. Without this work, struggle, and perseverance during each phase as it unfolds, the butterfly's wings would not receive the fluids, warmth, and exercise to render them strong enough to fully unfurl and become capable of flying into the sunlight as the butterfly seeks beauty and sweetness among the blossoms.

Similarly, the passages through loss, grief, pain, and suffering can cause a metamorphosis for us, whereby we often emerge feeling more reflective, compassionate, and understanding toward the human condition and all who grieve and suffer. These experiences typically require much in the way of emotional releases, reflection, processing, and integration over time. The physical death of a loved one, including the death of a beloved pet, tends to be the most painful loss for many. The journey of grief demands a vast number of inner resources, often impacting one's overall health and wellbeing. Great healing can occur by becoming gentle, loving, forgiving, and patient with oneself and others. At the end of physical life, a soul's Earthly work is done for now, and it leaves a human body as if removing a costume. The soul is released and transformed into the fullness of light and love in the soul realm, much like a butterfly leaving its chrysalis and dancing in the splendor of nature. An LBL experience can instill clarity and reassurance that the soul goes on.

Transformations occur through a journey through loss, grief, pain, and suffering. We are not the same person we were before the loss. While some people shut down emotionally, many others go on to heal with enriched lives and guidance toward a "new normal." As you will read in the following case stories, Life Between Lives spiritual regression therapy can significantly help this process by uncovering the meanings behind any kind of loss. Some clients even meet with the souls of loved ones who have transitioned into spirit. Gaining higher perspectives, deeper understandings and a sense of purpose mitigate existential angst and offer comfort.

Elizabeth Lockhart
Editor

# WHY ME?

## Dr. Teoh Hooi-Meng

As others affectionately call him, Uncle Lim is a jovial and well-respected man in his fifties who has been a close acquaintance since our early days.

He knew about my hypnotherapy practice but has never shown any interest in my work, as he has always been skeptical about the validity of a hypnotherapy session. All this changed about a year ago when his only son, Roger, whom he enjoyed a very close relationship with, passed away unexpectedly in a freak car accident. He fell into a deep depression, and when I shared my experience about LBL, he begged me to conduct a LBL session for him so that he might understand and heal the misery of losing his son at this time.

Since the untimely passing of Roger, many times while in great grief, my client had a strong feeling that his son was still around and reaching out to him. However, the more he wished to communicate with his son, the more he felt his heart was closed to such messages. With proper guidance, he hoped to enter this sacred spiritual realm so that he could have the opportunity to communicate with his son, understand why the son left him so suddenly, and, most important of all, establish a link so that the father and son relationship could be continued.

Another question he wanted to clarify was about his son's friend, Jay, whom he had never been fond of but who was the co-driver during the freak accident.

He harbored anger and hatred toward Jay for his son's death. This case concerns the complex emotions of sadness and anger closing the heart. I hoped the LBL session would enable Uncle Lim to accept reality and live on happily, experiencing peace that I knew would be part of the process. Preparing him for LBL was a painstaking process as we needed to clear many hurdles. The past life regression (PLR) proved to be a very successful session when he realized the past life relationships between himself and his son and the healing process that ensued afterward.

My client experienced a past life as a beautiful young woman who was sentenced to death because she was regarded as a witch for practicing "Black magic". She believed her ability to heal people was a gift from God, and, for a time, her loving husband protected her well. Her husband warned her against healing in public for fear of attracting unnecessary complaints from the neighborhood.

F: (At the Death Scene) Who do you wish to reach out to at this moment of death?

C: My beloved husband! I am in front of him now. He looks so sad. He must be worried about me because I was taken to death row without his knowledge.

F: How do you reach out and comfort him?

C: I am caressing his face, but he doesn't seem to notice it at all.

F: Do you have any thoughts on this life that passed?

C: It is so unfair for these people to pass judgment on me just because I can do something they are unable to do. I hated them for that!

F: As you move upwards into the loving realm of an all-knowing spiritual awareness, I want you to look at your husband and tell me if he feels like someone you know in this present lifetime.

C: Oh, my goodness! He is Roger! The look in his eyes reminds me of Roger's stare whenever he was in deep thought. It is just like looking into emptiness. No wonder I always have this deep, strange feeling for him.

Upon meeting his soul group and identifying the members, we explore further.

F: Of all the souls we had just identified, who are in your life today?

C: The one at 3 o'clock, the blue energy, a male-appearing figure, he felt familiar and full of loving energy.

F: Please focus on this energy and tell me, as you fix on this energy, who comes into your mind?

C: It's Roger! (becoming emotional and sobbing).

F: Do you communicate with him and ask him whatever you wish to find out? I know some conversations may be private and confidential, but are you receiving anything telepathically?

My client appeared to be in profound thought, and his voice suddenly sounded calm and composed.

C: Yes. Hi Daddy, I am so sorry to have left you so suddenly. I didn't mean to hurt you this way, but our time in this current life has come to an end. Remember the last time we were together, and you did not follow my advice and ended up hurting yourself? Well, this time around, I am doing the same thing to you to make you feel the same way as I did.

F: What exactly is it that Uncle Lim needs to learn so that he can let go of the hurt and live happily?

C: Everything in this spiritual realm is about love. Although he is feeling the pain and hurt, it is necessary for him to feel it to evolve spiritually. If he can understand the dynamic of this learning, then he can have closure. I have confidence in him that he will redirect his love for me and use it wisely to serve mankind for the remaining part of his current life.

F: Uncle Lim, do you understand now?

C: Yeah, I believe it is necessary for me to feel this pain to remind me to always listen to our loved ones. I never realized the importance of listening, as I have been so self-centered all these years. As I heed his advice, I am now aware of my urge to direct my time to charity work.

F: What type of work?

C: I have always enjoyed working with kids and will now devote my time to the orphanage.

F: Good for you! What about the role of Jay?

Can you check with the soul group?

C: It's funny. Why do I hear laughter?

F: Where is this laughter coming from?

C: It is from behind me. The androgynous being behind me is smirking at me.

F: Please check with this being.

He hesitates for a second and then starts to talk.

C: It's Jay! How can he be in my Soul Group? Aren't soul group members supposed to help each other?

F: Please allow this soul to speak through you now.

C: Well, my role, although it seems negative, is necessary for him (Uncle Lim) to accept and let go. He has been rather arrogant, and before he re-incarnated into this current life, he asked me to help him to learn something different about love. I needed him to transmute his emotions from anger and hatred so that he could embrace true love!

The session lasted about four hours, and upon awakening, Uncle Lim had tears in his eyes but seemed calm and glowing with positive energy. It took him a while to process the information obtained during the session, but he felt lighter during our discussion.

He explained that he realized that life is about learning, and everything that happens to us is a learning process that we must experience and evolve. He could accept Roger's parting as a lesson about listening to his feelings. He also understood that Jay had come into this life to remind him about the other aspect of love; that is, despite anger and hatred, true love may transcend those emotions!

The passing of Roger was painful to Uncle Lim as a human but was a great learning experience for his soul. In his past life, Uncle Lim did not learn because he was overwhelmed with anger, and that is why his son came with him into his current life to teach him about listening to one's heart.

Sometimes, things may seem negative and harmful to our human perceptions, like Jay's role, but in the spiritual world, this may be an experience that we have chosen for the soul to evolve. If we can accept this and find peace, I believe we all will be able to live a better and happier life.

# No Longer Bound by
# the Glue of Grief

## Toby Evans

In mid-October 2018, I was contacted by an enthusiastic 63-year-old man named Brett. Brett had obsessively researched, read, watched, or listened to countless hours of information about various metaphysical subjects. After reading Dr. Michael Newton's books, he was driven to set up a Past Life and Life Between Lives Regression to fit together some of his unexplained soul pieces.

One of his questions pertained to a recurring 'death dream' in which he would die in a variety of horrendous ways connected to a dangerous work environment. When he began work at the steel mill, he immediately recognized it as the 'death setting' of his dreams. Of course, he was interested in discovering the message his subconscious was trying to relay to him. He also shared that he suffered from allergies and a chronic lung disorder that began in childhood with severe bouts that resulted in him coughing up blood. He questioned if his condition had originated in another lifetime.

Coming through the tunnel and into his past life experience, we had this exchange.

> F: Get your bearings by looking all around you and describe whatever you are noticing.
>
> C: There's a fence, a barn, green moss, an old white 1800s farmhouse with tall windows, and a wrap-around porch.
>
> F: Great. Now, look down at your feet and tell me what, if anything, you are wearing.
>
> C: I do not see any feet. I do not see anybody. There is nothing there.
>
> F: That's fine. See if you can go inside the house and keep giving me your impressions.
>
> C: Wow, I thought about being inside, and I am automatically there without needing to use the door. I can move easily throughout the house. It looks familiar, but no one seems to live here because everything is covered in dust. The piano, the fireplace, all the furniture, everything is under a layer of dust.

Brett's attention is drawn outside, and he sees a man holding a shotgun standing near the woods. He reports that the man killed a deer and has it hanging in the old barn. I direct him to move toward him to get more information.

> C: Well, I am instantly there. I thought he was my cousin, but he is my friend Sam. He isn't saying a word. I am sure he can't see me. He is cleaning the deer.

F: And what are you doing?

C: Nothing. I am just watching him. All I can do is observe. I don't know why I am here.

F: Let's go back in time and see if we can fill in some pieces.

C: I see a very pretty young lady wearing a long puffy blue and white dress with a short black jacket and little black hat and white gloves. She is sitting in a two-wheel buggy in front of the same house. It is pulled by a well-groomed buckskin horse.

F: Do you know who she is and why she is there?

C: It's Rachael, and she is waiting for me. I'm coming out of the house dressed in a black suit with a silver vest, and I get in. We are going to town.

F: What is your relationship to her and what name does she call you?

C: My name is Rob. We must be newlyweds. When we get to the church, people stare at us, and young girls giggle and whisper.

I move Rob forward in his lifetime.

C: I am shoveling coal in a very dark coal mine. I am covered in black coal dust. It is so depressing, and there is no light. I can barely breathe! I hate this!

F: Let's move to another significant moment.

C: I am in bed at home coughing up blood, and Rachael is caring for me. I am only in my mid-30s and do not want to die. Later, I am still in bed, but much worse, coughing up blood and gasping for air. Rachael is holding my hand when I die.

115

Once out of the body, Rob observes what is occurring.

C: Rachael is weeping over me. She leans across my dead body and places her cheek on my chest. She is sobbing. I am completely filled with sorrow, not because I am dead, but because I literally feel her pain, and it is awful knowing I am causing it. I only want to be with her, to hold her in my arms and comfort her, but she can't feel me, and I can't hold her!

Brett is overcome with emotion and needs a moment to take all of this in.

F: Now that you are out of the body, do you understand or have insights about this life?

C: I worked in the coal mines to provide for my love. I wanted to make her happy and buy her the nicest things. I wanted the very best for her, but times were hard, and jobs were very limited, so I worked in a place I hated. I did it for my Rachael. But in the end, I saw she didn't care about the money; she just wanted me.

F: Now, are you ready to cross over to the World of Light, where you will receive an understanding of why your life was so short and what you were learning here?

C: I still feel like I am being pulled by the raw emotions like it is still happening, and I can't stop the pain.

Caught in the sticky glue of his grief, Rob cannot see a way out of this self-punishing situation and feels obligated to remain there for Rachael.

> F: We are going to help you leave this place, only taking with you what you learned. We are laying down the image of a labyrinth in the grass by the barn. All you must do is walk it. When we reach the center, a portal of light will be visible to you, as well as light beings who will serve as your escorts to the World of Light.

In 1995, I mowed the paths of a seven-circuit labyrinth into native prairie grass on my land, discovering that moving through the design had the potential to open a portal for Earthbound souls. I reasoned that the seven paths corresponded to the energy centers of the body, the chakras. Rob was able to use this image to help him release the chakra-related issues that are holding him back – through the heart center, which includes the lungs. My client shared his perspectives afterward.

> C: Now it makes sense that when the session started, I was seeing things from Rob's Earthbound view after he had already died. Rob could not go into the Light because of the overwhelming grief of not being able to comfort Rachael. He couldn't leave her when he completely took on her pain, feeling responsible for it. Yet, staying did not change it. His friend Sam took care of Rachael, but when she died, Rob was still stuck there, remaining – just like the dust. It was as if Rob was pulling on Brett's energy to come back and make the needed connections to free them both.

Brett's current job is in the same workplace depicted in his dreams. After coughing up blood a few years ago, he now wears a mask to prevent hazardous materials from getting into his lungs. His dreams warn him that he is repeating Rob's pattern, placing himself in another extremely dangerous environment, which can potentially kill him in a variety of ways. Awareness of Rob gives Brett expanded insight to question the distorted belief that he must sacrifice his health and safety to provide his wife a higher standard of living. Rob's experience can help him see that self-sacrifice is not needed to prove his love and only brings more pain and sorrow.

Brett had also brought other questions to his LBL session: "Why don't I fit into this world, including my family? How do you truly forgive someone? Even when my intention is good, thoughts about past transgressions trigger my old feelings of hurt and anger. Have the people in my life who have died crossed over, including two stepsons, many family members, and specific friends?

After having an out-of-body experience (OBE) in 1973, I became so frightened that I stopped meditating. Is it possible to regain this feeling again?"

Upon entering LBL, Brett viewed the Gateway as a big white door with an ivory handle.

C: Everything is bright. I am heading across white clouds. My whole body is tingling. There is a beacon of light beaming at my third eye. The higher vibration is the mechanism of where we need to be. There is no harm here. There is no fear. Universal Love is the source of this vibration. It is always here for everyone. There is a Presence all around me.

The Presence, a primary guide, gives Brett telepathic information that he begins relaying to me.

> C: I chose the family I was born into because it was the 'standard' of what exists on Earth in the third density level.

Brett begins crying, stating how sad this 'lower' consciousness is.

> F: What density level did you come from?
> C: Five or six ... I do not normally incarnate on Earth. On my home planet, there is no disharmony or division like there is here. I am what some call a 'Wanderer' with a built-in desire to help anyone in need. I feel connected to almost everyone, even when my caring and love are not reciprocated.
> F: Why did you come to Earth?
> C: To help raise the vibration level of people and the planet, to help those in need, and also to learn about forgiveness – of myself and others. On my planet, there is nothing to be forgiven. Everyone is in perfect harmony.

He is then reminded of times he has been negative, sending out ripples that decreased the vibrational level, bringing harm to those around him, due to his negative energy. In feeling the harm, Brett starts crying, knowing how contrary this is to his soul's desire to be of service to others. Additional information comes from his guide.

> C: I realize I made contracts with souls in my

group before this incarnation. They agreed to be adversaries for lessons of forgiveness.

Brett gives the example of three failed marriages, which included instances of terrible unfaithfulness by his first wife and, even more devastating, the suicide of a close friend who was involved with his second wife when the adultery came to light.

C: I am being shown these individuals were from my soul group, agreeing to play these roles, to help me learn forgiveness and learn to set boundaries. The deeper the hurt, the higher the level of forgiveness, and the greater the LOVE. I can view the offender now, not as an enemy, but as a dear friend, giving me the chance to forgive them while still learning self-love.

F: What gifts did you bring with you that can help you as you go forward?

C: As an empath, I sense what others are feeling as a way to help them. I feel a certain intuitive vibration that gives me immediate information.

F: Can you use that vibration to determine if the people from your life who have died have successfully crossed over?

C: Out of all of them on my list, only two have crossed over. Everyone else is still hanging around the Earth.

F: You have already made this journey to the light so you can use your vibrational awareness to guide them across. The energy presence that surrounds you will help them connect to their spiritual escorts and help them on their journey.

Brett's description and takeaway of what occurred was interesting.

> C: I cannot do justice in my descriptions of the vibrations I received during this event. The closest I have been was what I felt many years ago during my OBE when I saw my body below in the bed while I was a white ball of energy, brighter than the sun but not blinding. When the souls crossed over, there was a huge ball of energy, maybe 8 feet wide and 12 feet high, compared to my OBE, when I was the size of a softball. After this group went through the portal, Toby invited any other souls who were attached to me, from this life or any other lives, to also move through, as well as Earthbound souls who may have been observing what we were doing. It was like the HEAVENS opened and were vibrating. I felt hundreds of souls. The vibrations were so intense it was as if I was being shocked electrically but without the pain. Toby saw this and asked if I was in any discomfort, and I assured her it was totally exhilarating. The vibrations continued even after the session was over. I am not sure if it was just an after-effect, but as an empath, I believe they were still coming through 30 minutes later. I am totally convinced all of my family and friends, as well as countless others, crossed over that day.
>
> My guide encouraged me to meditate every day until I could carry the meditative state into my waking hours. By doing this I will be ready to experience OBE's again. I was also instructed not to eat such large portions of food at one time as it reduces the

vibrations in my body. I was encouraged to eat more fresh fruit and veggies.

Brett reported that since the regression, his current wife and he have started having meaningful conversations, which had been non-existent for many years, and she is showing interest in learning about spiritual things too. He no longer attempts to change her; rather, he changes himself and shows gratitude and respect for the adversary she has been for him. He now knows that it takes a special kind of love for a soul mate to agree to play an adversarial role, knowing full well the type of pain it will cause while incarnating.

Brett states that "The biggest change is in me! I feel as if I have just walked through a door in my mind that opens a level of peace and harmony that I have always wanted and could never acquire. I don't think there is anything anyone can do to me that could make me lose the wonder of awakening that I now have."

# So Confused

## Diana Paque

Valerie, age 60, came to see me in a state of exhaustion. She led a very complicated life, with work playing a major role. In addition, she was in the process of moving and renovating a house, having an active family life, and trying to decide on her path and what she should do next. She affirmed in our first meeting that she was a Christian woman and that her faith was a big support for her; however, she was looking for different answers than she received through her faith, and she needed some help to find a path forward. She had always had a strong bond with her father, who had passed, and she was concerned about her mother, who had recently died of dementia. She reported a fear of heights, an ongoing issue with migraines, and wanted to know about the roles of various people in her life.

Valerie wanted to know her purpose and the reasons she chose to incarnate now. She is currently married to Thomas and was interested in knowing about their journey together and how she could support him on his path.

She felt she was her father's twin and wanted to find out if this was true. She also had questions about her spirit guide and her connections to family, both alive and those who had passed, and strong concerns about her career choice and how she was to spend her energies in this lifetime.

Valerie easily regressed through this lifetime, noting that as I counted down the years, she saw episodes in her life pop up, causing her to giggle at things she had forgotten. At the age of 12, Valerie stood on the sidewalk in front of an upholstery store. She shared a room with her sister, a cool, purple room with black-light posters of an African queen with a leopard, Santana, and pompoms. The room was messy, with clothes everywhere.

At age 6, Valerie remembered the group of hippies gathered on the front porch of her parents' duplex. She shared a bedroom with her sister, her best friend, back then too and they enjoyed making mud pies in the backyard and playing with other kids.

In her mom's womb, her head hurts badly, and her nose is squished. Mom is upset while rubbing the baby's head and trying to keep her still. Her soul feels tight in Valerie's body, having entered through her stomach. While the fetus was in the womb, Valerie's soul didn't want to go into the baby or the womb itself and waited until the last minute. However, she stated that she was ultimately excited to be in this body and ready to dance. She's eager to begin!

During her preliminary past life session, Valerie entered the body of a white man named Hafiz. As a child, he once dented a big barrel, and his father told him to fix it. He did a really good job, though he never went to school because he worked with his dad. He wanted to work for himself, so he lived and worked in the same place, far from his family. In his free time, he enjoyed drinking and dancing, even though there were no women around when Hafiz danced.

He progressed into his 40s with wrinkled, dirty, and worn hands from working. He wore work clothes and worked with metal. He smoked a pipe and lived and worked in a barn. He was a solitary person who worked mostly by himself and lived simply. Over the course of his life, he increasingly developed carpentry and other construction skills. He had shielded himself from interactions with people, preferring his own company and keeping life simple.

At a point during middle age, Hafiz started a project at the home of a woman named Berdette. The woman's name might have been "Berdette", though Bernadette and Marie also come to mind. She was a widow who was gentle and compassionate and who developed a deep caring for Hafiz. She called him by his last name, Hafiz, and he thought she was pretty. He enjoyed working on her house, but he didn't feel he had anything to offer her. She brought him food, and he knew she liked him. He learned to open his heart to her, and his life expanded with this relationship, which resulted in the two living together.

Taking Valerie to an older age of Hafiz, Valerie started to cry. They were deeply in love but only for a short time. He felt both loving and loved, and their relationship flourished until her sudden death about a year into their living together. The woman had died, and Hafiz lived alone in the house. He was devastated to lose her and retreated into his shell for the remainder of his life. At 70, Hafiz felt too old to do anything, though he wasn't sick. He was sad and lonely, reflecting on the good life they had together, despite having no children. He learned about the bliss and heartache of being open to love, and this was what he shared with Valerie.

> C: I learned to live in a very small world because I could control it. I was so afraid of losing control, particularly over my emotions. As Hafiz, I felt love in a new way that encouraged me to be open to Berdette and no longer fear. But the loss of her was devastating. I wanted to follow her and was so happy to be reunited with her and feel the joy of that connection.
>
> F: What can you share with Valerie about your life lessons?
>
> C: I restricted my environment to keep life simple for me and to keep from feeling. Don't place these restrictions on your heart and choose work over being with people you love because you will miss so much. Had I been more open, I might have met Bernadette earlier and had more time with her. As it was, I experienced love and emotions I had kept myself from feeling from knowing, and I didn't need to be so self-protective. In the end, it hurt even more when I lost her. Don't do this to you.

Awake now, Valerie reflected on Hafiz's hard work. His father thought he was punishing Hafiz for jumping, kicking, and hitting the barrel until it broke. He gave Hafiz tools to fix it, and Hafiz repaired it better than before. This impressed his father, who began giving Hafiz more tasks to develop his skills. Hafiz had dirty hands with creases filled with dirt and wore a jacket that looked like a suit jacket but wasn't.

The woman really liked Hafiz and brought love into his life. Hafiz, focused on his work, initially didn't recognize her loving actions. She introduced him to kindness and warmth, persistently bringing food to him when he wouldn't come inside to eat. Despite Hafiz's grumpiness, her patience and kindness eventually brought joy and balance into his life. When she died, Hafiz was devastated. He thought she was so pretty, and Hafiz felt empty without her, not wanting to live anymore. They had no children together. Valerie becomes emotional as she remembers this and begins to cry.

Valerie then acknowledges her workaholic tendencies, often doing too much at once and multi-tasking excessively. She has taught her children to work as hard as she does but realizes the need for more balance in her life.

Valerie's takeaways include recognizing her current husband's kindness, gentleness, and love. When her father died, he advised her to stop working and just breathe, giving her permission to pause. Valerie values self-sufficiency but understands the need for balance. She loves dancing, just like Hafiz, and suffers from migraines. She feels she entered her mother's womb right before birth, initially excited about being born.

The journey brought back joyful memories of Elvis for Valerie. She remembered dancing and playing 45s with her older sister and their shared love for Kentucky Fried Chicken's banana cream pie.

In her most recent past life, Valerie was a 36-year-old Caucasian woman named Claudene, living down south in the year 1876. She was happy, pretty, and liked having a good time. With her hair curled and a southern twang in her voice, Claudene wore a long, ruffled dress made by her mother, who was a skilled seamstress.

Claudene lived with her mother in a big house down south, surrounded by big, fluffy trees that provided lots of shade. Her mother was a talented seamstress and made all the beautiful dresses Claudene and all the ladies in town wore. For Claudene, her mother was the most important person in her life. She didn't know what had happened to her father. While attending a Christmas party at her boyfriend's house, she seemed to be unbothered when the boyfriend ignored her. Claudene remained single throughout her life and wouldn't reveal the reason. Claudene finds joy in dancing.

Claudene is now 42, and her mother has passed away, leaving her feeling extremely lonely. Claudene never learned how to sew, she had no children, no sisters, no brothers. A kind black man named Buck has been helping her mother for a long time, taking care of the house and grounds, though he doesn't live there. He insists Claudene keep her mother's sewing machine, recognizing its sentimental value. Claudene appreciates his presence and sees him often, finding some comfort in his company. While she knows how to sew a little, she isn't as skilled as her mother and is not happy. Still living in the house and feeling sad, Claudene realizes she needs to figure out her life.

Claudene is now in her late 50s, around 57 or 58, and still living in the house. Buck remains by her side, helping her manage things. She has started renting out rooms, though she doesn't enjoy it. Despite this, Buck's presence makes life better. He works for Claudene, guiding her and reminding her of who she is, often bringing to mind memories of her mother. Claudene has become a self-made woman, running a boarding house, though she misses having children in this lifetime.

Now 73 or 74, Claudene feels tired all the time. Buck has already passed away, and things have become messy without him. She no longer rents rooms but still lives in the house.

On the last day of her life, Claudene sits on the porch in a chair. When she passed, her mother came for her, and she peacefully went with her and left her body behind. As her spirit left Claudene's body and entered her spiritual home, she felt the contact with her mother Hazel, and her guide, Alfred, who arrived at the gateway. Soon she found herself in touch with family. What was notable about this life initially was that Claudene's mother was Valerie's mother in her current lifetime, and as she engaged more with that life, she could see synchronicity between that life and this one. Claudene wanted to have a family but could not, so she engaged in working with others to support their needs through her service. She was a very spiritual and religious person, which helped her to handle working with the pain and suffering of others. Valerie saw that as Claudene died, there were many unresolved issues and desires that had bled into her current life.

Valerie's soul needs rest and is free from Claudene's physical body. In the distance, two lights appear. Her soul is now moving toward the lights; she feels a comforting warmth. Her guide told her to relax. Valerie's mother, Hazel, is there, and Valerie begins to cry with joy. Her mother offers comfort, filling Valerie with even more happiness. Guided by her mother, Valerie's spirit is led to its next destination, bringing her immense joy.

Valerie starts laughing when she sees her guide, and he starts saying that he's never left her. Her guide reassures her, saying she's got this and that he's always there for her. Although Valerie can't see him, she feels his presence strongly, which brings her comfort. When asked for his name, Valerie puckers her lips and blows out air.

Valerie feels the urge to move forward and stay active.

Valerie can see that Hazel is doing very well since passing and is happy. Hazel loves Valerie deeply and was there waiting for Valerie to find her body when she passed away. Hazel was giggling from above when Valerie tried to bring light into the room after she passed, because Hazel was already in the light. "This is so Valerie", Hazel says.

C: I am so happy that Mom made it. I can see her laughing and telling me that she thought Thomas and I were so funny.

F: What is she telling you?

C: She was watching us from the ceiling above her body, happy to be released. She is having a hard time talking because she is laughing so hard. Now she is saying how silly we looked as we were jumping around, trying to open up the light for her so she could pass.

F: So, the dementia didn't get in the way?

C: Not at all. She's saying that she passed out of her body and was swept into the light and felt an immediate relief of being whole again. I'm so happy for her. (Begins to cry.)

Valerie connects with her dad, Billy Ray, feeling his presence. Valerie's father often mentioned that he thought Valerie was his twin who had died in the womb. He confirmed that only a part of Valerie was his twin and that her fetus had died before birth. Because of their contract with each other, she was then conceived and born as his daughter. She's comforted to know he's alright. Valerie starts to cry, feeling his love. She begins having a conversation with her father, saying, "I am, I promise. I love you". Determined, she tells him, "I can do this", and continues talking inaudibly with her father. Emotion fills her as she silently communicates with him. Valerie was pleased to have this connection explained and confirmed.

Valerie didn't feel the need to talk to her sister, Charlotte, which was surprising because Valerie expressed an urgent need to communicate with her sister when first entering the session.

Valerie then sought out her mother-in-law to learn how she was and how to support her husband in his journey. Willie Mae advises her to give gentle nudges to her son, as she raised him right and appreciates Valerie. Willie Mae is very busy but expresses her fondness for Valerie.

> C: Willie Mae is telling me I'm being too controlling, too directive. I need to reinforce his efforts rather than be so critical. I'm still not sure how to motivate him. Now she's saying that he's hearing me, and he's resisting because of how I'm telling him. She's telling me to relax and let him grow at his own speed.

Valerie's visit to her Council came next. This was a joyous reunion with much joking and laughter. The Council tells her that she's doing too much and trying to make up for things she doesn't need to. They tell her to stop trying to make up for the past. Valerie listens intently, repeating, "Uh-huh", as she understands their messages. She acknowledges that her happiness now comes from her children and feels blessed to have them in this lifetime. To help Trevor, Valerie's son, Valerie needs to focus on her own life and accept that he will make mistakes. Regarding Triona, Valerie's niece, she realizes she must focus on herself and let go of trying to control her path. Repeating, "Okay, I've got it. I must focus on me". Valerie comprehends the Council's advice.

When Valerie asks why she sees spirits, the Council replies, "Get used to it". They explain that she has the capacity to see them, and it will always be a part of her life.

The Council advises Valerie to simplify and meditate to connect with them.

Valerie reiterates her happiness at having children. She realizes that Reggie is there to help her, and Willie Mae smiles in approval. Valerie feels grateful and understands that he is here to support her when needed.

C: They keep repeating the same message over and over: Simplify! I can see that I am trying to live Claudene's life and mine and make up for what she was unable to do, and it is so complicated.

F: What are you trying to complete for her?

C: Claudene felt she let people down because she didn't finish her plans to support them. I feel the same way, which is why I have been thinking about opening a day program for the elderly. My guides are telling me that I don't need to live Claudene's life; I just need to embrace mine.

F: So, what are you to focus on?

C: Family. Claudene didn't have children and I do, and they are my priority. If I focus on what is important to me in this lifetime, it should be my family first. After all, Claudene didn't have one beyond her mother, and I do.

F: So, where does work fit into your plans?

C: I need to balance work with the time I devote

to Reggie and my children and grandchildren. I see that they are the most important things in my life now. I will still always want to help people, but I can't do it at the expense of what is most important to me, which is what I have been doing.

As Valerie reviewed her questions concerning her life, one message came through over and over: Simplify! As she reviewed her choices, she was reminded of what is important in this lifetime – her family, the well-being of those with whom she is close, and her faith. Her guides pointed out that she seemed to be continuing Claudene's life into her life, which was unnecessary. While Claudene had plans for working with needy people at the time of her death, Valerie did not need to act on them. In fact, Valerie could release all of Claudene's life goals and simply live her life now.

Upon emerging from hypnosis, Valerie initially wishes to return, then laughs. She looks back at the session and realizes that she had been trying to compensate for not having children in her past life and for lacking social skills and sewing knowledge. The Council's message to move forward resonates with her. Valerie learned to sew from her mother, Hazel, in this life because she hadn't as Claudene. She also enjoys hosting big parties but recognizes her need for solitude and rest. It is time to simplify so she can receive more guidance while focusing on her own life. Valerie understands now what she didn't before. She kept her mother's sewing machine in this life, symbolizing her acceptance and growth.

Approximately a year after our sessions, I received a call from Valerie. She and her husband had just returned from Paris, where they visited places, her mother loved. Valerie had wanted to leave small amounts of her mother's ashes at her favorite places. In Paris, she visited a bookstore her mother always visited when she was there. Valerie found a crack alongside a staircase that was not likely to be disturbed. She dropped a small amount of her mother's ashes in the crack, said a prayer, and took a picture of the staircase as a memento. When she returned home, she looked at the pictures and then called me to tell me about this experience.

As she looked at the staircase photo, she saw a framed poem hanging on the wall. She enlarged the picture to read it and was blown away. The poem was by the Persian poet Hafez. He wrote inspirational poems about the limitations of human life and perception and the limitless joy of God and the world beyond life. She remembered her first past life experience as Hafiz and the amazing similarities of the name and the message: life's pains can get in the way of what is real, and when we open to love, we are able to receive more than we can imagine.

Valerie told me about her experience and the poem and how it made her sessions mean so much more. Finding this poem reinforced to her how right it was to follow her path and to be reflective. Discovering there really was a Hafez, though spelled differently, reinforced to her that she was paying attention to messages and gifts she was receiving for the continued enjoyment of her life in this lifetime, letting go of the sorrows and regrets of other times in other bodies. She mentioned that she was very happy and that her relationship with her husband and children was great. She had been following the path of simplification. Life was so much better and smoother for her and her husband, who was also simplifying his path. Valerie reinforced how important these sessions had been to her in shifting her priorities to what matters now – family.

At the time I am writing this narrative, I have just learned from Valerie that her 27-year-old son Trevor was killed recently. She has been devastated by his loss. She was grateful to have refocused her energies on her children and grandchildren instead of persisting in working towards external goals that drew her time and energy away from them. Her letting-go of life goals that were not from this lifetime freed her to be more present and loving in this lifetime.

# LIFE FROM DIFFERENT PERSPECTIVES

## Lisbeth Lysdal

Three years after the death of her older brother, Clara is still experiencing her grief. In every aspect of her life, she feels something important is missing. At the age of 68, she had lost other family members and a few friends. This time it was different, and she still does not understand why. Her brother, Peter, made a lot of choices in his life that she did not understand, and part of her always felt sorry for him. During their adult lives, they spent very little time together. She had always felt a strong connection to Peter, even stronger than to her twin brother, Carl.

She hoped that an LBL session would bring clarity and help her to let go of the grief and the empty void inside of her.

For a lot of people, the loss of a family member is what brings them to an LBL session. For Clara, who believes firmly in the existence of a spiritual realm, this is why she came.

Clara wanted to gain knowledge and understanding from the session to enhance the choices she made. Throughout her life, she has made choices she felt were necessary, even if they were not considered normal or even acceptable. She uses her intuition and feels guided, and yet she does not understand the challenges life has brought her. She grew up always feeling protected and safe with her twin brother, with whom she shared most of her early life. She really wanted to understand her connection to her brothers, especially to Peter. Often meeting with a lost loved one in an LBL session brings peace and makes it easier to come to terms with that loss. In this case, it turned out to be more than that. Clara was reconnected to herself and her brother in a way we had not expected.

The session brought Clara back to a warm, safe, and secure time with her brother, Carl, in the womb. She felt a certainty that this life was going to be a nice break from the steep learning curve she had chosen in other lifetimes.

When moving back further to her previous life, she is just a baby, almost 8 months old. Her name is Anita, and she is looking at her mother from the stroller. Her mother is crying. She feels instinctively that she is the reason her mother is upset. Her mother is poor and cannot afford to raise a baby on her own. At that moment, the mother pushes the stroller over the edge of a cliff, and Anita falls. People are rushing toward the mother, but it is too late. Anita leaves the small body, feeling at peace with what just happened. She knew it was the plan, and she could let go. She feels sorry for her mother but knows she is supposed to move on. She also feels relieved that this short life is over. As she moves on and up, she sees arms of every skin color reaching to bring her home. Upon entering the spirit realm, she is greeted by her mother in her current lifetime.

F: Do you recognize anyone?

C: I recognize them. It is my mother, Clara's mother. She is beautiful with soft blue eyes and milky white skin. She tells me that I saw her just after she died. She did not have to take the form of my mother because she knew I would recognize her. I asked her if she was with Peter, and she was. My brother Peter is here too. She tells me that being together is different here. She tells me everything is as it should be.

F: Do you recognize the next soul coming to greet you?

C: No. He is violet. Oh, it is Mutar, and he is coming to show me something. He leads me to a meadow. It feels like we are moving in slow motion. The meadow is full of flowers; the sky is blue with small white clouds. The sun is shining, and there are butterflies. Butterflies are everywhere. It is a wonderful place. We move towards a large gate and lights are emerging from the cracks in it.

Mutar brings Xani (Clara's soul name) through a landscape of mountains and rivers that represent the feelings from previous lifetimes. After the guided tour of her past lives, he takes her to three different places to experience three different states of being. In the first she experiences freedom, then independence and finally, harmony.

Then Mutar tells Xani, it is time to visit the Council.

F: Do you want to go there now?

C: I am already there. The light is dim, and I

have this floating sensation. I can see entities in a line in front of me. It's the Elders. You can ask their advice, though you do not have to use the guidance you receive. I meet with them when I am in doubt or need direction. Five of them are waiting for me – 3 in the front row and 2 behind them. I stand in front of them. They have similar features and are all wearing the same kind of cape. They are always loving and kind. The one in the middle of the front row greets me with, 'Welcome back!' They know everything.

F: What do they have to say?

C: I have a question for them. I would really like to know whether I have to go back. Am I supposed to live another life after the life as Clara? Oh. They tell me that it is really up to me, my choice. They are quite satisfied with the way I live my life as Clara. They even tell me that they are happy with the insights I have gained in this life. The life as Clara was meant to be an easy one. A life of rest and play, yet I have immersed myself in topics I learned about in previous lifetimes. I am told to remember that this life is a break and what I need to know will come to me when needed.

F: Do they have anything to say about the life as Anita?

C: I needed that short life. We needed it, Anita's mother and me. There was a connection between us. A connection from a life we shared where the love between us was impossible. We were tied to religious expectations, and that made our love impossible. Impossible. We were nuns, and we fell in love. This was hundreds of years ago. We had to break free and be able to move on during our incarnations. We had to let go of the belief that in physical life, love is impossible.

F: Do the elders have anything to say about impossible love?

C: They say love is always possible. There are many kinds of love, but none of them are impossible. I know this. I know it in the life of Clara. I lived it in my marriage to a man that turned out to be a homosexual. They tell me there are no levels, no grades; it is not a competition. There are insights and just different aspects of insights.

F: Why are they telling you this?

C: It is about my relationship with my friend. We experienced being on a journey together. I let go of his pace, which is faster than mine. He does not yet understand that it is all about the experience, not the pace.

F: Do they have anything else for you Xani?

C: It is like my mother told me in the beginning. Everything is as it should be.

F: Tell me Xani, is it possible for you to meet Peter on this journey?

C: He is already here. Oh, I have missed him so much. We did not see each other a lot, but I really miss him like crazy. He says it was supposed to happen, that he should die so quickly.

F: Can he tell you what the reason was for him to leave the incarnation as Peter?

C: He was supposed to learn to stand his ground, even if it had consequences. Now he has gained the insights he needed.

140

F: Xani can you tell me his spiritual name, the name of this soul?

C: We are the same. It is like we are the same soul, but we are not the same. We are the same soul!

F: What percentage of your soul energy was incarnated as Peter, Xani?

C: 40%, the same as Clara. Even if you are one, you can be two. I asked the Elders, and they told me that the same soul can incarnate in several bodies. However, you do not always know the other person. Peter and I did.

It helped me learn and understand. I always understood his way of behaving and the things he did. Even when he hurt my family, I understood at a deeper level.

No matter how you grow up, no matter what circumstances, life is made up from the choices you make. You have to trust and follow what you know is right. As Clara, I did that, followed my intuition, and broke free. Peter remained stuck. It is important to understand that both options exist and understand and accept the choices made by each.

The session went on to integrate the soul parts into one connected soul with different experiences. The turn the session took was unexpected, and yet the deep soul connection between the siblings explains the severe grief. The session brought about an intense understanding that every choice is a way to gain an experience. Every experience is inherently valuable. The visit to the past life as Anita and the deep connection to another soul that had to be concluded was a beautiful way of illustrating the difference between two connected souls and a single soul incarnated in different bodies. This session serves as a wonderful reminder that we should let go of our assumptions, as we do not know the whole story until we explore further.

# Concluding Insights
## on Understanding Loss & Grief

L oss and grief are universal experiences that deeply impact our lives, challenging our sense of identity and purpose.

Grief encompasses a range of emotions and can manifest physically, cognitively, and spiritually.

Healing from grief is challenging but transformative, requiring acknowledgment and acceptance of emotions.

Self-care practices, such as mindfulness and connection with loved ones, play a crucial role in the healing process.

Ultimately, healing from grief involves finding meaning and purpose in our experiences, honoring the memory of loved ones, and embracing life with gratitude and appreciation.

"During hypnosis, my subjects do recall frustration at being unable to effectively use their energy to mentally touch a human being who is unreceptive due to shock and grief. Emotional trauma of the living may overwhelm their inner minds to such an extent that their mental capabilities to communicate with souls are inhibited. When a newly departed soul finds a way to give solace to them however briefly, they usually are satisfied and want to move on quickly away from Earth's astral plane".[6]

Sanela Čović
Editor

---

# CHAPTER FOUR

## ON HEALING

# INTRODUCTION
## on Healing

L BL sessions can offer physical, psychological, emotional, and spiritual healing opportunities. Remaining open to all possibilities and accepting what is freely offered helps to manifest healing in the soul realm and here on Earth. What better way is there for us, as incarnated beings in a physical dimension, to choose paths of awareness and restoration toward wholeness and to maximize our chances for healing while experiencing, exploring, and learning through our humanity?

For our clients, the gift of healing exemplifies the loving care that Source, the Council, spirit guides, soul group members, and the soul realm itself willingly bestow during an LBL session and beyond. Feeling a profound sense of belonging and of being unconditionally loved and accepted can be healing in and of itself. Knowing we are never alone and are always supported by the spiritual realm is of great comfort. Trust in the process of life is inspired to unfold naturally like the petals of a beautiful flower. Understanding oneself, issues one is working on, others and relationship dynamics on a deeper level can cultivate a level of wisdom virtually unattainable through the intellect alone. Great restoration can occur within the blessing of these higher perspectives in the soul realm and be actualized by their transferability and application in physicality.

Clients often ask to be healed during an LBL session, and even if they don't, the soul realm freely offers healing interventions. Because a physical incarnation often leaves residual denseness or debris in a soul as it leaves Earth's plane, in the soul state, a spirit guide typically shows them to a "chamber of light," a "waterfall of light," or a "fountain of healing crystalline light." Sometimes, it appears as a clear spring or pool. This light may appear as physical water yet is not wet; it can have a distinct color or be white, known for containing all colors. The idea is to immerse one's soul in this light to become cleansed, restored and whole. Spirit guides, Council members, or other souls may envelop a soul with their healing, loving light. Other souls say they are going to their place of "healing," "restoration," or "renewal," unique for them.

These experiences are authentic because of the client's physical sensations, such as tingling or vibrating, and the visible glow they often exhibit emanating from their body. Healing in the soul realm may be accompanied by shaking, trembling, and tears. Clients frequently become extremely hot at this point, and blankets are kicked and tossed off. Practitioners can feel a shift in energy within the room. At times, there is a fresh and ethereal aroma like newly fallen snow. Post-session interviews with clients over time typically report that some noticeable form of healing has transpired.

Although commonalities are found in the healing experiences that occur in the soul realm during an LBL, there can also be differences. For example, some souls immerse themselves in a realm of sound, tones, or music to access different frequencies and renew their energies. Other souls go to a "healing team" or group of souls whose focus is the dissolution of wounds or restoration. LBL therapy can inspire and support clients to heal and release whatever does not serve them and to gently remove blocks or whatever holds them back in the highest multidimensional ways. While healing is usually an ongoing process or journey in one's lifetime and involves continued development or evolution as a soul, experiencing an LBL session, which provides new perspectives, spiritual resources, encouragement, support, guidance, and most of all, unconditional love in its purest form, can be invaluable.

As souls, healing and wholeness are our birthright. During an LBL session, we are made more aware of this by experientially recognizing we are part of a greater whole: we are One with Source or Creator. As we navigate in our purified form through the soul realm, we can explore wounds of any nature, note our reasons for choosing them, understand and learn what we need to, and access deep and lasting healing simply by seeking or asking for it. At times a spirit guide may indicate that an issue needs further work, yet the support and guidance are lovingly provided. As the mystic Rumi has been quoted to say, "The wound is the place where the Light enters you." Here, Rumi helps us to remember that even our deepest wounds, which may imprint on our souls' energies from lifetime to lifetime, can guide us to an experience of spiritual awakening. Additionally, we can offer healing to each other on Earth and beyond.

Elizabeth Lockhart
Editor

# DEEP HEALING:
## A Shift in Perception Away

### Eric J. Christopher

Emily came to me at age 65 in need of healing as well as answers as to why she had incarnated into her abusive current life family. She was a therapist herself who had experienced a lot of healing modalities in her life ever since intense memories of trauma surfaced in her early 30s. She felt bitter, angry, and in a dark, stuck place from her life experience of growing up in a home saturated with physical, emotional, and sexual abuse. She had a termination of pregnancy at age 12 after being molested. Her words were, "I feel a deep sense of hopelessness. My life was taken from me. How do I get it back? I've never felt supported, ever. I feel I've pushed myself through my lifetime and have no push left. Why is it like this?"

She set the intention to see a life that could most help her heal before going into the life beyond. She experienced her past life as a young girl named Elizabeth, who was raised in a very loving family. She felt confident and excited about being in the world. She loved school and eventually became a teacher before marrying a loving and supportive man and having two children. They ultimately moved in with her parents, who were there to help raise her children while Elizabeth and her husband took over the family farm. After her death, she was struck by how bonded her family was. She explained, "Such connectedness – communication was always there!"

As she drifted deeper into the spirit world, she was surrounded by loving beings and, soon after, a sense of oneness.

> F: What are you noticing or experiencing at this moment?
>
> C: I'm surrounded by different energies, and I am being filled up … now I'm diffusing into formlessness. There's a symphony of beautiful colors and sounds, and I'm all of it … not even separate … pure "beingness" … being with that from which everything arises! I see sacred geometry and feel the different energies of these shapes, and I am the space within which it all happens – a universe unto myself. I am Home!

Eventually, Emily experienced a deep communion with her main guide. I asked what could be known about her decision to incarnate into her current family. Her guide responded to her, and then Emily shared her insights: "To achieve what you did and will do, you had to experience the worst of humanity. Otherwise, you would have settled for breadcrumbs."

C: Emily had to lose herself to gain herself back again. She would have settled for so much less. Someone in the lineage had to make a bold move. I committed I wouldn't pass on the abuse. I had to swim in the toxicity until I figured a way out. I chose it – someone had to –to heal the generational line. With awareness, I can now be a conduit to send the healing energy up and down the line.

F: What will living your life from this new level of consciousness look like and feel like?

C: Wholeness. I can now bring the energies of Home back to my current life. I won't feel empty anymore. I will be filled with something that sustains me and enlivens others. There is more than enough substance of my True Self to fill me and everyone else in my life so it will no longer feel like I never really existed.

Two days after the session, Emily shared in an email about how healing and shifting it was to feel the effects of growing up in a loving and supportive family … quite the opposite of what she lived through in her current life:

*A door has been opened that was never available to me. I tapped into what it felt like to experience the effects of being raised in a family where mom and dad radiated love and acceptance to each other and their children, where my thoughts and feelings were hopeful and anticipatory of good because of the prevailing trust between me and my parents, where the looks in the eyes of my family beamed 'I am here for you – I am hearing you – I am listening' and the sense of being a whole person unto myself who got to have her ideas and beliefs, and experiment with what was possible. It was as familiar as having blood flow through my body. A life experience of that is now available to me.*

Ten days after the session, I received a further email from Emily. She wrote,

> *My life has been altered in a miraculous manner—there's no other way for me to say it. I was guided to a miraculous outcome. I thought there was no way out. I've been liberated and have come to know how to love, forgive, and accept myself.*

Emily wrote four months after the session:

> *I replayed the recording of the LBL session again and felt the energies of 'Home' flood through me again.*

We are multidimensional beings, and so deep healing can be a perception shift away. Sometimes, all it takes is to go on a deep inner journey into the higher dimensions of the spirit realm and our own "more permanent" being. Following her session, Emily no longer identified solely with the body/mind personality of her current life. She described her LBL experience as one of the greatest gifts she could ever experience.

# CHILL AND GLOW

## Diana Paque, PhD

**M**arly bounced into my office, ready for her past life and Life Between Lives journeys. She is a 25-year-old entrepreneurial coach who embodies enthusiasm and life force. She was encouraged to see me by her mentor, who helped her learn more about aspects of herself beyond this incarnation and supported her in her choices of direction in this life.

Marly's questions coming into her sessions were about where she should live and work. While she was born and has continuing connections in the Netherlands, she is international in her work and currently resides in Tenerife.

She is attempting to decide about her work, relationships, and where and how to focus her energies over the next several years. She is surrounded by intense light energy and hopefulness that she knows only a little about, so she wants to understand more about those aspects of her being. She has always felt that she is "a bit more" than others and wants to

154

know about the energies she perceives and feels in her body and world.

As we went into her first past life, she became Michael, a 34-year-old man. He regressed into childhood, aware of being alone but with a single mom who works. He moved quickly through childhood to 16 years old and felt life unfolded for him. He feels invisible in society but has a clear sense of himself. He has spent time by himself, invested in his studies and science, and is very cerebral. He lives in his head for the most part, although he appears to have normal social relationships and interacts in normal ways with others in his living environment.

As he ages, he finds himself living in an apartment with a view of the park. He spends a lot of time in the park, exercising and interacting with others. He also has good relations with his building neighbors, although none of these are intimate relationships. At 34, he spends most of his time in his apartment and his head. His apartment is devoid of clutter, which suits him, and he finds peace in the minimalism surrounding him as he works. Most of his time, he reads and synthesizes the works of others, writing his findings and thoughts – his work consumes him and his energies. Also, at 34, he has a scientific epiphany that opens up his understanding of his conceptualization of the whole of his work and connections. This seems to have been enhanced by a woman with whom he had recently begun to share his work and with whom he gained an increased vision of the scope of his findings and concepts.

He reaches 40 and dies suddenly. He has no negative feelings about dying so young except for the impact that it has on people in his world. He had not developed an interest in intimate relationships until he met his now friend and colleague Maria, with whom he learned he could share his trueness. She encouraged him to think beyond himself and be open to additional input into his conceptualizations, and, as a result, they developed a deeper and more intimate bond. He regrets that it took him to the end of his life to experience this and sees how grateful he is to have experienced both the passion of his work and the intimacy of a deep relationship.

Marly came the next day for her LBL session. We moved quickly into her most immediate past life. She noticed that most of her awareness was on a feeling level without many visual details. She became a 45-year-old man who is very muscular and appears to be someone who does physical labor. She notes that he has a wife and children but can't give much detail. We take him back to childhood; he is eight years old in Argentina, surrounded by a big family living on a ranch – a very charismatic mom and many people at the dinner table. Family is an essential element of Luis' life – he says he is in school, but he's not the smartest, but he appreciates that he is quite funny. He lives on a ranch with an extended family, and life is based on the ranch and the family.

As he grows older, he says he was 14 and was in school, but he didn't feel it was his place. He likes being outside on the ranch and is stimulated by being part of the family and supporting their common goals. When asked about his passions, he says he's never thought about them—he stays present in life as it is and is good with animals.

He moves to 25 years old and is quite strong now, still going outside and working; life is still the same, except he is thinking about getting married at some point, although he isn't chasing anyone. "I'm a loyal guy."

F: What is life about?

156

C: It's about family, about helping others, mostly about being there and doing what I can, taking care of my people and my environment.

At 45, he has his own children and loves being a father. It's so nice to see them grow and to teach them about life. He has three children—two boys and a girl. He and his wife, Joy, are very compatible—she is caring and takes care of the cleaning; he feels that she is caring and soft, comfortable, and sweet. He has a good relationship with Joy.

He still lives on the ranch but is in his own house with his family, and his parents are still around. He says he is religious as they always pray before meals, and that's something that he's done his entire life. Connecting with God is part of something he learned growing up; it feels safe.

F: What thoughts do you have about this life you are living? What do you think about those things?

C: How can I make life the best for my children, get food on the table for them, and teach them life's lessons?

His life is relatively peaceful—it's not so close to politics that the world doesn't heavily impact it outside his immediate world.

F: Is there anything missing in your life?

C: Well, it is a bit mundane; in a way, I feel my children's joy, which is most important to me. The connections with my family are peaceful. I work with my heart through the ups and downs, but life is ok.

I'm 53. I have worked hard all my life, but now

I have a cloud over me. My children are older—they are good kids and have taken over more of the work. They have the load, and I'm no longer burdened. I take more time to do other things, help my wife, and play with my grandkids.

Physically, I am strong, but the sun has darkened my skin, and I am just noticing this as I slow down. I wear glasses now, but otherwise, I'm good.

As he ages, he sees himself at 67, 69 and 74. Life is much the same with others doing most of the work, and he likes sharing his knowledge. He's spending time reflecting.

C: I'm happy, satisfied, and peaceful.

Working for the common good of your family, putting your energy into places that count, and giving your love through your work. He feels so grateful for having a large family that has stayed together in this natural setting.

On the last day of his life, he's in bed, and the house is quiet. He's in a wide bed, and only his wife is there. He wanted it this way.

C: I'm an old guy, and my body is failing.

His wife has back problems but is otherwise well. The family knows he's leaving but is giving them space. He floats away from his body and to the top of the room.

C: My wife is holding my hand and crying, but I see only her – we wanted to be alone together at this point.

Everyone is sad, but they also have positive memories of him. He says goodbye to his wife and that everything is all right. He then goes and says goodbye to his boys. He sees many of the people he touched are around to say goodbye.

C: I feel dragged away but I feel like staying forever.

F: What do you choose to do now?

C: I have a hard time choosing because of all the love around me.

I remind him that he can continue to be with them in spirit and still go home. I remind him that his guide is there to support him and is surrounding him with the light and love of home.

As he moves into the light, he releases the Earth to go with his guide.

C: Rafi is a very funny guy. He is charismatic. He wears a purple wizard's hat with stars and a robe. He is a serious person, but he likes to make fun—to show his smartness but make fun of it.

As Marly begins to review Luis's life with Rafi, his guide, he finds that it was very positive and that there were lots of compliments—what can you learn? It's about living this life well.

Luis liked the person he was. He saw himself as a part of the family, and there was always love surrounding him and the work of life.

C: Rafi is saying, "Welcome home, brother."

F: What is he showing you, sharing with you first?

C: There are lots of hugs welcoming me in – lots of compliments and pride for a life well lived.

F: They're happy you're home.

C: I'm happy I'm back too! I want to go to see the rest of my group so I'm asking Rafi how to see them again.

Laughing, he takes Marly to the others in a big room with a big wooden table.

C: There are people cheering for me as I return. They're all happy for me and happy I'm back and hugging me. They're all individuals that I have different relationships with all of them, and some of them I am particularly happy to see. I have a very strong feeling that there is one of them in my life right now.

F: How does he respond to you? Does he know he is in your current life?

C: He is the one with the biggest heart and hug – the longest one. It's funny but I have this idea that there are 8. I feel happiness and connection in the room, very safe and comfortable, but nothing specific beyond this. I have a strong feeling of Michael, and he is very present in the room as a guide – he is my guide in Marly's life. He is here to guide me, to give trust and a sense of rest.

As Marly's soul moves further, she calls on her guide, Rafi. He joins the group and brings her somewhere else—he has this idea of a learning part yet to do, so he is now taking her on a walk.

C: I have this idea that Rafi is teaching me while we are walking – asking me broad questions that make me think – about my life and values – the big questions. Learning comes both through talking and silence. The goal is the walk rather than the destination.

They sit down at the end of the walk, and Marly asks him questions about her life and journey in this incarnation. It's evident to her that he puts on a video with a funny voice that is more extreme about being frenetic and full of activity.

C: CHILL! He tells her. He makes it not uncomfortable – it's funny. He is old and knows the enthusiasm but also knows what it is like to live longer. He is making fun of it in a situational way but not criticizing or being judgmental. There is warmth and peacefulness. He has a warm, deep, and wise voice.

F: Can he tell you about directions along the path that Marly is going?

C: He is very proud that she is doing good, but she just has to trust time and herself.

F: What about other people in Marly's life? Is marriage something upcoming or later.

C: There will be a man who may already be there, who will bring peace and joy, and she will feel it when he is there. She needs to trust her gut – she has a lot of thoughts and stuff, but she knows she needs to trust herself and her intuition.

F: Can he tell you why you were born in this life?

C: Marly wants to know the whole picture, but he is only showing one piece. Marly is very good at connecting with people, and she is here to impact them.

F: How can she impact people?

C: She is doing it already. She has this idea that she needs to be further and faster, but she is already there even more than she realizes.

When he held up a mirror in front of her, she gasped as she saw a picture of her grandmother, who is very old.

F: Anything else he has to share with you?

C: The only thing is he is holding his arm around me. He's always there to protect me.

F: How can you access him in your everyday life?

C: There is a really strange person in Marly's life who I don't really know well who comes up now. I have the feeling that there are many Rafi's on this Earth, so there are many people who are around me to get this support. I'm always supported, always with people with super intention who are here to give me a sense of patience, rest, and safety – they are very grounded and relaxed people who surround me with their safety and peace.

F: Why this family and life for Marly?

C: Lots of similarities with the people at the table: warm, supportive, loving. I think I had lots of doubt when I came in and Rafi sees that I'm so good at what I'm here to do, but I needed safety – given support and safety that I needed right from the beginning.

F: Are you ready to see your Council?

C: Rafi says it's time as well.

As she invites her Council to join her, she has the thought and is there.

C: It's a bit scary like I'm going to American Idol – there are 4 of them, but there is a woman who is super pointy. Three is energy, and she is also energy but different.

I explain that they are here to support you, so they know you have these doubts and fears. And I then asked for Council input.

C: They feel that I feel judged, and they want to remind me that there's no reason to be fearful, so they start to give compliments, and I feel more comfortable.

F: Are they far away?

C: Maybe 3 meters.

F: Are you the same size?

C: Yes

F: Anything they want Marly to know? To be a bit less loud? What is their concern about loudness? There is some sort of dynamic between fear and trust. I feel fear and disappointment, but that isn't what they mean. They are talking about the dynamics between joy and working too hard. Joy is the superpower, and there is a limit; it's like a fireball that glitters and spirals around and leaves glitter, and if there is too much joy, it feels like a job. So, it's something to be supported as part of who you are, not what you do. It isn't meant to be work but simply an expression of Marly.

As Marly engages with this superpower of Joy, she begins to sense it in her body and feel it in her being. She also begins to connect with her memories in other dimensions, where she was glowing energy and glittering in her being, without needing to perform or do anything out of the ordinary. She is beginning to learn that in previous incarnations in other life forms, this is what she is; yet, coming into human form, she lost the clarity and simplicity of Joy for its state of being and has pursued it as work rather than as part of her beingness.

I ask her about her purpose in this lifetime.

She responds that she is to enjoy the joy, not about giving it first, which is also what she is here to do.

C: When I enjoy it, it will be more contagious, as before.

F: And Marly's purpose?

C: Be the joy and let other people feel it within themselves – it's obvious.

F: When do you know it's good enough? Does it need to be perfect before sharing?

C: They say that there's always more than enough – limitless joy, and when they say this, I also shift within the space that I am, and I transfer from a little girl to a wise woman. It's funny they're giving me a feeling of this shift that I can feel in my body. The colors that I see are gold and purple. Like Rafi. (She giggles)

F: How can Marly find balance in her life with work, service, and life and relationships?

C: Discover your heart of joy – the more joy, the more it all makes sense. There is no such thing as balance, so when you are joyful, it is all whole.

F: Marly is concerned about when things happen. What can they share with you?

C: It seems very contradictory to Marly right now, but everything is about relationships. And the fun thing is that they are already in her life. In the end it is about the other people, and she will draw them to her when she is joy; it is very obvious somehow.

F: Are there different spaces for relationships of various kinds?

C: Yes.

F: Where do they fit in her life and on her path?

C: It's unclear. It seems like they are giving me a picture with golden glitter, and there are some levels with some people closer and further away from the source. It is from very far away as if I were in the air, so I can't see distinctly.

F: Then your Council isn't worried about this?

C: Yes, that's right, and they are sure it will happen.

F: What about where she lives and works?

C: They're snickering, you'll figure it out – they're laughing at the smallness of the question – it's part of being human to ask these stupid human questions – Rafi is laughing in the background. They say one word with sarcasm: "Sure, live where you are present."

F: Are there experiences or lessons she is here to work on?

C: Yes, it is unclear, but there is a very strong picture filled with golden glitter, and I'm in the sky looking at the effect of this joy on everything. It is also about a feeling of acceptance—not a cloud of pink, but golden glitter. I'm here to bring true joy—Marly should have more joy doing this. She is meant to be super fun and joyful and in a personal space of joy. She has time to be this; it's all alright.

F: Do you have any questions for them?

C: How could Marly have more fun? They're laughing again – you ask all these obvious questions, even the pointy lady ... you know how to have fun ... you don't need to worry about these things. They're anchoring Marly's whole lifetime again and designed Marly to have a strong gut feeling as a compass. They are reinforcing these tools and resources. These are parts of me from before that Marly needs to use now.

F: What about the pointy lady? She is different from the others.

C: She is here to help with the details. Like what? She isn't clear, and she says things that I don't understand. It makes me feel like a little kid, and I know that I am a wise lady. I don't understand her way of communication yet.

F: Can they give you a clue about your soul's journey and your progress on that journey as Marly?

C: It's about making it easier and more fun. They are giving her a feeling of what she is. I'm trying to connect the dots among the lives, and when I try, the feelings disappear. The soul wants to teach others to be okay without teaching; it encourages learning without teaching, opening up opportunities to learn rather than teaching coming from who you are in your highest self.

As Marly finishes her journey and discussions with her Council, she returns to her current incarnation, with a greater sense of the glitter she felt around her but now permeating her being. She expresses relief and excitement about the "work" that lies ahead of her and expresses the differences in her sense of herself as she now recognizes parts of her from other times and dimensions that are very much part of her in this lifetime.

As she left, she commented that she would have to learn how to chill and simply be joyous without working at it like a job that took all the fun out of the experience. And she floated out of the room with a glittery glow of connection that made her seem even younger than her actual 25 years.

# A MESSAGE FOR LIFE
## Purpose & Healing a Long-term Illness

### Jerry Joseph, PhD

Melanie, an attractive woman in her early forties, asked for an LBL session because she had been dealing with chronic Lyme disease since she was fourteen, and she had twice started law school only to drop out because of her health. She was still determining whether this was the path she was supposed to be on. She had worked in a number of jobs in different states in the U.S., and she was now starting training in Reiki. She also wondered whether a friendship with a man she had met some years before when he was married would blossom into a relationship now that he had divorced and had reached out to her.

In the past life session two weeks before her LBL session, she saw herself as a man who was part of a theatrical troupe supported by a noblewoman who lived in a nearby castle during medieval times. In this lifetime, he lost his father when he was quite young and then lost his mother only a few years later. He missed them terribly, but then he joined the acting troupe soon after he had lost his mother, and they had provided him with companionship. When he was young, he married another troupe member, and they had a baby. During this time, he was the happiest he had ever been. Then they lost the baby, and during the following year, he lost his wife from heartbreak. Although he remained alone and sad, he stayed with the acting troupe until he died in his early fifties. Members of the troupe, and even the noblewoman, had tried to involve him in life again, but he remained unhappy and alone steadfastly.

Melanie then returned for her LBL session. The past life Melanie went to as the prelude to her LBL experience appeared to take place in a frontier period in the U.S., and she saw herself as a 10-year-old girl, happily helping her mother cook supper in a log cabin. In three subsequent scenes, she saw that she had an older brother who she liked and helped her father with his fur trapping work. In the second scene, her brother leaves to work in a different area that offers more opportunities, which saddens her. In the third scene, when she is now eighteen, he returns to see the family, and they celebrate, although he is leaving again. She said the celebration made her happy, but it was tinged with sadness because she knew he wouldn't stay long. In the final scene, which occurred only a year or so later, she was in the attic of a cabin looking for something (she wasn't sure what it was) when the attic door jammed, and she couldn't get out. She looked out the window and saw a forest fire approaching her. She moved toward a far corner, where she died from smoke inhalation rather than being burned.

After she passed, she said that she felt herself moving away from the cabin where she had died. She then told me that she had stopped moving. I suggested that she ask for assistance from her guide, and she said that a spirit being had shown up. She said he feels "like a friend, familiar, but not close". He was asking her whether she was "ready to go". I suggested that she say yes, and then she found herself in a classroom setting with this being whom she now recognized as her guide. He gave her information about her brother, who had life just passed, saying that they had incarnated together before. Then, they began discussing her current life as Melanie. She was told that a woman would come into her life who would help her. As a sign, the woman would be wearing a quartz necklace. Also, she was told that her health would improve if she would eat more berries. When the discussion ended, I asked what color she saw when she looked at her guide. She said that he was giving off a green energy, and I said that would indicate that he was a spirit interested in healing. I suggested that this would appear appropriate since Melanie was told she was a healer. Then I asked if there was another place that she might go to get additional guidance about her current life as Melanie.

C: We're going toward a building that looks like a courthouse.

F: Okay, keep going and tell me what happens there.

C: There are three spirit beings on some kind of dais.

F: This appears to be your Council of Elders. What do they look like?

C: They're very old-looking and dressed in whitish robes.

F: Is your guide with you?

C: He is here somewhere, but not right beside me.

F: Okay, tell me what they tell you.

In the ensuing conversation that lasted nearly an hour and a half with the Council, which is somewhat unusual in its length, they proceeded to tell Melanie that the chronic Lyme Disease she suffered from was needed so that her health problems could be used to keep her away from a career in law which was not what she should be doing in this life. They told her that she had been a healer in some of her past lives, and healing was the vocation that would be best for her in this life. They laughed at her efforts to get back into law school a second time when they had worked so hard to keep her from attending law school the first time. They said that she would not have felt happy and fulfilled in the law profession but would be happy and fulfilled doing healing work.

During the conversation, the Council showed her different problems and issues she had encountered so far in her current life and how they helped her work her way through them. They said they had allowed her to learn how to work through her difficulties, but they had pulled her back when the difficulties would have been too problematic. They went on to say that she should continue her training in Reiki, that she should remain aware of opportunities to expand her work to reach a larger population, and that her relationship with the man who had now reappeared in her life might or might not develop into a deeper relationship, but that they would always be friends. They also said that if she continued the healing regimen she had started for her health, she would be healed completely.

When this session with her Council appeared to be over, her guide reappeared beside her, and I asked if she would like to see some people close to her in her current life. She said that she would like to do that. In the following conversations, she met with her mother, who gave her support and encouragement; her grandmother, who talked about some recipes (Melanie got a chuckle out of this); and her brother from her life in the cabin, who also gave her encouragement. A close friend in this life also showed up, and Melanie believed that this person was the baby who had died in medieval life. I asked if his wife from that time was in her current life, and Melanie said that it did not appear so.

At this point, I could tell that Melanie seemed to be getting a little tired, so I asked if there was somewhere else that she wanted to go or if she thought that she had gotten what she needed. She responded that she believed she had learned what she needed to learn, and she was ready to end the session.

After bringing her back into the present, we processed what she had seen and heard in the session. She said that her guide had been helpful and supportive. She then relayed that the conversation with her Council had been excellent. They had connected so many things and, in the process of making the connections, had explained the reasons for many events and challenges in her life. She said that she was now comfortable with where she was in her life and was looking forward to moving toward the many avenues of healing that she believed would unfold.

# Karma Manifests Physically

## Gayle Barklie

When a woman in her early 60s entered my office, intensity was the word that described her best. She was a Type A overachiever, wanting to evaluate her life and quickly resolve a lengthy list of issues. She had concerns about her marriage's future and was living separately from her husband. It was a challenge to connect emotionally, and she sensed that his primary reason for marriage over a decade ago was to have a stepmother to his four teenage children.

Birdie is a semi-retired botanist who presented with anxiety and depression, manifesting as sleep issues. As a three-year-old, she contracted polio, but there were no physical disabilities remaining from it. However, she has a lingering 'post-polio mindset,' believing she needs to prove herself strong, constantly fighting to survive.

Birdie opened the session, listing several questions.

"I'm curious as to how polio shaped my life because I'm sure I'm carrying residual effects from it. Also, why do I respond to my 90-year-old father as if I'm still a teenager? I want to understand why I can't seem to connect with my husband."

I explained the regression process and led her into a hypnotic state. Dropping through different ages easily, she zeroed in on details from her current life.

"I'm six months old, and I'm being held by my mother. I can smell her breast milk. I feel so deeply bonded with her," she said somewhat wistfully.

I asked her to remember anything about being in utero.

"I see my mother walking in a snowstorm. There is power in her stride. I'm in awe of her," she contemplates this moment with reverie. "I'm there with her, as a spirit, and I'm influencing her. She knows she's having a baby girl and is so joyous!"

I directed her to focus on the body she chose to inhabit.

"It's a good, strong body. It's going to assist in balancing everything I'm going to go through in the future. It's small with big challenges, but there's a good brain/body connection. I chose to experience polio; it feels karmic, but my soul is ready."

She then described being a three-year-old recovering from polio. "It was so restrictive, but I see that it created fortitude and endurance. I decided that hard work equals results. I feel challenged being female like I have more dominant male energy. I've taken on many male roles with this body."

She realized that her 'can do' attitude was getting in the way of her marriage.

"I need to be softer with him since he is all about strength and control. We butt heads being so similar."

Suddenly, she described a reddish-brown male she calls a "tree person". He offered personal advice: "You've been rushing into things. You need to explore the side paths; they might be more interesting!"

"This spirit is well-rooted; he's grounding me and has guided me through many lives," she explained.

This entity led her to remember a lifetime in Paris as a large man wearing pinstriped pants. It's the turn of the century, Revolutionary War time, and he's walking on a bridge going over the River Seine.

"There's a woman with her hand on my left arm holding a parasol. We're close but not intimate. I have a sense of prominence, as if I'm someone important. I'm too independent to let myself get close to this woman. We enjoy being together, but I'm more confident than she is. I'm very protective. In fact, I decided that being bold means being protective and I've been living that belief ever since!"

Birdie went back and forth through various periods and saw other lifetimes in different roles, always with this same woman. She realized that this person is her grown stepdaughter in this lifetime.

"I'm back in the 1800's lifetime, sitting at a large desk. I'm a banker wearing Louis the 14th couture and I'm quite wealthy, privileged, very formal. I'm in charge of determining who is worthy of receiving a loan, and I'm quite harsh about who I choose.

I'm married to the woman I was walking with, but there's no passion, just loyalty."

I directed her to move to the last day of that life.

"I was a good partner, a good provider. It's sad to say goodbye to my wife. She's with me; I'm glad I'm not alone. She served my needs, and I served hers. What an indifferent thing to be thinking!" She felt acceptance about dying but also detached.

What were the lessons from that life?

"Because I was so disconnected, I brought the need to connect into my current life. Since I was judgmental and dismissive of those of lower standings, determining worthiness, I needed to learn humility and compassion. Choosing to have polio taught me that. Plus, it brought loyalty, determination, and strength, and that's how I move through life now."

She continued: "In my current life, it's hard to be around people; they interrupt my peaceful place. I'm always trying to recreate that feeling and never can."

She spontaneously slipped into another memory as a Native American making a fire.

"I'm in nature, and it feels good and peaceful. I'm not happy or sad; I'm just connected to Earth. Man has disconnected from the world, making himself more important than other beings. I just want to be working in harmony with nature, to just BE, working at my own pace, effortlessly. I understand now why I chose my botany career."

Acknowledging those yearnings, the tree person spirit re-emerges.

"Just be in harmony; don't worry," he instructed. He showed her a gathering of colorful stones and called them sacred glass treasures to remind her of this tribal life. "Don't let yourself drift apart. Be a caretaker, a guardian of truth. Use the rocks as symbols of connecting with nature. Remember: Life is about being, not doing."

She pondered his advice and appreciated his important messages.

She was then led to meet her Soul Group, people with whom she repeatedly reincarnated in different roles and learned various lessons.

"I'm seeing my current husband as part of my Soul Group. He's windy, blowing strongly, but needs to learn to be softer. I need to duck from his wind! Like doing tai chi, deflecting and transmuting."

A spirit flashed before her, a friend who passed five years ago. His name was Skee Mai, and he, too, offered advice: "Follow a path of heart, beauty, and spirit. Be rooted and stay true to it. Some detours are okay, but let your heart be your guide. This path will lead to grandmotherhood, your wisdom born of life experiences that will help hold that space for others."

Leaving, he said, "Your spirit's name is Jami, which means firmly planted, connected to Earth, won't blow over." Smiling, he added: "It's okay to take a break from your husband!"

She then met with her Spirit Council, consisting of six females.

"Birdie, remember that truth spoken softly is better received—universal truth than individual, personal truths. Your tendency to overthink can be turned into creativity. There are times when it's good to be engaged and times for solitude. Pick and choose wisely and remember to be happy!"

They instruct her about her tendency to be judgmental.

"You believe that being judgmental equals survival and safety. When your panic button is pushed, sit back and listen. See both sides; find the value in both. Expand your bubble of love and light and listen to the wisdom of the grandmothers."

Birdie asked the Council to report as to whether she's doing okay. They laugh at the absurdity of her question, seeing things from the perspective that life is about learning.

"You are more than exceeding our expectations in this life. Make sure to garden daily to remind you of the importance of nature. Be an example of being strongly rooted. Dance daily and sit quietly two times a day for five minutes."

They also offered suggestions about taking care of herself.

"Be gentle on yourself. Listen to your body. Eat when needed, two or three times daily. Drink more water. Remember to aim for peace with your husband, and most importantly, learn ease!"

At the three-month follow-up, the intense energy Birdie had arrived with had vanished. She reported immense ease in situations that had previously brought stress.

"It's effortless! I feel more at peace taking care of my aging parents, especially my dad. I don't get upset with him anymore. He's just being himself!"

She realized that having two homes generates harmony with her husband.

"We are much better partners living separately!"

Many pieces of her life came together from understanding previous and between lifetimes. Knowing that having polio was a lesson, she came here to learn offered freedom and self-forgiveness. A lifetime focused on doing shifted into being, nurturing grandmother's wisdom to pass on to future generations.

Getting words of wisdom and life advice from those with a spiritual perspective gives so much value to all who are privileged to receive it. Birdie took it to heart and her life transformed dramatically.

# HEALING MUSIC FROM HOME

## Elisa Shine

Claire was experiencing a life transition when she came to see me for an LBL. She had been married and was separating from her current husband. Retired at age 59 from a career of working therapeutically with children and parents as a Family Counselor, Claire had previously experienced two past life regressions with me. She had prepared a list of questions for her LBL, including a curiosity about the feeling of needing to rush from one thing to the next that she'd been experiencing her entire life. Claire hoped to find peace with her decision to separate from her husband and receive insight into their soul agreements. She also wished to know what was most important for her to focus her energy on at this stage of her life.

Claire was familiar with the process and went quickly into a deep, relaxed, hypnotic state, through age regression, into the womb, and transitioned easily into a recent past life.

She entered the past life as a man named Amar, a soldier from Rome stationed in Britain. He was in a position of authority, focusing on strategizing to fight the British. He led many men into battles, and there were repeated casualties. He was in a constant state of survival and grew very weary. His death came at the hands of three British men in battle. After leaving the body, his spirit hovered over the battle scene, and he reported feeling shocked at seeing "lots of dead people" and that there were other spirits that had left the bodies of the soldiers along with him. He heard a woman's voice calling his name, and he began to rise, leaving the Earth plane.

The transition into the spirit realm was described as him being magnetically pulled upwards from his heart. He was aware of other soldiers traveling toward the Gateway simultaneously. As he approached, he and the others were surrounded in a circle by etheric beings with feminine energy. He stated, "They are healers, and it is their job to greet men who have died in war." One being came forward and put her arms around Amar and the other soldiers, and he heard the message, "Welcome, it's all okay. Everything that happened was okay. There are no mistakes. No bad people." Amar wept with relief and said he didn't feel judged for his actions.

After this initial contact, Amar's Spirit Guide "Andi" came forward as a bluish light with masculine energy. The guide asked Amar how he liked his past life "as a man with all of those muscles" because he usually prefers to incarnate as a woman. Amar responded, "I appreciated the contrast, experiencing physical strength." The guide then addressed Amar by his eternal soul's name and led him to a healing pool of water. The healing occurred on multiple levels, helping Amar to shed the trappings of density from the past life body and become his light body. He witnessed light beings caring for the physical energy body from the past life by wrapping it ceremonially and sending it back to the Source.

My client's soul began traveling toward a light with her guide, Andi. She reported needing to stop periodically to acclimate to the new levels she was traveling through. As they moved along, her guide encouraged her not to hurry and to take her time.

When asked what more she could learn about her feeling of the need to hurry in her current life, her guide responded:

> C: The feeling of rushing is from the past life as Amar and is linked to life and death, rescue, and protection. In their current life, she is excited and filled with anticipation about her life purpose, and the importance of it sometimes feels like life and death. In her current life, she is a facilitator to help make things easier for those who need help and protection, but the lesson in this life is the opposite of that past life, and she is meant to go slow, build trust with people, and not to approach it as a battle.

An imprint connected to urgency was in her stomach area, and she could release it by sending energy to that area with the help of her spirit guide.

Next, her soul met with a Council of 6 beings, 6 of whom appeared as an etheric muted white color and one more prominent purple being. We were able to ask many of Claire's prepared questions. The following contains some important questions she wished to have answered.

> F: Claire is curious about what is most important

for her to focus on. She's involved with many things in her current life: Indigenous people, justice, and there's interest in writing a book. Please ask the Council what is most important to focus upon in the current life.

C: The answer I'm getting is that it's not any particular action. It's how I am in the action. I can do any of those things and it would be fine, but it's how I'm doing those things that matters. They are telling me, "Integrity, impeccability with your speech, listening to your heart and mind, and most importantly, waiting for the divine right timing, which you cannot see from where you are. Impatience doesn't help. It's not life and death.

Everything that's meant to happen will happen.

F: Is there anything else you sense is important? Please ask the council to tell you.

C: Well, one thing they're saying is that I have medicine songs, and when I sing certain songs, they're actually medicine songs.

F: Please tell me more; do these medicine songs benefit you or someone else?

C: I like it, and nature really likes it when I sing.

F: And how do you feel about what you've been told?

C: It really makes sense. It feels right. It strengthens me … and they're happy that I'm getting more in touch with my joy. They are telling me, "One of your gifts is to bring joy. So, you need to do that, and people respond when you do that. It's been shut down for a while, and it's coming back." They're really honoring that playfulness is such a potent energy.

They are saying, "Less trying means more being. Just be yourself, and you'll be where you need to be. You'll be doing what you need to do."

They are also reassuring me, "You'll get the support you need; you'll get the information you need to get; you'll get the resources you need to do it, but you don't have to try so hard or worry. You don't have to worry so much." And now they are showing me that there's a layer of my being that's conditioned and that I don't need anymore.

F: I see. Would it be appropriate to release this layer right now?

C: Yes. There are a couple of little angels coming to me. Wait, they're kind of checking my head. They take out the bits that are contaminated.It's their specialty!

F: And how does that feel?

C: It feels nice. They have these little satchels that they're putting all the contaminated thoughts into, and they're going to take it all away to its next highest evolution, whatever those unhelpful programming thoughts are.

F: And how are you feeling now?

C: I feel so good. My head feels really clear.

The Council continued to answer Claire's other questions. It provided detailed insight into why her previous husband had been important in her development and the lessons and agreements made before coming to Earth. She reported feeling "deeply moved and filled with love," feeling at peace with the decision to be in a relationship and to separate later when the agreement was fulfilled. In addition, she received a critical understanding regarding the separation from her current husband.

C: There were options, and separation was one of them. And the other option was to grow emotionally and psychologically together. But Stefan, my current husband, couldn't do it, and that didn't happen. I don't need to know the reasons why, but this was also another option, to separate. And this is also still good.

F: Is there anything you want to ask about what you've been told here?

C: They say being who you are is more important than trying to fit into an uncomfortable situation that's not going forward, and it would be wise to keep that as the most important thing, whether you're in a relationship or not. To be yourself. Because the world needs you how you are, not dimmed down, not smaller.

F: So, you need to stay true to who you really are, and how do they feel you're doing in your current life?

C: They're joking. They're like, we'll give her a letter grade. Well, they think I'm learning a lot of lessons that I was meant to learn, and there are more, but on the whole, I'm learning what I wanted to learn.

F: And what was it that your soul wanted to learn in the life of Claire?

C: How to be in a relationship with others but still be myself. I also wanted to learn to use power in a good way to help relationships. To help indigenous people. To help children. To use the privilege that I have and to make things better, very different than how I used power in the life as Amar.

After leaving the Council, her guide took her to a bench and put his hands on her head, eyes, heart, and feet, telling her, "It's much gentler here, and we don't rush into things. It's a lot to leave the body and acclimatize here, and I can help with this." She reported that it helped her to attune to how much love there is in that place, which is so different from Earth, which is dense.

Next, her guide took her to a place that she called "the viewing room": an area with a large, curved viewing screen. Here, she connected with the soul energy of two of her sons in her current life. She was shown a starry region that represented her people, and with the help of her guide, she was told that they were from a planet called Hadar. With great emotion, she went on to explain more.

> C: This is home; I can feel it in my heart! It's unconditionally loving there, and they know about the power of music. They use music for healing; there's so much harmony. They know about the power of honoring our interconnectedness, how powerful that is, and the three of us wanted to bring that energy to Earth.

My client is shown different aspects of the energy she and her sons are bringing to Earth, including a recent life on Earth where they used their voices and sound to uplift and shift energy. She is reminded that singing or toning out in nature can animate, energize, and clear space. It is also a way of connecting to their home planet. She remembers that she has songs within her that are medicine songs, and this is one of the gifts that she is bringing to Earth.

The last advice she received before leaving the spirit realm was, "Everything that is yours will come. Just be yourself. You are on your path."

When I spoke with Claire a few weeks following the session, she said she felt at ease with her decision to separate from her husband. The healing energy of the LBL experience remains with her, and she has had several beautiful dreams with visits from light beings who have provided healing to her heart in the weeks following. The impatience that she had been experiencing is gone, and she expressed that she feels steady in her focus on using her knowledge and experience to "bring good to the world." Claire told me that she and her eldest son had the opportunity to sing together before an audience, and she said that the harmonies were perfect, the energy moving through her was profound, and the audience's response was "wild with joy!"

# Concluding Insights
## on Healing

The healing journey is as unique as each individual, shaped by personal experiences, beliefs, and aspirations.

By embracing the interconnected dimensions of mind, body, and soul, we embark on a path of self-discovery, resilience, and renewal.

Through acts of self-care, compassion, and inner exploration, we honor the inherent capacity for healing within ourselves and cultivate a deeper sense of wholeness and well-being.

In nurturing the art of healing, we not only transform our own lives but also contribute to the collective journey toward a more compassionate, resilient, and harmonious world.

*Pain in life is especially insidious because it can block the healing power of our souls, especially if we have not accepted what is happening to us as a preordained trial.*
*Yet, throughout life, our karma is designed so that*

*each trial will not be too great for us to endure. At a wat temple in the mountains of Northern Thailand, a Buddhist teacher once reminded me of a simple truth. 'Life,' he said, 'is offered as a means of self-expression, only giving us what we seek when we listen to the heart.'*

*The highest forms of this expression are acts of kindness. Our souls may travel away from a permanent home, but we are not just tourists. We bear responsibility for the evolution of a higher consciousness for ourselves and others in life. Thus, our journey is a collective one.*

*We are divine but imperfect beings who exist in material and spiritual worlds. Our destiny is to travel between their universes through space and time while we learn to master ourselves and acquire knowledge. We must trust in this process with patience and determination.*

*Our essence is not fully knowable in most physical hosts, but the Self is never lost because we always remain connected to both worlds.*[7]

Spiritual healing transcends religious dogma, inviting us to connect with a more profound sense of meaning, purpose, and interconnectedness.

The Life Between Lives session often becomes a bridge that connects us with our ultimate life and soul purpose and helps us live a life of compassion, purpose, and kindness.

Sanela Čović
Editor

---

7    Michael Newton "Journey of Souls"

# CHAPTER FIVE
## ON CONNECTION & ONENESS

# INTRODUCTION
## on Connection & Oneness

*The first piece, which is the most important, is that which comes within the souls of people when they realize their relationship, their oneness with the Universe and all its powers and when they realize that at the center of the Universe dwells the Great Spirit and that this center is really everywhere, it is within each of us.* [8]

What does oneness and connection to this oneness really mean? We're all connected in both visible and invisible ways. As human beings in the physical realm of Earth and according to Maslow's hierarchy of needs, our common needs range from biological or physiological like air, water food and shelter; up to safety, protection and security; up to belongingness and love as is found in family and relationships; up to esteem as through achievement and responsibility; up to cognitive desires such as knowledge, meaning and self-

---

8    Black Elk, Oglala Sioux

awareness; up to aesthetic needs like beauty, balance and form; up to personal growth, self-actualization and self-fulfillment; and ultimately up to transcendence, when one has achieved a level of morality, creativity, and reaching of one's full potential, and whereupon one is able to help others self-actualize. Transcendence also involves freedom from the material world and its constraints and is often regarded as a spiritual experience of rising above it all.

As souls we are all created by Source or Spirit, although this Creative Force is called by different names. This Divine Energy, or Consciousness, as Seth via the author Jane Roberts might describe it, dwells within us and within everything in the Universe as "units of consciousness." We can never be separated from it, for we are part of it. Quantum physics has revealed that all matter, both seen and unseen, is made up of energy, or vibrational frequencies and patterns. Earth and physicality tend to contain denser, lower and slower vibrations, and the spirit world typically contains faster, higher frequency vibrations.

Human beings are more sensitive to vibrational frequencies within our range of perceptibility, using any of our five physical senses; however, some who are highly sensitive such as psychic mediums and intuitive healers, can perceive even those vibrational frequencies beyond the normal physical sense ranges of sight, sound, smell, taste, and touch. While we all possess intuitive and psychic abilities and can tune into various vibrational frequencies unnoticed by our physical senses, most don't develop these skills or use them much, often mistrusting or fearing them for various reasons. Many other animal species are highly perceptive and do use senses beyond the physical that can often warn them of storms or other approaching threats.

Emotions we experience as humans also carry vibrational frequencies, as do our thoughts. What we may refer to as negative emotions or related thoughts such as anger, resentment, sadness or disgust carry much lower frequency vibrations than the positive emotions and thoughts of love, reverence, hope, gratitude, peace and joy. All emotions and thoughts not only affect us but affect other beings and our environment, rippling outward like the ripples after a rock is tossed into still water. These vibrational frequencies can even extend out into space, as far as the sun and well beyond, and can even permeate other dimensions.

Everything and everyone are connected through Source and carry this energy as part of one enormous experience of oneness and expansion through creativity. Many humans have similar needs and desires to achieve transcendence, as guided by their souls, though not all dwell at the same levels of Maslow's hierarchy of needs. When one is concerned about having food, water, and safety, it's difficult to achieve some of the higher levels of existence and consciousness. All of life's experiences at any level of development are valuable for the soul's learning and growth, however.

Life Between Lives sessions can help reconnect us with our soul selves, with one another on a soul level, with our environment, and with the oneness of our Creator Source. This is possible by moving beyond our human egos, costumes, and dramas, and into a beautiful expansion of consciousness and convergence. All of this can be applied in various ways toward enhancing our experience of our human lives, as you will read in the following case stories.

It's vital that we remember everything that connects us in this Earthly realm and beyond. We are all souls having human experiences of an emotional, psychological, physical, and spiritual nature. The idea of being separate and having amnesia as we enter Earth's plane is an illusion to allow us space for creativity, rediscovery, growth, and soul development. This is an ingenious and divine gift! Ultimately, each of us returns everything we create and are to the Whole or to All That Is.

"Our harmonious feelings of love, compassion, gratitude, or appreciation, provide us with a direct way to align ourselves with what physicist Mark Comings refers to as the multidimensional 'sea of radiance' which unites everything. When we align ourselves in such a manner, we are remembering what has always been so. Nothing can be outside of everything – we are a part of All That Is."[9]

Elizabeth Lockhart
Editor

---

9    Spirit Walking: A Course in Shamanic Power

# ELEVATE

## Sanela Čović

Nico is a 36-year-old psychotherapist and researcher who wants to understand more about the energy he has been feeling recently and how to use this energy to help and serve humanity.

He wants to get more clarity about his mission in this life as Nico, what it is that he came here to do, as well as to know where his soul comes from.

He is studying new ways of connecting with energy and helping people on their path of spirituality.

His scientific mind has led him to start this journey of self-realization and connection with his soul self.

During the age regression portion of the past life regression session, we visited 3 happy childhood memories, and we explored the soul's connection with the fetus while in his mother's womb. The moment before my client's birth offered so much information about this time and the way his soul connects with the fetus. His soul observes the fetus

194

from outside before connecting with it. The soul energy softly surrounds the fetus, like a loving hug, and slowly enters the body.

In this incarnation the soul is inside and outside of the body at the same time during the development of the fetus. The reason why part of the soul's energy is on the outside is for the protection, which is related to the past life we are about to visit. After exploring the time in the womb, we continue our journey back in time.

Nico regresses to a past life of a priest, George, who lived a modest life in a temple in the north of Scandinavia in the 12th Century.

> F: Let me know where you are.
> C: I am praying…
> F: What or whom are you praying to?
> C: To the light that is shining above me.

He lifts his right arm and offers the light received from above to everyone. His life was dedicated to bringing light and love to the people who lived in the area, after he received the light from above. He further explained that he was not only George, he could be a bird, but he described it as a flow.

He is outside of the temple, there is no need for the temple. He travels through different realities and dimensions during his life of the priest and ends up in a wooden cabin.

> C: They were not ready to understand this.

During the next scene, George was ill in bed, and he was concerned that he would not be able to continue writing the book that was lying on the table. The book is very important because it contains the wisdom he was offering to people, the wisdom about the light and love.

In the last scene of this lifetime George is decapitated.

> F: Help me understand why?
> C: Anger, fear, they didn´t understand this; they were not ready.

Unfortunately, people became afraid of what George was offering, they didn´t understand it, and they decided to decapitate him.

Next, we were working on energy healing and recovering the lost parts after a very traumatic end of life.

Since Nico had a successful past life regression, we met again to journey into the Life Between Lives.

In another past lifetime, Nico as Ka sa fa is a woman living in Japan; there is a lake, and the sky and trees are reflected in the water. She is alone and it is raining.

> C: There is a tunnel, I am running through the tunnel.
> F: What happens next?
> C: Elevation. I am rising, ascending.

Ka sa fa is a 20-year-old woman, and she experiences the elevation often.

We move to the last day in Ka sa fa's lifetime.

> C: My hands form a triangle, and I am praying.
> F: How do you know that this is your last day as Ka sa fa?
> C: I am going back home.

F: How old are you?

C: I am 90 years old.

F: Is there anyone around you or are you alone?

C: There are many people around me. They are praying too.

F: What kind of prayer?

C: Silence. Silence.

Ka sa fa's life comes to an end, and she is surrounded by many people praying for an easy transition.

C: I am a drop that rises up, ascending.

Ka sa fa's soul is moving upwards, noticing red and blue oscillating lights, like a plasma.

C: They surround me, they dance, embrace me. I feel light. I continue ascending, and on my left, I can see an explosion. This space is like cotton; it integrates me into the plasma. I am that plasma, without shape. I expand, white, there are feathers, wings, white wings. There are colorful feathers. Peacocks. Beautiful.

F: Help me understand what this place is.

C: It's like a cosmic garden. Rainbows, spirals, they open, like a fountain.

F: What colors do you perceive there?

C: Rainbowlike colors. I am going up through the stream of light.

F: What is the meaning of this stream of light?

C: It is about continued ascension, I am in a flower of light, and the fountain of colors and rainbows. The flowers are like the mandala, I am blue. The flowers' purpose is where the nectar is created and I jump around the pollen, a blue, tiny creature jumping in circles. There are more like me. There are thousands of tiny particles of colors, bright red, blue, green. All the colors in one.

F: What is it that you do in this place?

C: I can create forms with light, rainbows.

F: Help me understand who usually comes to this place?

C: Boddhisattva.

He describes his soul self with long black hair, strong, blue. It is a male energy.

C: I can call him Shiva. He says that we all are Shiva. This location would be in the center of the universe, like a dot. Around this center is everything, spheres, I am sitting in the center of the circle with my flowers, there are spheres around me. It´s a small place but contains the potential of everything.

F: Are there more like you sitting in the circle or is it just you?

C: It is just me, but I am many.

Any name is fine, and we agree that I can call him Shiva. We receive the answers to the questions Nico prepared for this session.

C: This is the last cycle for everyone.

F: What does this mean?

C: Everything should end to start again. The only way is through the light.

F: How is Nico being prepared to help so many people?

C: Through challenge, suffering, anxiety, depression, desperation, hope, discovery, transformation, transcendence, service.

F: Is there something that Nico needs in this moment?

C: Calm, devotion, self-confidence, acceptance.

F: How will this help Nico achieve what he needs to do?

C: There is nothing that should be done because it's done. It's a process, there will be resistance, it's meant to be, he is ready. The world is ready too.

F: Nico wanted to know where his soul comes from?

C: From me. It's a journey, to gain, learn, explore, create, transform, become, come back.

F: Is this place located in our known universe or somewhere else?

C: I am the universe. Everything is in me. He is remembering, it's happening, everything is inside of him.

F: What is it that he needs to remember?

C: He is my son, he is me.

There is stillness ...

C: Don't get trapped in distractions, entertaining your mind, don't lose the focus.

He then continues.

C: The snake becomes the flower, the creature goes from multiple to one, from anima to Buddha. The pathway is always up, back to the nectar, garden, to Shiva, going down again to go up. I am here to dissipate the illusion, wake them up, show the glimpse of the absolute, through direct experience, they will see it, once you feel it you cannot deny it. The river is the sea, just flow, go back to the source.

The client received all the answers to his questions, healing and insights that will assist him for the remainder of his life.

Mastering the art of ascension, light and love are still present in this life as Nico, and he will continue to offer this gift to humanity.

He could connect with his soul-self, the Shiva consciousness and could remember all that he was, is and will be.

This is just a glimpse of the magnificence of every human being. We all are a part of Oneness and we come to this life being one, forgetting it when born, and remembering it again as we evolve on our spiritual journey.

"The river is the sea, just flow, go back to the source."

This is such a beautiful way of describing the never-ending cycle of reconnection with the source, with Oneness, with what we truly are.

When we live true to our essence, we truly bring light, love, and unity to all living beings.

# A LOVE FOR DOGS

## Tatjana Braun

I had known Maria for some time, and she has had the experience of both meditation and hypnotherapy before.

From the start of our session, Maria achieved a deep state of trance. This allowed her to describe fluently her happy and colorful childhood experiences. As we went further into the time before her birth, Maria spontaneously recalled the easy relationship with her mother. Even before she was born, she was full of anticipation for her new life.

After a smooth transition into a past life, Maria found herself as a strong 25-year-old man named Eskil, who lived in Greenland and was walking alone across an endless and silent snowy landscape.

He was befriended by a family who welcomed him into their lives and invited him to join them for fishing. As all this unfolded for Eskil, he formed a strong emotional connection to the six huskies who pulled their sleds.

The remainder of his life was shown as Eskil living with

and looking after the dogs. On the last day of his life, he passed peacefully away in his igloo in the company of two of his dogs, Pit and Fiö.

As Maria left the life of Eskil, she felt her heart had been opened widely as she moved into the spirit world.

She offered an emotive description of a beautiful rainbow made of yellow, red, orange, and violet.

On the right upper edge of this rainbow, Maria perceived an older man in black and white colors, who smiled at her very lovingly, emanating kindness. She introduced him as the Archangel Michael. In these moments the room had been filled by the energy of love and light, and Maria received the following messages from Michael, her spiritual guide:

C: You have fulfilled your task very well as Eskil. It was to connect consciously with nature, to find peace in the silence and isolation. Also, your task, to help animals with love and care, has been carried out wonderfully.

Maria was told that her spirit's name is "Loop" and that she has recognized and mastered the previous tasks in her current incarnation very well. Maria (Loop) was deeply touched by these messages.

Her life as a pilot had enabled her to acquire discipline and consistency and brought the opportunities to develop a rational mind and display courage – these being natural characteristics of her soul.

Michael mentioned as well with great appreciation, that in Loop's current life as Maria, she has provided a loving home for dogs who had experienced trauma.

Then some familiar souls came forward which was very

moving for Loop.

Many sparkling, small points of light formed a star just in front of her, which radiated bright and warming energy. Individual points of that star (her father, her grandfather, and a good friend) started to communicate to help Loop understand how indescribably loved, and appreciated she is.

Her friend who is also a pilot in this life said, "Here in the Spiritual World you can fly in the most perfect and pure form, without any restriction." As Loop heard this it brought a big smile to Maria's face.

The group then dissolved, and a luminous carpet unfolded before Loop, upon which were all the dogs that had passed over in Maria's lifetime and they were now healthy and happy. They jumped and ran, so full of fun all over the carpet and as Loop (Maria) watched intently, she was again deeply touched. She received such strong gratitude towards her from the souls of the dogs she had helped and understood that their connection would last forever, and they would meet again in the spirit world.

I asked Loop, what activities she undertakes in the spirit world, and she talked about flying through all the different places in order to understand the different possibilities and develop them further within the sphere of the spiritual realm.

When she returned from the spiritual realm, Maria radiated deep inner peace, happiness, and joy. She described her journey and interactions with her soulmates, her guide and the souls of her dogs as absolutely pure, loving and bright moments. These feelings, thoughts and images would continually accompany her for the rest of her life. She would now know with deep certainty that endless love comes to us from the spirit world and awaits us there at the end of this lifetime.

# DEVELOPING LOVE

## Elisabeth Iwona Röpcke (Kupisz)

My client, a 32-year-old Polish woman, has studied philosophy, but her career is directed towards working with people in healing and raising awareness. She learned about LBL and Dr. Newton by channeling. She read the books and handed them over to her mum, who also became interested in them. Fascinated by LBL, she decided to contact me, having found me on the Institute website.

She came to the LBL session to see herself in a larger light spectrum, find out why she needs so much alone time, and explore the possibility of expanding her practice toward working more with groups. She works with two different energies, combining them and assessing whether something else is missing. As part of the session, she wants to know where these energies come from?

Her mum is loving. Her father, now deceased, was an alcoholic. When she was 10, he tried to commit suicide by cutting himself with a broken bottle. As a child, she tried to take responsibility for her parents. She witnessed how her father beat her mother, but she couldn't do anything about it. She learned that not everyone can be helped. At the age of 14, she realized that she needed to do something special in her life. She wasn't sure what that should be, though. She was interested in working with energy and cured herself of asthma. Working with childhood trauma, she has used different techniques. She receives messages from the spiritual world. She is alone a lot. She communicates with an entity named Ethi from Sirius. Throughout her life she has experienced a lack of emotional contact. She has learned to support people in a way that does not strain her own energy and to take care of herself without remorse that she gave too little.

After the induction, my client was at the beginning point in the session where I was suggesting that she return to the past, using the image of descending white stairs. She expresses a desire to run down them. She stops when she was on step 16, corresponding to age16.

F: There is an argument. Dad is beating Mum.

My client is crying. When she calms down, she runs down the stairs until she was 7 years old. She does not want to go to school, so she jumps down to the 3-year-old step. She then says that she wants to move directly on to her mother's womb.

F: Move to the ninth month in the womb.
C: I feel mum's love. I know what awaits me, I look at what will be and what was. There are flashbacks. I'm still collecting information. I put it all together. There will be a lot of action. I'm receiving different energies and information. A lot, like being

at an intersection. I pick, I take, I ask for more. Yellow energy arrives. That was missing. This is it. That was what I needed. It flows through me to Mummy. I support Mum with the energy, and she is calm. She's worried, but for daddy. She is strong. She loves me so much.

F: Let's move back to the sixth month of pregnancy.

C: I'm examining the mind. Checking. I wanted this body and mind so much, but I want to be very sure of this. I go in and out. I'm adjusting. I check. It is a weird feeling. It is as if I'm not touching, penetrating, and touching without touching and going out. Oh! At first, it is difficult, as if I am entering a dense liquid. Entering and exiting in fine-tuning. Then it is lighter and lighter. I want to be sure this body suits me. I check so that there are no surprises. The body is fast, volatile and without problems. But the most important thing is to have a good mind in order to have an easy life and not be distracted by ordinary matters.

(pause) Mum's energy is love and support. Dad's energy conveys an uncompromising attitude. They are to balance each other.

I take her back out of the womb and go through the suggestions to enter a prior life. She was a very sick woman named Adele living in the sixteenth century in Europe. Her disease was unknown and incurable. At the age of about 30 years she was sent to a center where she survived to the age of 60. I moved her back to her childhood when she was healthy.

C: I am 11 years old, and I am very energetic.

My parents are with me. Dad has a very big hat. Dad is cheerful. Mom is sad. (The client begins breathing hard.) We sit at the table with a richly plated silver platter. The staff serves us.

F: Go to the time when you first fell ill.

C: I am 7 years old and coughing up blood. The doctor says that everything will be okay. The drugs weaken me, I have no appetite.

F: What did you study? Where were you playing?

C: I learned numbers. I played with my cousin. Not far from the house there were ruins of a castle. They do not let me get away, though. I was like in jail. I could not play as I wanted. I wanted to move, explore, and search. My mom was jerking my arm around, bringing me home. (In relating this she exhibits physical pain.) She forbade me to play outside.

F: What else do you find?

C: I'm older now. I'm 16 years old. What a life! I do not see the point in living here. I cannot move anywhere. I do not have strength for anything. My parents are sad. Uncle does not visit us. This is probably my fault. No one knows what is wrong with me. They want to isolate me. I'm alone much of the time.

She was put into a health center, and no one visited her. Everyone was afraid of her. They were helpless. There she met a very sick boy. She was fascinated by his strength. She met three other people; however, she did not care about them.

F: Go to the last day of life in that incarnation

and tell me what you are experiencing. (She then moves through her passing.)

C: I did not use this life. I should have been happier, despite the illness. I should have enjoyed my life and the fact that I was alive. I should have enjoyed what is, not looking and thinking about what is not. The three people I did not notice in the health center could have helped me. Because of sadness, I did not make any decisions. It was a lesson. Only this boy fascinated me, and it was a success.

F: Compare that incarnation with this current one. What do you have to pay attention to now?

C: I need to be careful of my feelings. I should not sink into sadness. Not so deep, just touch it and do not fall into it. Do not be a victim. From this perspective now, it does not make sense, because I am now free. I should have felt more joy of existence. To be in the here and now. I had some strength, but I did not use it. I was sick, but I was to use the strength that I had available. To keep going. That was my job. I was to trust in whatever happened. When I do not have confidence, then there are only emotions left. I shall pay attention to the environment around me and to how I feel so that I will be able to pick up the information that comes to me.

Passing through the tunnel, she enters the golden gate to the Soul World. At first, her dad welcomes her.

C: As I enter, our energies merge into a vortex. I knew it would be difficult, but I knew that it would help me to grow and go on. He tells me that I was brave. Then he pats me on the head. He has a calm energy here. He helps release my sadness by pulling something out of my throat, telling me that I didn't need it. He also tells me that I am free and that he is too. The energy between us is flowing from the heart. That had been missing. We are holding hands, and a group of souls are supporting us. He adds: Follow your soul desires, be strong, trust, do not give up and after this life (her current one) we will meet again.

(After a pause)

Mom and Dad are not angry with each other. They joke. They want to make me laugh. They are happy. They succeeded.

Her guide appears.

F: Describe the look of your guide.

C: He showed up as purple energy surrounded by yellow. Blue-white aura with elements of intense magenta, very intense violet inside. He has a lot of peace, stability, and knowledge.

F: See yourself standing in front of a mirror. Describe your reflection.

C: I look like him. Just inside I'm white, outside yellow, blue and magenta, shining intensely from the inside. The outer colors penetrate. It's a little green turquoise.

F: What color does the group radiate?

C: Yellow and blue. One stands out. His color is purple. He will change the group.

F: What is the group working on?

C: On not giving up on the emotions. It's important, but difficult. Finding out all about yourself and having fun. It's so difficult sometimes.

The client receives a message which she relays.

C: The element of working with emotions is learning to express what you feel and to allow it to go away and not go down, not to fall. Everyone has the task of expressing oneself in love and passing it on.

I laugh and say to my dad: It was a good challenge you gave me! This is the message. This challenge is for everyone.

F: Describe what you do in the spirit world?

C: There are two places. One is a laboratory where we mix different ingredients and look for something. The energy is in a pure form. Most versatile. Healing energy. The second is the lecture room. We exchange what we think and experience what works best. It's about proportions. We have all kinds of energy available and create a ball of energy between our hands.

F: How do you transport it to Earth?

C: Energy flows through us through the solar plexus, but it does not have to be this place. It emanates from us, but this energy is in the plexus. First, we test ourselves. The point is that we have to emanate it. It's going to expand. We have chosen it to support people, their innermost, purest vibrations. What is in them, the purest truth. This is a kind of vibration that supports another vibration in others.

This ball has different vibrations and is designed to match us. When we radiate from the solar plexus, it adjusts individually. It's the same as how the soul adjusts to the body. As shoes, only other sizes. We are working hard on this ball. There are fifteen of us. The group is good, lively, and busy. Everyone has ideas.

During the session, we find that when choosing this incarnation, she discussed with her guide the likely difficulties she would face. He asked if she was sure about this life because it would be tough with her parents. She wanted to see if she was able to pass healing on to others using the energy they were working on in her group.

F: How did you plan to transmit this energy?

C: Love harmonizes with the solar plexus. Healing power is a connection with love. I have to learn it. Develop love and compassion for yourself, and further to others. If it did not work, then it would be a very good incarnation anyway. I am not worried. I decorate the energy ball like a cake, where there is no more room for decorations. I work with the energy, and how to pass it on. The beginning will be very intense, then it will be better. Mind has to harmonize this energy with love.

She begins talking again about her discussion with her guide about what to expect from her current life if she chose it.

C: The guide asked again if I was sure about what I am choosing to do. There are lighter variants. I could have had more peace and still have development. The childhood I will have is enough, though. The rest is an additional bonus for development. I do not have to, but I really want to do it. He says you have a choice. I should not have remorse. He does not require it. However, I demand it from myself. He says I can rest now. He gives me violet energy. He says to ask if I need support.

I already know that energy in the solar plexus is one energy, through the hands is the second, the third element is love in itself. Energies are given. Love develops in itself. This is very important! It is about developing a deep love that goes beyond the love of two people. It takes in everything and heals. I develop this element, and it works with these energies. It can do anything. It's like a fractal. Endless and multiplying. It can cover the universe. This is my individual part. I work with the combination of energy from the solar plexus, from the hands, and love. The energy of the hands flows best when I feel love. I use it without borders.

I lead her to the Akashic Library where she learns that in previous incarnations she worked with energy and was a healer, and a priestess in ancient temples. It was in bright ethereal worlds where nature was an energy that could not be touched.

F: What are your challenges now?
C: I have done a lot. What is left is to expand the theme of all-encompassing love. This segment is left. And then I will go on.

In her meeting with her Elder Council, she is told that she is on the right track. That she is on target. She is to develop that love which embraces everything. This is not generic. It is very specific.

When she decides for the future and accepts it, then what was has been will be erased. As soon as she sees the future and is sure of it, the past will be erased. She decides on where she wants to be, and she will be and must have unshakeable confidence. They emphasize this.

She is in the process of creating a new technique of working with energy, and it is good. She must trust it, and the signpost to it is the certainty that this is the moment.

She is developing an all-embracing love that fuses into unity. She needs something for it, and it is what she has been working on in her group of souls.

Regarding expressing oneself in relationships with others, the Council of Elders gives her a final, inspirational message: "Every single person who develops love is like a drop in the sea and changes it."

# A COMPLETE RENEWAL

## Ricardo Mones González

A Life Between Lives (LBL) therapy session in Mexico is an uncommon occurrence, particularly in small cities in our country.

Mina comes from a small city. She is 55 years old, a doctor by profession, separated and a mother to three children. She explained in our initial telephone conversation that she'd had a difficult life, beginning with her childhood. She studied medicine, not out of conviction, but because her parents convinced her of it. She never really practiced because she worried that conventional medicine seemed insufficient to effect true healing and so she entered the world of naturopathic medicine. She married young and went to live in North America and there she dedicated many years to healing others with natural medicine. Four years ago, her mother became ill, so she had to return to Mexico leaving her already self-sufficient children in the United States. After her mother's death, she began a process of spiritual awakening.

214

She contacted me and explained her main intention is to learn more about the desires of her soul and find a path to follow, since allopathic medicine does not fill her, and naturopathic medicine also seems incomplete. This would be her moment to define her future.

Before the preparation session to explore a past life, I had the impression she was shy, but the session showed the complete opposite. She remembered a past life of great solitude. She quickly found herself in the afterlife and a guide appeared. She was able to have a very long and clear dialogue with her guide, with lots of information and messages. The main lesson was to realize that she chose that life of solitude. Her guide says, "You are a soul who likes strong challenges, and you always choose difficult things." Recognizing that her life's challenges were of her own choosing left a strong impression after the session.

When she returned for her LBL session, she did not bring the list of important people in her life, as she felt she didn't want to have spiritual contact with people who caused her depression and anguish. I explained that what comes up in the session is what her guides want her to know for her own benefit.

She progressed in her LBL showing an impressive connection with spirit and clarity throughout her session. Her past life revealed a strong man who spent much of his life at war as a leader. He returned home to find his family was lost. Alone and overcome with grief, he died.

Very soon after death, Mina enters the spiritual realm. She is reconfiguring her energy and enjoying the experience enormously.

C: I am a very bright light and from my center

comes a lot of energy that fires like rays of light in all directions, thousands of rays that arise from the center of me.

She is impressed with how she looks and feels amazed at that experience.

C: And I can make them grow. If I concentrate on what I feel, the rays grow, giving more intense light. If I remember my physical state, the rays become smaller. I can handle this energy.

For a long time, she continues to experience her own energy, remembering this perfect state.

C: I would like to remain here always, but also, I want to continue advancing in my evolution, so I accept incarnating on Earth, because I want to get beyond this. I know there is more, and I want that. I know that I want to return to the Source that created me, and the only way is to grow in experience and challenges. And I know that the Source that created me waits for me with open arms and tells me to take my time, that I have a lot of time, so be patient. But I also realize that when I incarnated, I didn't advance as much as I wanted.

After that time of reflection, she observes that other lights are approaching. There are between eight and ten lights, some bigger and others smaller than her.

C: They come to meet me and surround me in a

circle. It's as if they give me a big hug and tell me "We know what you've been through, we're here to comfort you, and let you know you're not the only one, there are many of us who want to move forward and we're a team that supports each other." This makes my energy and my rays grow more. I feel like this is a hug of love, understanding, support and brotherhood. I feel that WE ARE ALL ONE. I thought that only I was fighting for my cause but now I see that we are together.

Among them is my guide and he gets close to me, he calls me in a way that I can't pronounce, something like Cravisha (Soul name of Mina), and he tells me that he has always been with me. He tells me that on Earth we forget and that is why I have felt alone but he has always been close to me. He tells me that these other lights are my companions with whom I decided to experience this life.

Here Cravisha makes an expression of concern and says:

C: But I wouldn't want to know who they are, I wouldn't want to identify them.

F: What does your guide say about that? Because maybe Mina's mind is set against meeting anyone from her current life, but Cravisha wants this to happen.

C: He says to some yes and others no, because I'm not ready.

F: So, tell him to introduce the ones you can identify.

C: There are my children (of her current life). They are beings of light who come to accompany me with their love and understanding. They know why I went through it all. They are my teachers. There is also my friend Marcela. She came to accompany me in the most difficult moment of my life when Mama was ill. She has helped me a lot in this process.

And as always happens in an LBL session, the magic appears in small details. At the point where she might encounter the Souls of those who had hurt her in this life, Mina is unsure. I suggest she asks her guide if he would help her.

After a few moments of silence, she receives information from her guide about her brother, sister, mother, father, and ex-husband. It was not a direct meeting with those souls, but her guide was giving her information about why things happened as they happened and why her relationship with them was as it was. After that came a clear understanding of her successes and failures in managing those relationships.

Mina's conclusion was, "In my eagerness to bring love and meet the needs of others I have made decisions even against my own happiness."

Now renewed by this spiritual process, there would no longer be pain but understanding.

After that, I suggest:

F: Ask your guide what is coming next?
C: He asks me if I am prepared to know why I chose the life I chose. I answer that I am ready.

The following is a summary of the information Mina receives:

C: He lets me see the options I had, they are like movies, I could have been a man, but I chose to be a woman. In this life I have sometimes felt like man in a woman's body. He tells me that for many lives I have preferred to be a man. That's why I chose my parents, they would be hard on me and make me strong because I did not want to be a fragile girl. I chose a more balanced life between my masculine and feminine energy. I chose to be feminine, yet strong.

In this life I have been very rude and sometimes I behave like a rude man inside a female body and I have had problems with that. I put emotions aside and decide with my mind and not with my heart. My guide says that this is my main challenge of this life. The plan was for me to be a strong female without engaging the male part. That's why I often have internal conflicts about this. In my past lives I have preferred to be a man many times and for me that is easier because I tend to be more strategic, practical. That's why I set myself the challenge of now doing what is difficult for me, which is to be more feminine. That's why I choose lives with high challenges as in this case.

Now I understand the relationship with my ex-husband. He was a weak and immature man, and I was the leader, the strong one, but sometimes I tried to act more feminine so as not to hurt his masculinity. And that led me into a serious depression. I was the leader, the strong one and it was like cutting off the wings of what I could be and do. My guide tells me that I set very tough goals because I want to move forward very quickly. My guide says I must not fight but accept and find a way to balance my energies. I am not two people; I am only one. I have to learn to accept myself in this duality without fighting. I must accept and embrace the fragility I don't like. My guide tells me that I must accept myself and seek that balance by understanding my inner being.

The dialogue continued with advice about her healing.

C: He tells me to listen to my heart. I can help others who are going through the same thing. I will be able to guide them back to their spiritual life. Now I have the full vision. Having been a doctor before has helped me to understand the human body, but I felt that something was missing. Now, if I can understand the spiritual part more, I will understand that all people have inner struggles between our inner self, our mind, and our body and those are very conflicting struggles. Now that I understand it, I can help those who come to me as a doctor, with a more complete vision, to help them heal from the three levels. I can help others to understand that balancing their body and mind with their soul will achieve a much simpler and more complete life. Things will then flow better, more naturally and be more beneficial to everyone.

At the end of the session Mina has renewed her feeling about her eternal soul and the intention to move forward and evolve. She has also renewed her perception about her current life and her difficult relationships.

Now there is no drama, but clarity and understanding about what has happened in her life. And finally, she can feel a knowing that there is an inner part that has led her to what she is today, a being that forms body, mind, and soul. Her life and her work can continue with renewed energy.

# Our Light is One

## Tianna Roser

During Sandy's past life regression, she visited just a couple of younger ages in the former life, where she had left her people and lived alone. Most of the regression was spent in the late years of that life. At first Sandy was surprised that she seemed happy and cared for. She didn't need to concern herself with how her needs would be met.

Delving further into the scene, she found herself in a circle of women, feeling free and connected. She began to sway uninhibitedly, experiencing great joy in her movements. There was a deep sense of community and support in which she felt free to express herself.

At the end of that lifetime, I asked what wisdom her former self would like to share with her current self. She was drawn to connect heads at the forehead as her two selves just melded into each other at that level. At that point Sandy said she felt relief.

We concluded the session and Sandy left to rest before

the Life Between Life regression the next day. Despite that beautiful experience, Sandy shared the next day that she hadn't felt quite ready to fully let go of the migraines. She didn't want to leave it behind with her former self. She was also concerned that the past life experience still felt a bit vague. She worried that she wouldn't have the vivid experience she desired.

As it happened, that wasn't a problem whatsoever. Although this time Sandy experienced a relatively uneventful past life in which she owned and worked on crops in a field, the life centered around loving family relationships. When asked what the main lesson from that life was, she replied "I accepted wonderful love, and I gave wonderful love."

At the death scene, an excited Sandy released the body and opened to the spirit realm, feeling big flows of energy. Her face began to itch quite a bit as the energy was just flowing and flowing. She found herself cocooned in an orb of radiant light. Slowly it came into awareness that the light above was her guide, always attached but separate. Her guide's light came over the top of her and down the sides, carrying her as they moved through the spirit realm. Sandy mentioned that with her guide, she felt protection, and she could just trust. "My head feels safe", she said.

Joining her soul group was an emotionally powerful experience, perhaps the most significant part of the session. As Sandy was greeted by her mother, her husband Jason and other family members, she cried tears of happiness.

C: At the moment of recognition (of Jason) I let out a cry of gratitude greater than anything I have ever experienced on this Earth. I cried and cried in utter joy to be with Jason. Our lights became one and we twirled together for an extended time. Our light is one. We are one. I'm so glad to be one with him again. It's euphoric.

Most of her LBL was spent with her soul family. These connections were the key to her healing and transformation. Her father was there, hugging her. Sandy stated that he says, "You don't need to keep that hurt, child."

C: I bless you, Dad. I love you. (She sensed that she was supposed to release him, which she did with gratitude.) I let you go. All is well. He is well.

Poignant moments from her childhood and throughout her current life continued to surface to now be re-experienced with greater insight. Her expanded awareness allowed these memories to fit into place in the bigger picture of her soul's existence in relation to these cherished souls.

As the session continued, we addressed the list of questions she brought in to be answered.

F: What is your soul's name?
C: Instead of hearing a soul name she heard, I am Light. I am the Light of the world! We all are!

Sandy proclaimed this, beaming with joy. The love she radiated was palpable. It seemed to fill up my office space. She shared a memory of being told that, by a pastor in her current life. It had been nice to be told that, but how much more powerful it was to finally feel the truth of those words. There were no doubts left.

Shifting into this higher state can be profoundly healing and insightful. In the higher spiritual awareness, we find that the differences in perspectives that separate us in the Earth realm fade as we uncover the deep love shared with these souls over many lifetimes. We remember that the true identity of ourselves and others is pure love and light.

After the session concluded, Sandy excused herself to the restroom. When she returned to the room, tears were flowing down her face as she gave me a deep hug of gratitude. She later shared with me that revelations have continued since the session.

Two months after the session, she was absolutely blown away with the sudden awareness that her relationship dream of greater intimacy with her husband was fulfilled. Since the regression, Sandy has been able to live from a place of lovingly letting go of her dad, which freed her for greater expansion of showing up in life. The migraines have become more subdued, and she knows they are no longer hers to have. Moving forward, she feels empowered to express herself, stepping more into who she is. Sandy knows that she's always safe and that she is indeed the light of the world.

# CONCLUDING INSIGHTS
## on Connection & Oneness

Beneath the surface of our individual identities lies a deeper unity that binds us all. It is a spiritual journey of awakening to the inherent divinity within us and the interconnected web of life that sustains us. The quest for oneness beckons us to transcend the illusion of separation and embrace the unity of existence.

At its essence, oneness is a shift in consciousness — a recognition that we are not isolated beings but integral threads in the fabric of creation. It is a realization that our actions reverberate across the cosmos, shaping the destiny of humanity and the planet we call home. In embracing oneness, we cultivate reverence for all life, honoring the interconnected web of relationships that sustain us and infusing our actions with wisdom, compassion, and love.

To experience oneness is a whole different story. We can think about it, contemplate it, but it is only when we experience it that we know what oneness really is. When we connect with our soul´s essence in the Life Between Lives session, we can experience the oneness and connection with all there is, the unconditional love, and healing. After such an experience in this human body, our lives are truly forever changed.

Sanela Čović
Editor

# CHAPTER SIX
## ON GUIDES &
## ADVANCED BEINGS

# Introduction

## on Guides & Advanced Beings

Among the most sacred connections clients make during an LBL are with their spirit guides. These may include advanced beings who have incarnated on Earth, angels, Elders, teachers, ancestors, spirit animals, otherworldly beings, and more. Although guides can appear visually or otherwise in many forms, they are often recognized by a patterned energy frequency and its emotional impact. While many guides are recognized immediately by a client's soul, others can be fun-loving and a bit inconsistent, playing hide-and-seek or presenting as a client's favorite rock star or religious figure. At times, spirit guides can seem to require clients' souls to work harder at entraining their energy to connect, allowing the whole experience of their meeting to unfold naturally and trusting what is revealed or conveyed to them.

While souls are typically greeted at the "Gateway" when crossing into the soul realm by a spirit guide or guides, often more experienced souls move where they know they need to go without guidance. Souls can sometimes be greeted by a soul mate or soul group, which tends to foster feelings of familiarity, welcome, belonging, and comfort. This Gateway greeting experience can be very individualized. Asking clients if they recognize a greeter and how a being's presence makes them feel can help with understanding the being's role in their existence as a soul. Having the client directly ask, "What is your relationship to me as a soul?" or often, "Are you one of my spirit guides?" will ensure the client meets with a higher source of guidance once confirmed. Because information transmitted by guides is most often telepathic, symbolic, metaphorical, or gestural in the soul realm, a client usually will receive information in these more subtle ways; however, clients do frequently report "hearing with their 'inner ears.'"

Generally, our main spirit guides greet us first. These beings have often been with us since our creation as souls. Sometimes, we may gain another guide or teacher, usually related to an area in which our souls are learning to specialize, such as healing, creating with energy, and more. Some guides may help us with special issues we are contending with in our current lifetime, such as grief or a pattern of unforgiveness from lifetime to lifetime. Some guides greet us after a traumatic lifetime to show us to a place of healing, and this is their primary function. Many clients report a sense of waiting for something or someone after time in a healing space of light before their main guides appear.

Since journeys into past lives and beyond to LBL are made with the intention of the highest healing good for the client, this helps to steer a session. Our guides tend to be unique, yet often emanate the familiar feelings of unconditional love, compassion, and support, along with complete acceptance of the soul it oversees. There is a companionate tenderness and softness toward the soul, although, at times, there may be sternness, seriousness, or an emphatic quality about essential issues. Guides are gifted with the ability to raise a soul's awareness without judging. Qualities such as profound wisdom, understanding, and keen insight are present in our guides, including our Council of Elders, who have known and helped guide us for eons since our creation. In human terms, much higher and more stable frequencies of feelings exist among these beings.

Spirit guides and other advanced beings can assist us in answering deep questions we have in our current lives and lovingly remind us of our soul's purpose for incarnating on Earth, helping us find and stay true to our inner light and the path we have chosen. They are comforting in times of sadness, distress, doubt, and fear. When we meet spirit guides in LBL sessions, we know we are never alone and are always loved and supported. Guides are there for us to offer help, inspiration, encouragement, higher perspectives, and clarity when our life's path grows dim. Occasionally, they insist that we know the answers to specific questions and urge us to discover information and decide for ourselves. Receiving such a message of their belief in us and then learning to trust ourselves spiritually facilitates soul growth.

LBL sessions can include finding out the names of guides or what they would like to be called, which can be a simple nickname such as "Fred" or "Grace" if their name is too complicated or obscure to say and spell. When pressed, guides may divulge that their identity is more a pattern of vibrational frequencies that the human tongue cannot pronounce but only recognized energetically; thus, a nickname can be helpful. During LBL sessions, it's highly desirable to discover the circumstances under which it is best to contact our guides. So often, the answer is during meditation, quiet moments, and time in nature, although guides will enter our dreams, hypnogogic states, or reach out spontaneously during waking hours. Another important question to have answered is how we will know our guides are with us and can they give us a physical sign to satisfy our human conscious mind. The responses to this query are usually a symbol such as a butterfly, a physical sensation like tingling in one's body, a gentle touch on the shoulder, or perhaps simply a strong intuitive knowing.

Encounters with spirit guides in whatever form are life changing. To experience firsthand the unlimited love, purity, and divinity these beings offer energizes our souls and offers us a vast expansion of consciousness and awareness, along with opportunities for extensive spiritual growth and development. All guides are inherently teachers and often transmit vast amounts of knowledge to clients energetically, sometimes described as a "download." Guides can and will frequently provide multidimensional healing when asked. If this request is better provided for in another location, such as a waterfall of energy or by a healing team of souls, they will lead a client's soul there. Spirit guides, in whatever form, ensure a soul receives precisely what it needs, whether through LBL, dreams, meditations, or by their presence in a physical life. Although guides don't require gratitude, they inspire reverence, awe, appreciation, and joy. One only needs to reach out and be trusting and receptive to what they offer.

Elizabeth Lockhart
Editor

# THE WHITE BOOKS

## Lisbeth Lysdal

Laura is an engineer, 42 years old, and the mother of two young children. For the last few years, she has been working on getting a new perspective on her life. She had no prior knowledge of Michael Newton's works but was inspired to explore LBL after a public talk. She has no previous experience with hypnosis except for the past life regression she did in preparation for the LBL session described in this article.

Her wish for the session was to enable her to be present and aware in everyday situations with her children, as she often found herself lost in thought and wanting to escape from her life.

In her youth, she dreamt of becoming an author. She fantasized about all the classes she would take, all the books she read, and all the experiences she wanted to have. She wanted to combine all this knowledge and write books that would benefit humanity. Her father told her that being an author does not make a living. She abandoned her dream and chose engineering, as she loved mathematics, chemistry, and biology.

Even if Laura's previous experience with trance was limited, she went into a very deep state, and this was maintained throughout the session.

The session started with a few visits to happy childhood memories, deep contemplation, and a feeling of fulfillment. The body is a good fit in the womb.

She notices that the brain seems small and notes that this will change as she grows up.

We went on to Laura's most recent past life in a world of clear, soft, flowing water, a soft, flowing world of harmony and understanding, a world that gives hope. In this world, her name is Jakara. She lives peacefully until the day her husband passes away. Because this world is happy and peaceful without physical pain, the feeling of loss and sorrow from his passing is even more profound than it is in human form. This is not supposed to happen. Jakara lives on and watches her children grow. In the end, she decides to let go and leaves her body.

She feels connected to a source of energy and describes a structure of energy that connects everything. She has heard about those connections in her life as Jakara and is fascinated to see and examine them. Traveling along those connections, she describes the space around her as free and unlimited.

While she is moving, she tells me her spiritual name is Jamara. She is met by her guide, Lamila. Lamila takes her to a pool of happiness and laughter and lets her swim in this place of healing until she is ready to continue.

Lamila asks her if she wants to see the library. He tells her, "There is a reason you are fond of libraries in the incarnation as Laura."

C: It feels like a gigantic, magnificent place. Every soul has its own book. I do not have the need to look in the books of other souls. It is peaceful, like an old library. There is a tall cube and a lot of light and shelves. Even if I do not want to look at single books, I am curious about how others live their lives, how their journey is progressing, and what else is possible. I look forward to meeting souls that will share their journey and exchange stories.

F: Do you receive any guidance here?

C: I talk to Lamila tell him I want to see something new, something others have not seen. He says all is known. We do not discover here; we get what we already know.

Jamara continues to discuss the workings of the library with her guide, Lamila.

She continues to describe the library.

C: Something is changing. On the right side, there is a curtain or a white veil. I pull it aside, and there is a little theatre behind it. It is a game of pretending. I can look at the way we live our lives. This is my special interest.

F: Do you have a special connection to this place?

C: I want to be a librarian. I feel at home with the books. I help the visiting souls to find the correct entries and access the relevant knowledge.

F: Do you share this interest with other souls, or do you have a special guide here?

Based on the previous statement and her guide's reference

to her fascination with libraries in her incarnation as Laura, I want to explore the possibility that Jamara is training to become a librarian. I also hope to get more information on the white books.

C: I help the souls to get information. But any soul can read those special books. Those books are shiny, white, and thin. They do not contain the full story of their lives. The books contain general teachings, messages, and the knowledge the souls need now in their present incarnation. There is half a shelf of these white books. These books are different from the books of individual souls, but I (Jamara) think they are interesting. They are special books, not personal books; the same message is meant for more than one. The information is still deeply personal as the book changes to suit the reader.

Those who have access can choose a theme and get the wisdom that applies to them.

F: Do you have a special relation to these books?

C: Yes, I am a caretaker for these books. They need loving attention. Taking care of them is being around them, paying attention, and being present. When someone comes to get knowledge, I choose the book most suitable for their purpose. This is the interesting part. Choosing the book and presenting the book to them. It feels good. I help people move on, and I understand their curiosity.

F: Is there a connection between these books and the books for an individual soul?

C: The white books are lighter and have a fine and simple energy. The books for each soul are old and voluminous, like encyclopedias. The white books are as if they are made of light. They do not hold experience but wisdom. They are books of light.

With Lamila's guidance, she realizes that she prefers white books and is not interested in her own book. Lamila insists, and they enter the main library to look at Jamara's book. It is old, large, and dusty. She fears the book, and Lamila instructs her to make the missing entries. She has been carrying a lot of fear because she neglected to look at her own book and her soul's story. She has not gained knowledge and wisdom from experiences in her lifetimes.

The session goes on, and Laura realizes that the knowledge and wisdom she wanted to use as an author in her youth are connected to her specialty at the soul level. She sincerely wants humanity to receive these books' original wisdom of light. She becomes aware that she has used her attention and presence to gain knowledge and understanding and neglected to be present and aware in her present life as Laura. Both she and her relations are suffering from this. Jamara receives instructions for Laura – from Lamila and the Council – detailing how to use her knowledge and wisdom to be present instead of losing herself in all the information accessible to her.

The existence of the white books described by Laura adds a dimension to the library that I hope will be interesting to all. The white books contain generic information applicable to all souls. These books differ from the books for individual souls in that they are accessible for all souls presently incarnated, and access is not restricted to a particular soul or soul working with the archives.

# SUPPORT FOR
# HUMANKIND

## Nino Borsari

Early in my LBL career, a client was a middle-aged woman with an intelligent, elegant, quirky sense of humor, and much curiosity came to see me. She expressed a lifelong passion for learning and helping others, including animals. She had traveled widely and worked in nonprofit organizations. She was experienced with yoga and meditation. She experienced one of the strangest past lives I've ever encountered.

She had already experienced five fascinating past life regression sessions before her Life-Between-Lives (LBL) session: three lives where she was involved in the healing and teaching arts in several locations on Earth, one of which occurred during World War I. In a fourth lifetime, she was a type of 'animal whisperer' during the mid 1800s in Australia. Her fifth past life was extraordinary. She asked for and received special dispensation from her Elders to incarnate into a koala's body in the early days of white men settling in Australia. She was so upset at how many of these gentle creatures were being shot by early settlers that she asked to incarnate into a dominant male koala body to start instilling the instinct to hide from this new species of humanity.

She began her LBL session and quickly regressed to being in the womb.

> F: Give me your impressions now you're in the body.
> C: The first half of this life will be difficult. But the second half will be big.
> F: Please expand on that realization.
> C: I sense there will be many disruptions as a child and teen. It will help the stable part of my personality to learn to deal with change. Also, quite a few different jobs initially will teach me to speak up and to trust myself. I don't enjoy entering bodies at this density, so I've recently had trouble in a few vessels (bodies). These quick-fire changes will help me to stay focused. I also have a nagging sense that I have a task. This is a significant life.

Early on, I will learn to adapt quickly, and then later in life, I will help others who are afraid of change to adapt as Earth changes begin. I will know how to teach people to go within, to feel that inner guidance, and to trust that help will be there during adversity.

The Earth needs strong souls at the moment. This time I will be of support to humankind and benefit others with my confidence. I've had extra preparation for this sojourn. I have a heightened ability to look into people's motives and also see what they need. This will develop later.

F: What about your family life? Do you know the souls of your family? Have you had any contact with them before you came into the fetus?

C: Yes, they do know about me. My mum is good, we've been friends before. Dad too. I will have a good relationship with both my parents. They love each other and are on a spiritual course. They are both sensitives. Both do advanced yoga. It will be a big family and fun at first. But there will also be chaos (crying). It will be tough at times for them.

F: Do you know why?

C: There will be unexpected disasters within the family (My client is upset, and there are more tears). I am firstborn, so they will need me to be strong for the younger ones to follow. I can feel their heartbreak. Some won't deal with turmoil well. But it will be okay and is good training.

F: Is there anything else you sense is important? Ask your guides to tell you.

C: I can hear my teacher saying don't forget I have good intuition and much compassion. Don't allow your self-doubt to stifle your gifts. It can hold you back. Stay true to your heart, and you will do much!

F: Can you go to the time of entry into this body and talk me through the process?

C: I enter through the back of the neck and head in a fine way; I spin as I enter. It helps distribute my particles into the cells, including the farthest parts. It helps infuse and balance the integration of the character (of the host body) with the incoming soul.

F: Any other impressions before you are born?

C: (Speaking about herself in the 3rd person, which sometimes happens) In the second part of her life, she will step into her leadership role through transitions. She will have people and teachers sent to help her take shape. To awaken the training she has done.

Plus, a soul mate will appear. He doesn't incarnate often anymore.

We then revisited her past life in WWI as a medic. She reported being in the final battle, most of her fellow soldiers have been gassed, many young souls are confused and are hanging around.

F: What do you notice?

C: Well, there's a private sitting in his lifeless body, trying to get it to move; he's quite disturbed by it all. Soldier! Come over here! Excuse me, I need to attend to a few of these men; I realize I'm here to help them make the transition without getting lost. It helps that I'm a sergeant.

My client then recalls rousing the confused souls and reassuring them they would get home. The session continues with my client accompanying these souls through the tunnel of light back to the receiving area, where their respective guides or loved ones greet them. My client is then free to carry on her journey.

C: I've done this so many times, my body and I already have a low fear of death anyway.

We can move on now.

F: Is there anyone in the arrival area to greet you?

C: No, I don't need that anymore. It was a short trip. But my group knows I'm back.

F: After a violent life or death, we are sometimes offered a healing. Do you need something like that?

C: No. I am aware that I volunteered to be on Earth during a big war and that my main mission would end with me separating (from the body) at a large battle at a young age. Quite a few of us went to Earth for this. I was to make sure we looked after the younger souls as they separated. It all went well. We didn't leave anyone behind. I completed my mission successfully so that we can move on. I volunteered to be on Earth to help bring the young souls home. When the war began, it's like a veil was lifted. I knew that I knew I should be involved at an easing-of-suffering level.

F: Can you explain more about this volunteering?

C: I can tell you that just prior to the dropping of the atom bombs in WWII, there was what you might compare to a 'Public Address' asking for as many volunteers as possible to assist at the arrival areas, as there was about to be a huge influx of confused souls who will need our comfort and guidance. As far as I know many thousands of volunteers appeared. I'm told it was a good result. We are guided by Great Minds to be where we need to be. In ways I cannot express … It's really a great orchestration!

F: Thank you. Now, we can move on. Tell me about your soul group, your spiritual family. Do you go home?

C: No, not yet. Many are doing important tasks, and we don't need to meet up after every return from a trip anymore. We will get together later. A couple of them send a 'Welcome Home' message. I do look forward to relaxing later with them.

F: Tell me a little about them.

C: My group is getting more serious now. We are seven. Many, as do I, are taking the opportunity to recycle quickly during these times on Earth. Some are moving in different directions, and we have newer specialty groups that we are a part of. But the primary soul group is always the most special one. We still have wonderful fun when we get together.

F: So, can you tell me what happens or where you go next?

C: I'm a student guide, and I'm also a teacher; I go to my class, and my students are very pleased to see me. (Smiling beatifically) I'm delighted to be with them again, too.

F: What do you teach?

C: I'm involved with sharing how to bring the heart and mind into balance on Earth. I'm helping them discuss why shorter lives on Earth may be beneficial to more advanced souls. We are asking if it's worth it. This discussion goes: we have all chosen to spend some incarnations on Earth to learn from its more extreme duality levels. But, because we forget who we really are when we are there, we basically have to start again when we are young. It can be difficult and scar us for a while. But, once the scars heal, the wisdom from these experiences remains burned into the soul's wisdom forever.

Thus, increased compassion is one potential benefit: by increasing our breadth of experiences (mind observation) and heart-fullness (compassion). So, we discuss the advantages and disadvantages of Earth, comparing with more harmonious places where you don't forget your origins, or scar as much.

F: What is your view?

C: I'm training to be a guide, so on my path, these experiences help me build up my depth of understanding of complex situations from multiple attempts. So, for me, yes. I return often now, even though I often rebel when I'm in the body. We do build up valuable experience here, not available on simpler dimensions, which then equates more deeply and quickly into wisdom (Mind) and compassion (Heart), when you've suffered for it.

F: What have you learned on Earth recently?

C: I tend to over empathize. I get too involved with the emotional side of lives. Compassion is good, but too much involvement can make it hard to make the wiser choices.

I'm training to be a leader, so we shouldn't try to solve the problems of our wards unless they're in a real dead-end. That tends to be when they pray for help the most and turn on their intuition, feel, and listen closer to spirit; it can awaken us more quickly.

In my lives I tend to block transmissions from my guides. I'm not a beginner anymore, so they sit back and watch me work through it. But they're always close if I want to feel them. We've agreed for them to be less hands-on now.

F: So, guides helping out isn't always a good thing?

C: If they do tell/show us the way out, then we may not be fully tested and may be forced to incarnate again to make sure we've learned our particular lesson properly. You can't trick your way through evolution.

It's not wise to make it too easy for our wards. In time, we learn to hint at guidance and consider different options from the same old ones, for example. But normally, we don't directly instruct nor show them the way out, especially more mature souls.

Too helpful is as unbalanced as not helpful enough. It must balance. Earth is a tough task-master school! When you're finished, you tell yourself, "It was all just a scary roller coaster ride!"

We continued this exceptional LBL session, revealing a much higher understanding of how souls work with their guides on Earth.

F: I'd like to enquire about your soul's light.

C: My colors are royal blue at the center, with yellow edges.

F: What do these colors mean?

C: The blue denotes a guide in training. The yellow is about my creative aspects that I like to work with.

We completed the session with more details about her current life. She later contacted me and explained she always knew she was here on Earth to 'give support.' Her LBL session had shown her that she was supporting younger souls and training to be a guide. The information in this session also taught me how much support, care, and guidance are there for us on this turbulent planet, even if we are unaware of it.

# STAYING CENTERED TO NURTURE OTHERS

## Dr. Tahmineh Nikookar

My client Helen is 54 years old, a single mother, and seems wise. When she contacted me, she explained that her primary purpose in doing an LBL would be to get more clarity about her current life so that she could enjoy life more and be more relaxed. She told me she believes in past lives. Her LBL session went very smoothly, and she seemed to be stepping onto a familiar road.

She regressed easily to age 12 and then age 7 in her current life, which allows for the necessary mental stretching exercises before accessing a past life. At age 7, she recalled the time that she was shooting with her dad at a gravel pit.

It was fun, and she loved it.

She regressed easily to her mother's womb, where she was quite comfortable, but she knew it would soon be the time just before her birth, the time to be born. She could feel her mother's emotions occasionally, but she couldn't influence her emotions. She expressed pleasure about the body that she would be born with, as it would be a good match with her soul's consciousness. The mind works well, is very intuitive, and is also logical. She said, "I need my body and brain to work well together; I can't have any handicaps or hindrances."

She went quickly to her most immediate past life and then to the last day of that life. She is female and 86 years old, lying comfortably in her bed in her bedroom. She had enough time to think of what life lessons she had learned: how to be happy.

C: I had a good life and a fun time and enjoyed what I did. When I cross over, I feel peaceful and a bit sad because I had a pleasant life, but I do not want to stay longer, and I am fine to go. I will hold on to that nice feeling and move away further to come home.

F: What do you see next?

C: Everything is bright. It is a beautiful day. Above me, I can see a large globe of light. I am connecting with the larger light. We are moving towards each other. Other lights are waiting, and I will meet them later. It is a white light, and it envelops me with loving energy.

F: Is this a guide energy or a loved one?

C: It is my guide, a female energy with beautiful blue eyes. We do not need names. We just know each other. I am told I did a really good job in my last life. Now, I am being taken to another place by my guide. I can see buildings and beings coming and going.

We walk through a street and then up a hill to a big open area, a busy place with pillars.

It seems like I am going to get an assignment on what I need to do next.

F: So, you are being shown your next life soon after arriving?

C: Yes, my last life was very pleasant, and the next one is not, and now it is time to do some serious work to prepare for my next life.

F: Tell me more.

C: It is simple. Like getting a job, and I agree to do it. I find out by connecting telepathically with my guide to learn everything about the nature of this job. I know that, in my next life, I must be strong and help all these people work through things. I will be a kind of catalyst, helping others work through all of their problems. This particular group of people is coming to Earth in my life. My job is to be the center of the wheel, a strong anchor for them, and help them to be connected and do their work.

F: Quite a responsibility.

C: Yes, and a lot of work. I wish it wasn't quite as much work. This next life is not as comfortable as my last one. Now I am to go and meet with my Soul group.

She quickly connects with her soul group, which numbers about 15 to 20. They are bunched up, standing in a circle, and she is in the middle of the circle. She feels supported and peaceful. She is in the center of a clock face, and her soul friends are positioned singly at 3:00, 6:00, 9:00, and 12:00, and the rest are anywhere in between. She recognizes three female friends from her current life but only one of her children.

C: I am a lavender color. This group I belong to is deeply concerned with nourishing things to grow and develop. We are all advancing at the same rate. I have a connection with my partner in this life, who is in another group, and their main characteristic is action. Together, we can experience different things. Our job is to go to other soul groups to help them progress. I get the impression our group is very old. Sometimes, we like to experience what other groups do, so we go there to participate, but this is not our main purpose.

At this moment, she says she wants to go to a special place—a garden—and gather something to take with her. As her next life is set to be lonely, she needs to take something from the garden and keep it with herself. She goes with her guide.

C: I am here to get energy; it is yellow. I also need to take something from the garden which is more tangible than the yellow energy. It is a rock. It is beautiful, something from the air, and fits in the palm of my hand. It has that energy that straightens up everything. I need to hold it in my hand, then put it in my heart, and it will always be there. I can't take it with me physically, but I can if it is in my heart.

After this, she wants to go to the library.

C: There are beings here; they know who you are and will bring you your book. It is a big and heavy book; the cover is leather, and a special flower is on

251

it. There are lots of pages. You open it up, and it has pages and pages of old writing. Some writings are black, dark, and damaged, and other pages have beautiful drawings. Towards the back, there are clean pages, but not that many. I can put my hand on the book and get energy. The energy flows out of the book, but I know everything that I need to know, and I don't need to read it because it is a part of me.

F: What are you learning or experiencing that relates to your current life?

C: I need to use the energy stored up in my soul to nurture me. There are people in my group, whom I get energy from in this life, and they are people who I come in contact with. There is a young member in the group who is the youngest, and she is one of my children.

Next, she wants to visit the Council with her guide. She calls them "Wise Beings."

C: It is a kind of library; you go out to a countryside with mist. It is a small open place, not like the Acropolis, though it has pillars, and they are sitting around a stone table.

Nine "Wise Beings" are waiting for me. I'm standing in front, and my guide is with me.

F: Describe them to me.

C: I count nine. I sense they are on the same level as me. They show me males and females. It looks like they are dressed in work clothes and wearing something long and glowing. They have an order but no Chairperson. I get the impression they all have different jobs, different roles—their number changes after each lifetime. The Council is a place to give jobs to be done, and they just check to make sure I have everything needed for it. I know I'm not being judged; I can say no to a job, but I also know there is important work to be done. I am permitted to ask them questions about my current life.

F: Go ahead and ask your questions.

C: I ask if there is any message that will help me in my current life. (Pause) I have everything I need and shouldn't spend so much time worrying about it. It is a big job, but I can do it. I am one of their trusted people. Next, I ask them what my purpose in this life is. (Pause) Just helping all these other beings to develop and to know that I am doing well, and I have a lot to learn, and I must not let their issues bother me. My job requires so much to learn and not to worry about.

F: And why does your current life have so much in it?

C: I am an experienced soul, and my job is to help all these other souls right from the time I get here and for my whole time here. They can get stability from me; I don't have to do anything; I'm just there for them. My challenge is remembering who I am.

F: Like the center of the wheel that you described earlier.

C: Yes, like that.

The session drew to a close. Before she left, she wanted to return to her group to replenish her energy. After replenishing her energy there, she was ready to leave the spiritual world.

In the discussion after the session, I was interested in understanding exactly what she had learned and what guidance resonated with her.

C: Knowing my purpose in life is helpful. Otherwise, I would spend my time trying to interact with these situations and thinking that I caused them. That's what my human personality is like. Now, I will not spend my energy and time on something that doesn't feel like it is from the heart. I always asked why things happened and believed I was responsible for the situation in my family life. I now get a sense that all my life struggles are connected with this job I'm doing. And I must take time each day to remember who I am and where I come from.

A few weeks after the session, I telephoned Helen to see how she was doing. I was pleased to hear her tell me how much she had gained from the LBL session. It helped her to find the answers to many of her difficult life situations, whereas before, she would stress about how to fix things, worry about who was at fault, and get worn down by all the feelings that went with thinking like that. The higher perspective of knowing she is doing an important job has allowed her to relax and reduce her stress. "I feel better as things don't stick to me and float off more."

# Kate's Wisdom

## Patricia Fares O'Malley

Kate is from an Eastern European country. Although she speaks English well, you may notice the accent in her sentence structure and use of words.

This case follows her LBL experience when meeting her guides. They have taken her to show her a Higher Realm. Kate is silent for a long time as she experiences the beauty of this realm. When I ask if she would like to share what she is experiencing – she says:

C: Love is here. Freedom is here. Creation is here. This is a place of Creation. The one thing we cannot create here is life. But we create flowers and the environment of this place. It is very neutral here. Creation has no emotion. Creation is satisfied with its own creation. It doesn't experience, it just creates. We experience for her. So, it's good, and there are no feelings here where I am. My other selves experience feelings.

F: Tell me more about that.

C: Here, life has been hard. This new creation brings more freedom and more light. The creation is beautiful; it is not ugly. But even if it's ugly – it is ok! Beauty lives and dies.

Ugliness is part of the cycle. Flowers are made beautiful and then will not be the same, but that is okay. Neutrality is part of the cycle.

F: How does this help Kate in her life now?

C: She has to know that she has an energy that attracts people to her. But she must now be alone – be neutral for a while. She has to be alone. To find peace in herself. She must not do too much of this – not too much of that. Focus on staying above circumstances – neutral.

(She is quiet for a long time … she seems to be coming to some decision … so I wait, and finally, I move forward.)

F: Is there more you'd like to share?

She interrupts me, and I stop to listen to what she has to say.

Now she seems to be "channeling" her guide/s rather than simply reporting her experiences. The energy has shifted into a higher vibration in the room, and her voice gets louder, faster, and deeper. This is the transcript of her channeling.

C: We can see her now—she can stay neutral for a while—but we want her not to call for love now. (Addressing Kate directly) You must be you now. You have so much more to share than you know now. We will make this happen for you. This is why you are here. We will help you. We will call her to where she needs to go. We share our wisdom with her. She has so much wisdom to share. She will go where we tell her, and she will help many people. The moment that she begins to speak to people, we will show her the magnificence of herself. We enjoy her. We want her to know that we are with her. She enjoys music; we are music. She enjoys the ocean; we are the ocean. We want her to know that she is with us – we are her, and she is us …

F: May I ask who is speaking to Kate at this time? Giving this information?

C: She is an Angel with us! She wants to uplift people, but people do not want her help. There are many Angels, and we all want to help – but people, they ask for help, but then they don't do anything with the help. So, people are suffering. It is so unnecessary for all this suffering. But people don't want help – so the Angels have stopped helping. Right now, we watch. It is so sad. People are suffering, and they will continue to suffer a lot. It's not because of others; it's because of their reality. They don't want to end the misery. Sometimes, they call for help, and we come to help – but they don't really want help. So, this time, in this era on this planet – we Angels are not going to help. We are going to watch you heal on your own. We gave you help, but you forgot. And if you call us and say, "I'm ready, I'm ready," then we will come. Now, we can only watch to see what you will do. This is the moment to rise above your own evolution.

Most of the people of this planet know that we are here. We know – we have given the power back to you. Nothing we can do ... except we watch you!

F: Thank you! Are you ready to return?

C: You are a good woman, too, now—a very good woman. You need to know that!

F: Thank you.

C: I can see you! I can see you! The children of this planet are very special, but your planet does not support them well. It is important to very much support the children. You have to reach the parents. These children ... these children ... if you don't destroy them, they will be able to guide – a step forward – the evolution of this planet.

F: Please help me to understand more about this.

C: Parents forget the reality – the reality is these children – and you know that already. Affirmations is part of the way to help them. So, when the children are sleeping, they get the message in their brain, and they will raise their own vibration. The parents ... the parents ... the parents ... there is no more time ... there is no more time ... The parents were taught to value "things". They teach these children these same values, and it is destroying them, so we need an evolution for the parents, the kids, the entire planet ...

One of the ways to help the planet is to give the kids affirmations – and then they can raise their own vibration. They can teach themselves to love themselves.

In nature, we see two animals fighting, and then the next minute, they are fine. They don't argue about it … they don't keep fighting … they fight, and then it goes away.

This teaches all of you. Your feelings are like tsunamis – so you fight – but the next minute, you can hug. The same with the children – to make the negative energy a big deal – makes it difficult to let go. Teach the children to know that they can fight, but then they can say I love you and go for a walk together. This is how nature is … (laughs) This is for Kate too – she was able to catch this now.

F: Thank you!

C: Kate is ready to come back now.

# Out of the Darkness Comes the Light

## Diana Paque

Corinne is an artist in her 70s who has been on a journey of spiritual emergence. Over the last several years, she has done intense psychological work on herself and was referred to me to support her in working on the soul plane. We have had several sessions previously, and today, Corinne is coming up with questions about resistance to her artistic work and strengthening relationships with her children and potential partners.

As this journey unfolds, Corinne begins to feel the energy of her guides surrounding us. I support her relaxation and opening to the loving energies surrounding her today.

F: Notice how your guides appear and what you notice as you enter this space.

C: Off to the left, I have women guides, and one

of them is that huge Celtic goddess I've seen before – she's HUGE. There is one who looks severe but seems more focused and has green gossamer wings; she's pointing to something in the distance. And one who is very faint and hazy. So that's the 3 of them – they don't feel as playful as usual.

F: So, what are they pointing you toward if they are more focused?

C: The goddess is pointing across me to my right – there are some buildings coming up. There's a gold path that's curling around the buildings that I am taking. The guides are just watching and following me. There's a huge courtyard in the middle of the buildings; there are lots of little people doing things like the munchkins. This feels like "follow the yellow brick road!"– the guide says no, that's not what's going on – that's wishful imagining on my part. There's something else that is there - I see a brown dirt area but I'm afraid to go into it.

F: Ask her if it's safe to go there.

C: It depends.

F: On what?

C: On my bravery. There's this huge roaring presence around me. It's meant to scare me off, but it doesn't. The big goddess is smiling because I'm not afraid. She knows it is energy that is powerful but not threatening. (After a few moments, Corinne goes on.) I've floated into space in the darkness.

F: What does that feel like? Is it purposeful to take this step?

C: The goddesses are behind me and with me. Nothing's happening – just floating.

F: Let's ask the goddess for direction or insight.

C: She keeps saying I need to go out there.

F: Perhaps it means opening to the energy of the space and receiving it so that it can open to you.

C: It's a huge open feeling – brilliant as it opens - it comes all in my chest. It's dark around me, but I feel peaceful.

F: What arrives to you?

C: I'm going to get some knowledge since I opened up. It's brilliant in this dark space, and I'm learning. I am now eligible for the knowledge. The courage comes from staying open to what is here. It's like a brilliant flower emerging out of my chest – I sort of like it. I like being brilliantly out there – that huge presence would have scared off someone else – personified dirt 100 feet tall screaming at me. I feel like I'm getting some information everywhere I turn, a big download coming in.

F: You need to be open to receiving without trying to process at the moment.

C: Everywhere I turn, there is more coming. I'm so happy to receive it and to be downloading it. Now, some bright and dark downloads. To my right is this bright navy-blue space that is coming in as I turn toward it. I feel brave, but it isn't going to hurt me.

F: What do your guides say about this?

C: It's part of my training to be a guide – they're adding to my knowledge – it's exciting! Now they want to have a little party! The third hazy figure is like a tiny Buddha figurine: regal, really still, and watching with interest. They said it's enough now and you've received it.

F: What next? What do they suggest now?

C: I need to just be with it, process it, and allow what it is.

F: Is this something for this current life as Corinne or your soul purpose?

C: It's for everything. It seems that it's more for the soul and instructing the soul to be a guide.

F: Does this have a specific relation to this current incarnation?

C: It will help me definitely, but it takes practice.

F: Do they have some suggestions you can practice in your human form?

C: They said get in touch with the guides, be open, and ask the guides to help bring it into the intellect and brain knowledge. So, engaging with the guides more regularly. I'd like to go up here more often – it feels so good!

F: You can open yourself and simply expand your heart chakra to open and receive this connection and practice this to access this space and energy.

C: Will I feel different now that I'm downloading? They say, "Yes, you're more expanded now." Feels exciting!

The guides tell her to open her crown chakra to add to her expansion to support this openness, to move down through her body and through each chakra to support this connection moving through her, to help know this expansiveness throughout her body.

C: It's like I've lost all the molecules in my body. The download is masking the body until the body absorbs and takes it in. They're saying to take my time with this; it's part of the process. The guides are still here watching me, and their task was to help me with this download and engaging with the energy coming in.

(After a few minutes) It feels like my whole body is just swarming, like rivers.

(After a long interlude) It's coming to an end – it's subtle and getting quiet. Feels a little complete right now.

F: Any communication from your guides?

C: They wanted me to go to the violet lights, and when I did, I saw hands clapping, welcoming me, happy for me. But then, off to the right are three guides I usually see, the tricksters. I feel like I grew taller in their presence – I grew physically! I feel joyful with this download, and it brings me a lot of joy.

F: What are your guides telling you about this, and what happens next?

C: I'll be able to use this in my life. I asked if it would help with my pain – they didn't answer but I got an excited feeling. So maybe it will.

F: Will it help you with relationships with others, your children?

C: No, not in this life. It's about soul-level connections, but not in this lifetime with a partner. And asked if there is a partner in my vicinity – yes, so we shall see. And what do I need to do to be open to receiving a partner in my life?

They answered to just stay soft and present and talk to those out there and be present – I see humor in everything right now – I can't take anything seriously!

It feels lighter.

F: As a guide of young souls, you have to take them lightly – people tend to see the dark side, so having some light and joy can bring light to others. Can your guides share anything about your daughter and her ability to have children?

C: They just said children, babies soon, though that could be anything with their timing (she laughs).

F: Is there anything you can do or be to facilitate this for her?

C: Love her and encourage her on her path.

F: Is that the same for your son?

C: Yes, but I wonder why I had him. He had to come through me and his father to be who he is, he is an innovative brilliant artist.

F: Is there work to be done on your contract with him?

C: Just stay in touch with him, and I'm going to have to do it because he doesn't reach out.

F: Is there anything you are meant to teach him now?

C: Self-care: taking care of himself which he doesn't do too well. Putting himself out there more. Everything always came to him, and he needs to learn how to promote himself. It's interesting to watch.

F: Is he here in your life to teach you to guide?

C: Yes, because many of the young souls have a stunted emotional life, and I need to learn how to deal with this without trying to fix or assist them. Set little examples, be supportive and not absorb his challenges as mine.

We discussed her role as a guide to young souls and learning to withhold projections, especially dealing with projections onto her daughter about finding happiness in work.

C: She has no intention of doing that; she hasn't found what she's here to do yet. She wants to move to Bali – I don't want to go to Bali – too hot and sunny. I feel fortunate I have both of them – they teach me things and being in their own lives in this society.

F: Anything the guides are advising now?

C: All I hear is start art, but I want something more. Can they tell me more? All this downloading will help with the art. I will be more pleased with what I see.

F: Can they support you in addressing the resistance? Scanning you to release it?

C: It's in my heart area. I felt a huge thump. One of the guides is pulling something out.

There's a little knot on the end of it, so he had to tug on the end of it. It's a yucky thing.

F: Can they heal where it was?

C: It's sort of healed.

F: As you think about painting, what does it feel like now as you consider painting?

C: Well, it feels like I don't know what I'm doing, but it also feels like more of a flow.

F: What do they suggest about getting started?

C: Be open to receiving from them and be open and have them with me as I get started to work. Feels very exciting. It feels like a solution to this problem I've had. (She paused and then went on) I see myself during the download and what I was experiencing – I just loved it. When can I do it again? They want me to come here now and again to develop greater skill at doing it on my own. Contact them more.

This is the first time I've had the women guides, so it appears like more of them even though I know they're energy. I feel more energized than I've felt – active but quiet – a flow rather than a bolt of high energy. I feel like I got something powerful today, and I don't realize the power yet. They say it was important that I got this today and have it. I need to be in contact with them to expand more so that I can open to what is here for me.

F: What can they tell you about the download?

C: There's no human word for it – wisdom, information, but no human construct for it. More than wisdom, knowing – much bigger and fuller.

F: You're developing a stronger connection with consciousness beyond human experience and limits, so the language doesn't explain this – it's too vast. Recognize this by the feeling rather than the language – what do you notice in your body?

C: I feel like I've had a transfusion. I feel like I don't have bones but brilliant golden light encased in my body. It feels beyond good – I feel like I can still function in human form, but the connection beyond is now expanded.

F: They seem to have been working on your soul connections today.

C: Yes, we can describe it a little bit, but not really: the feeling is just ... (takes a deep sigh)

Feeling the universe within you, flowing through

you, bigger than we are and not stagnant.

C: Too hard to talk about it. I had this vision of my body floating in dark space, myself outlined by a body but me being gold light; even though it's encased in the skin, it's so huge – no way to describe it. I'm so fortunate and lucky, yet I still feel so alone when I go home. I still struggle on a human level.

F: How can they help with this?

C: They said it's not going to be a problem, but you can be yourself: 2 things existing at once – the vastness of consciousness and the human body.

F: How can you learn to connect more comfortably with others on a human level?

C: Be more present, to show up and there's nothing more to be done. I will attract someone who is also showing up. That's what they always sort of say that I still have the same human information.

As Corinne returned to the room, we chatted about her experience and where it lies in the progress of her journeys. She knew already that she was in training to become a guide for young souls and that this life was meant to help her learn how to take on this role and what to do and be. Her art had reached a place where she was stagnant, and the message from today's journey was to invite her guides to be with her as she worked.

Following this session, Corinne moved from her house to another location. This move stimulated her art as she was in a location that was hers alone. In her previous home, she had engaged in art to dissociate from her failing marriage, and the physical move gave her space to enjoy art for its own sake and her pleasure.

Corinne came to see me for another few sessions, during which she worked with her guides to download and learn more about herself, her relationships, and her place in the Universe. She ultimately learned that she had received all the downloads to support her work, and her connection to her guides continues in her work and connections to her children and friends.

# CONCLUDING INSIGHTS
## on Guides & Advanced Beings

**G**uides and other advanced beings are often conceived of as non-physical entities that exist in higher dimensions of reality beyond the limitations of the material world.

In some traditions, guides are viewed as departed loved ones, ancestors, or ascended masters who continue to offer guidance and support from the spirit realm. Others conceive of guides as celestial beings, angels, spirit animals, or divine messengers entrusted with aiding humanity in its spiritual journey.

Regardless of their form or origin, guides possess profound wisdom, compassion, and insight, offering higher perspectives and assistance to those seeking guidance. Guides offer support and advice and may provide insights, inspiration, and intuitive nudges to help individuals navigate challenges, make important decisions, and align with their highest purpose. Guides serve as companions on the spiritual path, offering encouragement, comfort, and reassurance during times of doubt or uncertainty.

In addition to guides, individuals may encounter advanced beings such as enlightened masters, extraterrestrial beings, or entities of higher consciousness in their spiritual journey. They are often described as emanations of divine wisdom and love, embodying enlightenment, compassion, and universal harmony. Encounters with advanced beings can be profoundly transformative, catalyzing spiritual awakening, expanded awareness, and profound insights into the nature of ultimate reality. They may impart teachings, transmissions, or energetic blessings that accelerate the process of spiritual evolution and personal soul growth. Moreover, encounters with advanced beings often evoke awe, reverence, and interconnectedness, awakening a more profound sense of purpose and belonging in the cosmic tapestry of existence.

> *Our relationship with guides is one of students and teachers rather than defendants and judges. Our personal guides help us cope with the separateness and isolation that every soul inherits at birth, regardless of the degree of love extended by our family. Guides give us an affirmation of Self in a crowded world.*[10]

Guides may come in different shapes, colors, representations, and disguises. Yet, their energy will be immediately familiar; this is when we know we have reconnected with these divine beings.

Sanela Čović
Editor

---

10   Michael Newton *Journey of Souls*

# CHAPTER SEVEN
## ON DIVINE GUIDANCE

# INTRODUCTION
## on Divine Guidance

Spirit guides, angels, spiritual teachers, ascended masters, Council of Elders, spirit animals, healing teams, and other advanced beings can be integral to a Life Between Lives session. One or more guides meet most clients upon entering the soul realm after leaving a human incarnation through regression work, typically at the end of a past lifetime. At times, spirit guides are also present during one's childhood as an "imaginary friend" or during time in the womb, usually because a soul needs extra care and support. Embarking on an Earthly lifetime as a human can require large amounts of preparation, tenacity, and courage for a soul. Souls incarnate for special purposes or learning, ideally involving their expansion and growth; however, souls also work together for one another's benefit. A soul may feel ready for challenging circumstances in an upcoming incarnation but may harbor doubt, anxiety, and insecurity. Guides and other forms of Divine Guidance encourage and reassure our souls throughout their transition to and through Earthly sojourns.

Although our souls wish to remain deeply connected with the spirit realm and our unique intentions and purposes, we are challenged with amnesia upon reincarnating. The conditions on Earth can be highly distracting and seductive, sometimes luring us into hedonistic pursuits, self-gratification, and living a shallow life. Our souls and their intentions can become estranged and forgotten, usually until a human crisis opens our hearts and we turn inward to our soul selves and seek more purpose and meaning. There are several effective ways of accessing our souls and Divine Guidance and connection, such as meditation, prayer, hypnotherapy, contemplative activities, automatic writing, creative pursuits, time in nature, dreams, and more. Our guides and soul selves provide an essential source of wisdom and guidance and can help us find our way back and reconnect to our soul's purposes and intentions for our lives.

The soul often uses the human body as a finely tuned instrument for receiving information and connecting with higher wisdom. Seeking stillness, calm, and going within can facilitate these phenomena. In everyday life, information and guidance can be received as a "gut feeling," strong intuition, and inner knowing, and they can include what have been defined as our psychic senses (see below). These abilities can be strengthened over time with effort. Meditation and other techniques for becoming very still and receptive while expanding one's consciousness can allow information to flow more easily.

Clairvoyance is a clear sense of vision, i.e., psychic sight.

Clairgustance is a clear sense of taste, i.e., being able to detect psychic information orally

Clairsalience is a clear sense of smell, i.e., the ability to detect psychic information nasally.

Clairaudience is a clear sense of hearing, i.e., the ability to detect psychic information through the ears.

Claircognizance is a clear sense of knowing, i.e., psychic insight.

Clairsentience is a clear sense of feeling, i.e., the ability to detect psychic information through your body.

Clairempathy is a clear sense of emotional feeling, i.e., detecting psychic information through your emotions.

Clairtangency is a clear sense of touch, i.e., the ability to detect psychic information through your hands.

Learning to connect with and trust our soul's guidance and wisdom, along with other forms of Divine Guidance, such as our spirit guides, is crucial to living a soul-guided existence. Living in such a way allows us to overcome spiritual amnesia, discover our soul's purposes and intentions for coming to live on Earth, and courageously follow our path, ideally noting what Michael Newton referred to as "signposts" along the way. While fate and destiny are sketched out though unwritten, and souls are ever blessed with the power of choice, our lives are divinely inspired and guided creations.

Elizabeth Lockhart
Editor

# Finding the Next Purpose

## Jerry Joseph, PhD

This is the story about Larry, an older man's desire to learn what he might do in the remainder of his life. He has a PhD as a Licensed Clinical Counselor and has been an educator at a large state university. He had successfully experienced previous regressions, including one spontaneous regression. Having retired from his teaching position and essentially closing off his clinical counseling practice, he feels "… like a rudderless ship blown around with every change in the wind. Whenever I start thinking I know what I should be doing now at this stage of my life and start moving in that direction, a door slams in my face, or all my motivation drains away. I'm just sort of floundering, and my life has never been like this before (at least not in this lifetime)."

This was causing Larry much suffering, and he wanted to understand why.

Since he is out of state and we both feel comfortable with Zoom, we agreed to have a virtual session.

Larry indicated that he had been adopted as a baby, and he had a wonderful life until his adoptive father died when he was five. He had been very close with his adoptive father, who spent much time with him. Afterward, his adoptive mother, whom he loved, married two more times. He said that his first stepfather was abusive, and he and his siblings were glad when their mother divorced him. He said the next one, while not abusive, was, unfortunately, indifferent. When he had grown, he was able to find his biological mother, and they developed and maintained a positive relationship until her death. He went on to a successful career in counseling and teaching at a university.

Following the induction for an LBL, which led to a regression, it was suggested that he step into another life at another time. He was quiet for a moment.

F: What are you seeing or feeling?

C: Things are gray, and I seem to be a little confused. Anxious.

F: If you look at your feet, what do you see?

After a moment, Larry answers.

C: I'm wearing combat boots.

F: What do your clothes look like?

C: I'm wearing a green uniform. A military uniform, I think.

Larry pauses before answering.

278

C: I'm with a group of guys, and we're all in uniform. British, I think. Some have helmets, and some have aviator's headgear. There are biplanes and triplanes around. It appears that I was an aviator in World War I.

I am a machine gunner in the back seat of a biplane, and we are getting ready to go out on a mission. There is higher anxiety than usual because we are expected to encounter German planes, and one of the pilots is a renowned ace. When we meet the German planes, there is a chaotic dogfight, and my pilot was flying upside down in an evasive maneuver when everything seemed to go black. We had been hit, and the blackness was from my burning plane. We had parachutes, but I had been shot badly and couldn't bail out. I think my pilot might have been able to. I am going to crash and die.

I ask him to go to the time of his last breath.

C: I'm already out of my body. I'm watching the plane crash and burn with my body in it. I'm floating above it. I felt no pain. It wasn't as bad as I thought it would be.

F: What do you do now?

C: I'm hovering, watching the dogfight.

After a moment, he continues.

C: I'm worrying about my mother. She will be so upset. I want to go see her.

Larry pauses for a moment.

C: I'm there in my mother's house now. She doesn't know that I'm here, but I sense that she has a feeling of foreboding. I see that she got her Bible out this morning, and it is lying on the table. When she stepped outside for a moment, I turned the pages of the Bible to the passage [John 14:3], where it begins, 'And if I go and prepare a place for you...' She thinks the wind turned the pages, but later, the memory of this gave her comfort.

F: What do you want to do now?

C: There isn't any reason to stay around. There won't be a funeral. My body was burned too badly.

F: Okay, so what is happening now?

C: I hear music. I'm floating to the corner of the room where there appears to be a tunnel, and I float in. It was a little tight getting in, but then it expands.

Larry's happiness is evident.

C: There is my daddy. The one who died when I was five. He has been my father in a few other lives. He is going to go the rest of the way with me.

F: Okay, keep me updated.

C: We're stepping into the light. There are others here.

With happiness, Larry continues.

C: I now see that my adopted mother and father have been together a number of lifetimes, and I've been their child a number of times.

F: Who else do you see?

C: I see someone who I think is my guide. He looks like a Frenchman. Dark hair and a mustache. I call him 'High Self'. There was someone I wanted to see, but she isn't here.

After looking around, Larry takes a long pause and makes a statement rather morosely.

C: Oh, she's in another place in the universe. We may not be connected for a while, but later, we will.

F: Where do you go now?

C: My guide is leading me to something like a hot tub with reclining seats. He is turning on lights – all colors of the rainbow and beyond. I feel as if I'm a balloon with air being blown into me."

F: Well, enjoy yourself. Let me know when you are finished with having your energy replenished.

After a bit, Larry responds.

C: Okay, I'm finished now.

F: Where does your guide want you to go now?

C: He's taking me to a place where I'll be with my soul group and teachers. It is similar to a neighborhood with different sized houses. Ours is a large two-story house, and there are study rooms where teachers come.

F: Does your group have a particular characteristic or purpose?

C: We specialize in advancing spiritual knowledge and related information. There are other groups that we work with who have different specialties. This is interesting because in my current life, I worked for a while in a Baptist ministry.

F: To make it more comfortable for us, do you know your name and your guide's name?

C: It is coming that my guide's name is Akor, and my name seems to be Sanji.

I suggest that Larry ask Akor if this is a good time to ask more questions. He says that Akor says that it is, so I suggest he ask about feeling rudderless at this point in his life and what advice Akor might give.

C: Akor is pretending to be somewhat offended by the idea that I have been rudderless. He says that he hadn't abandoned me. Rather, he is the one who guided me to read the Newton books, and then he continued with this effort until I had contacted a facilitator. I agree that it was a good idea to find out about The Newton Institute and set up an LBL.

F: Is this a good time to ask more questions?

C: Akor says yes.

F: Okay. Ask him this question: What would he suggest you do with your life at this time? I know we talked about whether you would want to be a facilitator for The Newton Institute, so you can also ask about this.

C: Akor is saying that I could be a facilitator, or I could pick my counseling back up, but less clinical and more life supporting, or I could do some of both. He is saying that this is my choice, but any of the above choices can be fulfilling.

Larry had more personal conversations about two people who had entered his life during the last two years, and he received guidance about them.

F: Is there anywhere else that Akor thinks would be useful for you to get information that you can use in your current life?

C: Akor says that he always recommends visiting my Council of Elders. He is taking us there now.

F: What are you seeing?

C: I seem to see three entities, but they are a little blurry. At first, I saw one of them with the face of one of my male relatives, who I always thought was very wise. This threw me off a bit, and I shut it down.

F: Why don't you ask them why the entity appeared with this face?

C: The one who had the face is talking to me now. He said that it is to show that I will be receiving wisdom.

F: That sounds good. What are you being told?

C: He says that I need to integrate the energies of my head and heart. I need to listen to my heart more. I already listen to my head. My heart has different frequencies and different knowledge that will be beneficial to me. He then reinforces the need to keep on doing things for my physical health.

F: You might ask him what other information he could give you as guidance in your current life.

C: He is saying that I have made substantial progress in being less overbearing and more respectful of others' choices.

After a moment's reflection, Larry continues,

C: I probably had the tendency to be a bit overbearing when I was younger in my current life. He is also saying that I need to moderate my somewhat unreasonable tendency to not want to burden anyone in any way. He says that I need to gain balance in this aspect of life. There is no harm in getting some help from those who want to give it.

F: Anything else?

C: I am being told that this is not a full life review from my Council. This is the reason that their faces were blurred to me. They were fine with giving me a brief update, but a fuller review will take place at another time.

F: Is there anywhere else you feel that you want to go?

C: Actually, I think that I've received the information that I wanted. I'm ready to come out of the session.

After thanking Akor, I made the usual suggestions to return Larry to full consciousness and full recall of all he had seen and heard. A few days afterward, in a conversation to gain his approval for using his case as a case story, he said he was delighted with the information he had received.

# BECOMING
# INDEPENDENT

## Joy Nicholson

Sarah is a Sound Therapist and is currently studying BioAcoustics. She is 65 years old.

Her intent for our session, amongst other things, was to gain a deeper understanding of soul groups. She had been told in a previous LBL session that she did not have a 'fixed' soul group, and she wished to know more about this and to understand the process by which she chooses other souls to work with.

I was intrigued by the concept of not having fixed soul groups, as I understood (formed in my LBL experiences and from reading Dr Newton's books) that we are part of a soul group from the moment we are created to eternity.

Sarah has had a lot of experience in hypnosis and easily reached a deep trance, which was maintained throughout the session.

We visited several of her childhood memories and then progressed to her Mum's womb, where she became aware that she was a bit anxious about her body choice. On exploration of this, Sarah understood that she had chosen this body to learn 'about the power of being quiet, working on subtle levels and learning through observation.' She had chosen strong, tall bodies and learned through action in many previous incarnations.

We then went to Sarah's most recent Past Life, where she was an Australian soldier in WW2 called Joe. We entered Joe's life on his 21ˢᵗ birthday as he and his mates were on the Kokoda Trail in New Guinea in 1945, on their way to an allied outpost after many months of battling. Joe died that day with some of the other troops when a faulty bomb exploded at the outpost.

Sarah/Joe's soul was quickly released from Joe's body, and they felt a deep sense of peace. They were met by a being who carried the Caduceus and performed healing "after that life in a war-torn civilization so that all the sights and experiences of savagery are being put in perspective – being balanced so that I can look at them as they need to be seen and not cloaked in emotion, in preparation for reviewing what happened."

Layla's (Sarah/Joe's soul name) personal guide came forward and took her to meet with The Wise Ones, where several of Sarah's questions were answered on other topics she wished to understand. After this, Layla visited the library (Akashic Records), where Joe's life was reviewed. She learned that Joe's life was a lesson in maintaining, perfecting, and honing purity and innocence and seeing good in others (even those who had performed atrocities). Joe had done wonderfully well in this regard.

When I asked Layla where the best place was to go to

have Sarah's questions about soul groups answered, her guide took her back to The Wise Ones.

> F: What can they offer about Sarah's understanding that she doesn't have a fixed soul group?
>
> C: It's a certainty that I don't have a regular soul group, but they are showing me threads of light extending out to various other souls who I connect with and reincarnate with. They are saying, 'Because Layla is a softie, she always goes for the nice ones!'. What they are meaning is that our contracts are usually of a non-confrontational nature because of my nature. So, it's supportive, caring, and loving – not challenging.

The Wise Ones then assisted Layla in gaining understanding and insights into some of the contracts she has with souls she is currently incarnated with (which confirmed the supportive nature of these).

I then requested permission to ask The Wise Ones a question and was given the same. I asked why not all souls have a 'fixed' soul group.

The response was:

> "How reincarnation structures are formed is based on the needs of the human side of the equation and with increasing fracturing of – in the way western civilization structure their community, this has necessitated a lot more – having freer higher souls to enter into more fluid contracts in the human world so that – there are a lot more people now, a lot more souls – moving outside the soul group's structure so

they can experience more broadly and perhaps this is a sign of – the soul's evolution itself, that it doesn't – it's not so dependent on – on a soul family but it is now becoming independent. Each soul is stepping out independently and has the confidence to do that. So, the structural change has been – a reflection of the human structural changes to meet the needs, but it also reflects the development of the souls that are reincarnating."

I thanked The Wise Ones and commented that I assumed support was available to these independent souls. Indeed, was the answer and:

"That's part of the trust structure that is now so firmly in place that each independent soul needs to have a degree of trust that there is a support structure for it. There is a lot of support, but they need to have the wisdom and experience of reincarnation that allows them to be at a stage where they have enough remembrance of their soul – so that they know they have a soul. Therefore, they know that there are other souls they can call upon for support. So again, a sign of that evolution – because without having that remembrance of originating and being part of a soul and originating from a soul-based community – the suicide rate could be quite high. And that would not necessarily be productive. So again, a sign of soul evolution of those who are incarnating."

Sarah felt that she now has a real sense of 'where I fit in' both immediately after the session and several weeks later, which gives her much comfort and confirms her purpose and aims for this life. She was intrigued by how Joe's life achievements (perfecting and honing innocence and purity) were the perfect forerunners for her current life. She is pleased that she now understands how she chooses other souls to incarnate with.

As Sarah is a humble lady, she quietly accepted her level of soul evolution. On the other hand, I was doing star jumps from the beautiful information offered!

I chose this case because I feel the understanding and insights Sarah and I received from The Wise Ones regarding how a soul can and does evolve to become independent may interest readers.

# SUPPORT FOR
# BECOMING

## Elizabeth Lockhart

D ee is a client who was referred to me by a Reiki practitioner
friend. She is a 49-year-old electrolysis technician who
practices Reiki and offers crystal singing bowl meditations.
Dee desires to explore what seems to be holding her back
from expressing her "true self." While her electrolysis clients
appreciate her work, she has trouble accepting their praise and
appreciation. She has trained in various healing modalities
and yet feels she keeps getting in her way because she is afraid
to step out of her comfort zone and express her spiritual
beliefs. She has three children, two of whom have been
chronically ill, and the constant worry and financial strain
have been challenging for her and her family. Additionally,
she greatly misses her deceased mother, with whom she was
close and who was a significant source of emotional support.

This client's aims for the session center on becoming

"unstuck" regarding her life's purpose, living authentically, her career, and her family's health issues. Although this case has several interesting features, one of the most salient themes is Dee's fear of dying for her beliefs.

Her guide in the Hall of Records, her Soul Self, her Council of Elders, and her primary soul group, which includes her deceased mother from her current lifetime as Dee, readily offer support and encouragement.

Dee experienced a past lifetime in 1826 as a dark-skinned male in his late twenties, José. He was wearing rags and aboard a large fishing vessel, navigating through rough waters with a group of men who resembled "pirates" in their mannerisms. José felt fearful and thought he "doesn't belong" and "thought differently than them."

He is fulfilling a family obligation by working on this ship. His father is aboard the boat, and he expects José to conform to his adopted lifestyle, which creates tension between them. José's last day in this lifetime occurs around the same age as he is in the opening scene. His father, feeling betrayed by José's unwillingness to think and act as he does, abandons him on the beach of a strange, uninhabited island. José describes the oppression by his father and feels isolated, sad, and angry toward his father for leaving him. There is nothing but rocks, sand, sea, and sky. José is sitting on the rocks in this desolate place, feeling defeated, hopeless, hungry, thirsty, and weak.

He lies down and is waiting for death to come, almost welcoming it.

At the moment of death, José feels an intense energy coming in and lifting him out of his body. There is a feeling that everything will be okay, and soon, he leaves his body behind on the beach. He experiences a sensation of being pulled upward and continues to float further away, higher and higher, with no remorse. He describes a feeling of peace that he is dying for standing up for his beliefs and not giving in to what his father wanted, but instead doing what was right for himself.

José sees a column of light going straight up, pulling him upward. The space around him becomes even brighter, and he feels he is being cleansed in the column's pure, bright white light. After spending time there, he exits through a doorway and is greeted by a strong, wise, masculine guide named David, with whom he is familiar.

F: Describe to me where you go next.

C: I'm greeted by a man whom I've seen before as a guide.

F: Do you notice a color of light emanating from this man guide?

C: It's just more white light.

F: What do you call this man? You've known him before.

C: David. I feel like I'm standing at this door, preparing for another journey or adventure. I have a backpack and a walking stick, and it's like I'm needing to prepare for something. I don't know.

F: Just go wherever you're led and describe for me what happens next, where you go, what you might see or do.

C: We're just walking, and he feels very mortal-like.

F: How does it feel to be walking with David?

C: I feel very tentative; I'm kind of timid like I need time to assimilate or get used to where I am.

F: (After deepening) Look at David and tell me

what he looks like.

C: He is very handsome, short dark hair, blue eyes.

F: And he has been your guide before?

C: Yes. He's a very strong masculine presence, very educated. If you saw him in a room, you would think he was a lawyer. He is very wise. He's not a soft or emotional man.

F: Where do you go next with David?

C: I feel like I'm being taken back to a library; I assume that's what it is, which is where I first saw him—a building with books.

F: Books, yes. And as you go there, is there a special book that you're looking for?

C: Those answers to my life's path.

F: Is this book your book or a general type of book?

C: (Emphatically) My book!

F: Are you in the library now?

C: Yes.

F: How do you find your book?

C: David is leading me to it. The books all look like they're ... they don't look like regular books ... they look more like light beams ... more energetic than actual texts.

F: Yes, more like light beams or energetic books. What happens next?

C: I want to open it, but I'm afraid to ...

F: Tell me more about that ... why are you afraid to open your special energetic book?

C: Either I'm not going to like what's there, or I'm going to be afraid, or it will be too hard to see what's there.

F: What helps you overcome your fear so that you might examine your book?

C: He's telling me that it will be okay.

F: Please describe what happens next after he reassures you.

C: I can see the book on a table, and I've got it open, and it's super bright ... like bright light. I'm trying to read it, and it's not clear; there are no words to read. Maybe I need to feel it ... It's a different form of communication.

F: Yeah. Does David help you to tune in to your book?

C: I'm putting my hands on the book and just trying to feel the energy.

F: Yes, feeling the energy, trusting what comes. (After some time) Do you feel as though you are beginning to understand and connect with your book?

C: I definitely have a sense of where I'm supposed to be on my path, but being able to see anything beyond this moment in my lifetime on Earth now is not clear.

F: (Deepening) Do you have a sense of your soul's name – what does David call you?

C: It feels soft like an "s," soft and feminine sounding, and an "f" sound ... Sophie.

F: As you feel into your book, with the help of your guide, is there anything that stands out for you or grabs your attention?

C: He's bringing my attention back to my fear of death from other lifetimes for standing up for my convictions. Me being left to die because my beliefs were different from others.

F: Do you have a sense of where this fear is located in your body in this current incarnation?

C: In my heart.

F: Hmm, in your heart. Can we please ask David if there's a way that we can help you heal from that to become stronger and release this fear? (Note: I was holding my hand over her heart space with the intention of helping to move the energy using Reiki)

C: I'm feeling almost like he's kind of joking with me ... laughing, uh, saying I've been trying and that it's not something that's going to go away with a quick swipe of a hand (amazing!), but that I need to continue to do the work, to chip away at it, and that I am doing the work, it's just slow to dissolve.

F: Chip away at it, doing the work. Are there things that you might do in this current lifetime as Dee to assist in clearing this fear so that you can move forward?

C: Just continue to listen to other people telling you ... people who you've worked with or on, who tell you of their successes, and to trust them; listen to other people's voices and not your own so much.

F: So, to listen and trust these messages of success that come? And the messages within yourself; does David have ideas of how you might work on these yourself?

C: I'm not getting a clear answer ... (after some time) finding ways ... meditation, quiet time, connecting with David ... to help block out external negativity so that it doesn't filter into my own mindset.

F: Yes, so making time for meditation and

connecting with David, quiet time, letting in messages of success, and blocking out negativity? C: Yes.

When attempting to ask questions that Dee has brought with her, David "steps back a lot," and Sophie senses energetic beings nearby. There are three beings in all who emit green, purple, and blue lights, respectively. Sophie describes them as separate beings, yet the colors blend and flicker together in flame formation.

They seem to communicate together as one. I ask permission to refer to them as "wise beings", which is acceptable to all.

When asked how Sophie is doing on her soul's path, these wise beings tell her she is where she needs to be in her current life as Dee. Upon inquiring into Sophie's career path in her current life as Dee, they tell her that it is important for her to work with people and make them feel better in multiple ways.

Although Dee currently does this as an electrolysis technician, Reiki practitioner, and one who plays crystal singing bowls, she is told that she needs to "step out of her comfort zone." When asked what she might focus on as a next step, the wise beings convey "school, education, formal as in human services, as well as alternative." Much of what she is seeing/receiving are possibilities that Dee has imagined in this lifetime, so I deepen, in case there is more, at which point the wise beings fade.

Sophie notices that her mother, Joan, who was Dee in her current lifetime, appears. In this moving encounter, Joan tells her that she is being too hard on herself as Dee. Sophie admits that, like Dee, she has always been one to get in her way by overthinking and needing to prove more to other people.

Her mother answers questions regarding assisting Dee in her current lifetime to progress and become "unstuck" and offers, "Live in gratitude." Joan also wants to reassure Dee that "the kids will be fine," which is comforting and emotional. As Dee, Sophie feels her mother has pride in her and can use this in her present day to help validate, support, and encourage herself in overcoming some blocks. I confirm that Joan is part of Sophie's soul group, and Joan leads her there.

Joan leads Sophie to a park with grass, open space, gardens, flowers, statues, and water fountains to meet with her soul group. At first, she felt many energies around her and no one in particular, but then she expanded her consciousness at my suggestion and allowed soul group members to come forward. The first member is Dee's husband's grandmother, Louise, who calls her "Dear heart" and tells her that she is "amazing and that I should believe in myself."

Another family member comes forward whom Dee does not know in her current lifetime: a great-uncle named Ralph, who died very young and appears to emit blue light. He is adamant about being recognized and supports Sophie as Dee, encouraging her interest in genealogy, a shared passion.

She senses that many relatives are there to support her, yet they don't come forward individually. Questions about career path and purpose are answered collectively with, "to make people happy, and you already do that." Sophie, as Dee, realizes that in her current lifetime, she must internalize this message more fully and reduce negative chatter.

Regarding medically related financial stresses in her life, she hears from her father's grandfather, Tom, who was a disabled farmer and emits a light green color. He emphasizes that health is important, not money, and not to sacrifice health for the sake of money. Sophie feels more love and senses more individual energies around her that acknowledge and support her in her current lifetime as Dee. She states that this is her primary soul group, which also feels like her family, even those she does not notice—one last question posed in the soul realm concerns "next steps" regarding Dee's career. The responding guidance comes from Sophie to Dee and urges her to take any step to get her moving and unstuck, even if it's not in the "right" direction.

Dee was awed by being in the presence of "something bigger", including the soul realm itself, her spirit guide David, the wise beings, her soul self, and her soul group members. Reuniting with her mother's soul was especially poignant and meaningful. She was relieved by the realization that there was no need to "sweat the small stuff" from this higher perspective. Dee was reminded that she has much loving support from the soul realm, which can assist her in "becoming."

Awareness of the repeating theme of having died because of her convictions and the related fear of being her authentic self has helped her to understand herself more. Through experiencing her Soul-Self in these ways, she now notices a transformation from feeling stuck to being more hopeful and joyful.

Later, contact with her revealed that she is indeed "stepping out of her comfort zone," as the wise beings suggested. She is performing crystal singing bowl meditations for large groups, planning to take academic classes, and enjoying traveling with her family.

# THE DOME

## Sanela Čović

This story is based on the case study where my client will experience a beautiful healing place between the end of life and the Life Between Lives. I called this story "The Dome," honoring the space and time some souls need to heal and move on into the loving and caring realm of Life Between Lives.

My client is a young female therapist and mom of two who wants to understand more about her anxiety and what she needs to learn to reach a fulfilling life. She also wishes to visit her soul group and see if any of her soul mates are in her current life.

After a beautiful revisit to her childhood memories and taking time to explore the womb, we continue the journey into the past life.

It's a warm day, and Pavel is outside. He is a middle-aged man who wears brown formal shoes, trousers, a coat, and a hat. It was 1952, and he was in Surgut, Soviet Union. He is on his way home to his wife and daughters but feels lost.

He is looking for a bus that goes towards home. He had been in a business meeting with six other people. On the way home, after the meeting, he is upset.

Something went wrong in the meeting, and he had been told some things he did wrong.

Pavel is 45 on the last day of his life. He got drunk and died of the consequences of sickness. He feels sick, throws up, and cannot stop, and that is how he dies. He feels like he falls asleep. He got drunk, ill, and died. This was not a good life. It seems like a wasted life because he did something he didn't like and lived without much joy.

Now that this life is over, his soul moves fast toward the purple light above him. The purple light gets lighter and more prominent as he is moving. It is a sphere-like form.

# The Dome

He finds himself in a purple dome. He feels alone and lost. He has yet to learn that this is where he needs to recover from the previous life, contemplate, and heal enough to move on with his guide. It will take some time before his soul moves to the spirit world. He is afraid; he doesn't know what is happening.

After a considerable amount of time (in Earthly time), he moves again towards a bright light on the horizon. He is moving towards a light blue, medium-sized light. He is moving towards the lighter and endless space. There are many lights in the distance. Some are brighter, and others are less bright.

They are everywhere, above, beyond. It looks like an electrical grid but is in linear movement. He is in a horizontal position in relation to the grid. He is landing just like a plane would land at the airport. There is a lane in front of him with all the lights, and as he moves horizontally, he needs to change position and move vertically to land on the lane. He is in a hub surrounded by electric blue light. He follows that blue light. It looks like a vortex. This connection gets lost, and he finds himself back in the dome.

It looks like there is deep space above him, dark purple, deep sky. He is alone. He feels and sees nothing. He is waiting for something to happen, like the sky before sunrise. He doesn't feel lonely alone; he feels normal, not scared.

He stays here for a long time, in Earthly time. Time doesn't move; it is an interesting concept that he cannot grasp time. This dome is only for his soul: it is vast. It seems like some lights are moving on the perimeter but not approaching.

The purpose of being in the dome longer is to rest. This is a place to rest and think of his past life. He is thinking about his past life, which seems unhappy and wasted. It feels familiar being there.

Soon, he starts feeling positive energy from the outside source. It comes from above the dome. He can see this energy that looks like the sun. It is like seeing the sun from the Earth, but not too shiny. The sun-like energy lowers itself into the dome. Now it is in front of him, and he can see its oval and long shape: bigger than him in size. He feels much calmer and less empty. He feels hugged. It is Nashraf, his guide, who has male energy.

It is time to move on from the dome into the open space. He remembers his soul's name: Agrin.

A blue and white space is like a big sky, where the light is like sunshine and comes from everywhere. Some beings are floating and dancing all around. They are just moving through. It seems like they're on an excursion.

## At the playground

Soon enough, Agrin arrives at a familiar place where his soul group sits on the stairs of a large building.

C: There is a group of friends, who look like a group of students sitting in front of school/ university, on the stairs inside a large building. There are five stairs where one can sit. They are divided into different groups: a group of four are on the left side on the first stair, and the other two groups on the second stair a little further to the right. All of them are close to each other. This place is called the playground.

This is a place where Agrin usually goes between incarnations. He feels he belongs with them. It is like going to the first grade of school, where he needs to meet everyone again. Their colors are golden-yellow to orange and very warm.

Agrin has a triangular shape, wears layers of light fabric, and constantly moves. She is a female, quite tall, white and yellow with golden edges, inside white, then yellow, then darker golden edges.

## In the Park, aka
## The Contemplating Place

The Park is just next to this big building with the stairs. Everything here has more or less the same colors but no defined shapes. The park is bathed in reddish light in the setting sun. There are trees in the park, and one can take a walk, relax, contemplate, and think. There is a bench where

Agrin contemplates and thinks. This park is something private, not for meeting friends typically. There are similar places where other souls relax, think, and contemplate.

# The Wise Beings

Agrin is now in front of the tall building. The walls seem to be made of strings, which is why Agrin can see through them. She can see what is inside the building. There is a big hall, and it seems very tall.

Agrin stays outside. She can see inside, and it looks like a very serious place—a place of decisions and examination. She goes inside but not alone. Nashraf is behind Agrin on her left. It looks like a cathedral.

The Wise Ones invite her inside. It feels good. Agrin feels positive energy from them. There is a big table, and 5 Wise Beings are sitting behind it. The one in the middle stands out; his energy is male, and he looks like a warm, golden, very dense light, somehow resembling an older man. There is one female and three other male energies, too. The female one is on the Old Man's right side. She is purple. Her name is Eria.

Agrin is in front of the Wise Ones. Nashraf is behind her on the left and stands in front of them during her visit.

The number of the Wise Ones sometimes differs after incarnations; some are not always there. The number and composition of the Wise Ones depend on what they need to discuss.

They are quite serious, but they will not be hard on Agrin. All of them address her; they communicate telepathically. It seems that Agrin didn't do enough to enjoy life and her choices as Pavel were to go with the flow. Like Pavel, Agrin made easy decisions, which made her life difficult. In her current incarnation, however, she is making different choices.

At this moment, one of the Wise Ones, someone on the right side of the middle, sent a warm, white light towards Agrin. It filled her, giving her a positive charge and a good feeling. Allowing the light in, the positive light, made her feel good and more complete. He sent her this light as an encouragement. He is a male with long, light brown hair.

Here, we ask questions. Agrin, in her current incarnation, had prepared for this session. Eria answers the question about the anxiety disorder and says it is related to being uncomfortable. She confirmed that she needed to learn separation and not avoid negative emotions, not only in this lifetime. It has been an issue in past lives, too. Pavel's life was about avoiding all emotions. Agrin is doing quite ok; she is on a good path. She hasn't gotten an answer about her grandparents being incarnated yet. After just a few moments after answering the questions, the Wise Ones left.

Agrin is now back on the playground stairs. She is moving backward from the stairs and park, ready to incarnate.

# Back in The Dome

She is alone back in the purple dome. The dome seems like a place where you come and go. It's a stop-in-between and a place to begin the journey back into her current life.

My client wanted to understand her anxiety disorder, as well as to see her soul group and ask other questions that are important to her in this life.

Her past life as Pavel was disappointing, and it took her a long time to recover enough in the purple dome, the rejuvenation place, before she could meet her guide, Nashraf, and move on into the spirit world.

She managed to see her soul group, go to the contemplation place, meet the Council, and then return to the dome before incarnation.

She gained the understanding to look at things positively, to live a positive life, and not just sit and complain. She understands her life better now, and she needs to look at it from a positive point of view.

Possibilities are open, she is encouraged, and she has a positive feeling about the future.

This is the most important thing she needed to understand while remembering and feeling the otherworldly energy recharge from the Wise One.

# FROM DARKNESS TO LIGHT

## Janna Aidarkhanova

Cassie was one of my first online clients in the summer of 2020. An artist and a mother of two grown daughters, she was also training to become a past-life regressionist. Cassie had not experienced an LBL before but had heard about it, and in her pre-LBL session, womb, and birth trauma had to be cleared and understood from a higher perspective. Cassie had prepared a cast of characters and a list of questions for her LBL asking about the purpose of her life, her skin sensitivity, and possible relocation to another country from Greece, where she currently lives.

In the womb, Cassie gained a lot of insight into the sensitive, emotional system of the female body with which her soul was integrating. This client commented that while not in the fetus' body in the womb, her soul goes to visit the "other" family.

The client described in detail the last day of her past reincarnation as a soldier of the highly trained, elite parachute squad of the British Armed Forces in WWII. He was on a special mission that went awry. Once he jumped, the Past Life incarnation, Gregory Davis (Welsh), was shot in the legs from the ground, landed badly, and had to shoot himself to avoid being captured by the enemy. Upon his death, the client experienced a variety of emotions and deep pain: anger, sadness, disappointment, and thoughts of his mother and sweetheart.

Once out of the body and standing next to it, the soul's perspective quickly took over and shifted his feelings.

C: I feel relieved, proud. I managed to pull that trigger…

He went on to experience an impromptu past life review:

C: It was a heroic life. I enjoyed the strength of my body; was competitive, sportive, confident, popular. I had a nice, supportive family, parents, and a comfortable childhood; I loved my career in the Armed Forces, offered good outlets for my sports ambitions. I felt a great deal of integrity fighting for my country and people, for their freedom… put my mental gifts and powers to good use…"

After saying some goodbyes, he felt changes occurring.

C: There is a pulling upwards from the back … I'm looking back at Earth, which is becoming a blur … now turning to see where I am going.

The client described the crossing over in this way.

C: It's a frequency… I was expecting to be pulled into outer space, but it's a frequency… As a Soul, I am leaving the physical band of frequency… and the sense of movement comes as frequencies change into higher vibrational frequencies… so it's not really a physical movement; it's attuning…

F: Which frequency is your soul attuning to now?

C: I still have to move through some frequencies until I find the one that resonates with where I came from… Nice journey, a sense of going home… As I move through the frequencies, the ego personality must dissolve. At first, it feels as if I am alone, then the sense of separation diminishes. There is always the sense of individuality, but at the same time, the feeling of merging with the field, with the resonance itself, within the oneness of the resonance… I feel very comfortable, safe, familiar…

F: How do you perceive your body now?

C: It's an egg of energy, a sphere … it's not moving… the frequencies are changing … like an elevator, and the floors are moving …

F: How does the frequency of your final destination feel?

C: Like a very fine vibration…

After being greeted by the soul family in her spiritual home, Cassie met with her spirit guide to review the past life.

F: The insights and realizations from that past life have already started coming. Is there someone who can help you understand it better?

C: Yes, my teacher or guide, a mentor, comes to me. They are like from the next level and guide me as a soul between incarnations.

F: And who are they? Is there more than one?

C: One main one, he is always there.

F: Is he predominantly male?

C: He is whatever I want him to be.

F: What do you call him?

C: Khudrah.

F: And what does Khudrah call you?

C: (after a long pause) Leifing-la. It's hard to put it into words...

Khudrah offered an additional perspective on my client's past life as Gregory Davis in a private chat with Leifing-la:

C: Did ok, but a little too centered on self and heroism... Gregory's self-centeredness was not allowing... if he wasn't so beguiled by glory and gone into elite parachute, he could have found other ways to serve more usefully for other people and community.

However, he wanted to push his limits, and that's okay... (The guide said)

F: Has Khudrah given you any feedback about your future choices?

C: I get the feeling that I have to go back and... take some of those heroic qualities and courage, but next time, use them for the greater good, for the good of humanity and those who are close and those who I can touch and influence and be with... because I am very much concerned about this dark shadow over

Earth… We [Leifing-la and Khudrah] joined the others and there is a debrief on the way.

F: Are they the same group that you visited when you were in the womb?

C: Yes, they feel like home. A lot of us chose to reincarnate at that time of WWII, on all different sides: Japanese and German housewives… like we wanted to get the global human experience from this war, and now we are comparing notes … and some of us are still down there, still in it … some chose not to go at all … There is this discussion about the darkness, or shadow, over Earth … it's energetic but manifests as ideologies and belief systems, and then acted out by humans … So, what we are discussing is this energy. If it's a problem on Earth, will it bleed through to other frequency bands of existence … like a cancer? It's not all love and light in all spiritual realms either … there are also dangers and concerns…

F: Is your group specializing in something?

C: Honor, protection… (client laughing) We are a little bit like a parachute elite team.

Protection of the truth and the light and of all things good and right…

F: Do you specialize in this only on Earth or other frequencies?

C: Most of us specialize on Earth, but some are working on other frequencies of existence, who have been on Earth and are graduating in a way. That's why they leave the group to apply what they've learned in other frequencies of existence … Earth can accommodate all the levels of schooling depending on where one incarnates, when, and as who … We are all learning about honor, integrity, and courage. Once we learn about them on a basic level, we can demonstrate them in such a way that they can affect other souls in other incarnations. Still, ultimately, we serve the Godhead ... Earth is a tough school, and resilience and strength need to be built up, as there is such a strong illusion of separation from Source. Still, it is such a rich experience ... I get a sense of water and creatures of water – like the energy of dolphins and whales, but much more connected to Source, just getting used to being separate from Source.

Only very heroic souls can take a long detour from Source, and only if they wish...

F: What else do you do for recreation, learning, and regeneration?

C: We play the games of strategy, like a human chess board... but there are also moments when we need to immerse ourselves like in water... feels like a sensory deprivation. Like a void. It serves a purpose of reconnection to the Godhead or recognition of the Godhead within us ... checking in with Source without any distractions, free of constructs or games ...

I allowed the client to immerse herself in the void for a deep reconnection with Source.

The Place of Higher Wisdom for the client was the library, where Khudrah took Leifing-la.

C: It's a record place or Library but not with books, but frequencies again... all answers, knowledge is kept here. It's guarded by Guardians because it has to be … It's not like any building … don't perceive any boundaries. It feels like infinite space or outer space … Like water, it's a sea of knowledge that can hold infinite amounts of information … Khudrah has a pass because he has proven to be a mentor. I don't think I can go there without him. So, what happens is that you ask a question, and the filing system is such that the frequency of the question matches the frequency of the answer or the other way around. The frequencies arrange themselves according to whoever is in there, so it's a different experience for every soul that enters, so now it is just me and Khudrah.

F: Shall we try how it works?

C: Yes.


Then, I read all the client's questions, and as she answered, I wrote them down to provide them on a separate paper after the session. With the client's permission, here are some of her questions.


F: What is Cassie's main purpose for incarnating at this time?

C: To bring Light when there is darkness, to protect that Light. Be strong and brave; that's why she has warrior energy. By not backing down in the face of dark manipulations and demonstrating her own Light, she gives others the courage to stay within their power and inner Light.

F: How can Cassie best support her life purpose?

C: She is finally doing the right things by learning to work the Light Realm and transmute the darkness into Light. The therapy training will help people to release the low frequencies that they hold … Cassie went a bit off track for a while, but it wasn't a wasted journey as she learned many things – honor and integrity – and now she is doing her life purpose.

F: What are the main challenges in this life for Cassie?

C: Within all challenges lie the gifts … to uncover them, must go through the challenges. Self-doubt, also sensitivity – is a blessing and a challenge … with it comes the danger of being overwhelmed by the darker charge. Overcoming that is in itself a good learning that requires courage and strength and self-belief…

F: Where on the Earth is Cassie best placed to fulfill her life's purpose?

C: Doesn't really matter … Some places are less distracting than others for fulfillment of her life purpose. Greece is okay for now; it is a place of meetings and safety. There will be time, maybe in the near future, if Cassie chooses to leave … It's about frequency – whatever she does, wherever she does it. The whole bandwidth is moving up, and so her mission is to strengthen the top-end frequencies and dismantle the lower end … making them unstable. Many souls are being called to stabilize the higher frequencies. Her soul family is engaged and helping with that. Honor, courage, and strength of character are important to us.

The Earth is moving up to a high band or octave of frequency. Earth is an instigator of the frequency of the low. Earth consciousness has been comfortable in the low. As octaves move to a higher-end spectrum, the old resists with all its strength …

F: How can Cassie best support herself?

C: Staying focused and committed to the path she is walking now… Dropping those people, habits of a lower-end frequency… For example, she tries to help souls wishing to experience lower-end frequencies, thus wasting her time as they chose to experience those. Unless they expressly ask for help. Alleviating suffering is a fine quality to have, but the compulsion to help people can take away the experience from another; what they have chosen for themselves can tip over into control and backfire on the noble cause … Courage is required to let go. But Cassie is getting better at discerning … between those who really want to change and those who want the attention…

Before leaving and rejoining her soul family, the client suggested that Khudrah wanted to give her something as a gift.

C: It's a black beetle in my hand – meaning the knowledge of the dark sorcery … Knowing what it is – its weapons, attacks, manipulations – weakens its power and gives a better chance for neutralizing it.

F: Any other words of wisdom or advice from Khudrah? (still at the Library)

C: Be patient with yourself!

After the library visit, the client attended a Council meeting, where she received even further personal insight, guidance, and reconfirmation of her mission.

The Council supported Cassie's choice of reincarnation as

Cassie at these times on Earth and offered several viewpoints on the role of art in Cassie's life. They emphasized the importance of the artist's intention in creating and expressing their art to raise the collective's frequency. Cassie's life is unique; her mission is to help the shift.

C: It was a great challenge and honor to be here at this time … a good test of what I learned so far to demonstrate what I learned in other lifetimes.

The client was even able to formulate the role of the Council in the current shift.

C: It's a very fine balance (for the Council) between interference and assistance – very delicate, like a surgical procedure. They are assisting Earth by mitigating potential damage to Earth's life forms while respecting free will. However, the tipping point hasn't been reached to push the dark off, where it can't destroy anymore. The Earth is a mighty being. Some of these races are working with humans energetically through channeling and contacting humans telepathically and bringing messages and wisdom … and all of them are broadcasting frequencies, which are available for humanity to tune into.

After her session, Cassie was incredibly surprised and touched by the experience despite what looked like a familiar journey for her Soul and her natural navigation through spirit realms.

Cassie received many answers to her questions. She said post-session: "I already feel the richness of life. Misty mirror cleared …"

As a therapist, it was a rich and valuable experience that proved that an online video platform works as well as in-person facilitation for even a 5.5-hour session.

# Concluding Insights
## on Divine Guidance

**D**ivine guidance is central to facilitating spiritual growth, inner transformation, and alignment with one's soul's purpose. By attuning to the subtle whispers of intuition and the nudges of Divine inspiration, individuals can navigate life's challenges with greater clarity, discernment, and resilience. Divine guidance offers a compass for the soul, guiding individuals toward healing, self-discovery, and expanded consciousness.

Moreover, divine guidance fosters a deeper connection with the Divine Source of all creation, whether conceived of as God, the universe, or the higher self. Through prayer, meditation, and contemplative practices, individuals can cultivate a direct relationship with the Divine and open themselves to receiving guidance, wisdom, blessings, and grace from higher realms of consciousness.

*We are divine but imperfect beings who exist in*

*two worlds, material and spiritual. Our destiny is to travel between their universes through space and time while we learn to master ourselves and acquire knowledge. We must trust in this process with patience and determination. Our essence is not fully knowable in most physical hosts, but the Self is never lost because we always remain connected to both worlds.* [11]

Sanela Čović
Editor

---

11   Michael Newton *Journey of Souls*

# CHAPTER EIGHT
## ON HEALING THE EARTH

# INTRODUCTION
## on Healing the Earth

## Voices of Earth

We have not heard the music of the spheres,
The song of star to star, but there are sounds
More deep than human joy and human tears,
That Nature uses in her common rounds;
The fall of streams, the cry of winds that strain
The oak, the roaring of the sea's surge, might
Of thunder breaking afar off, or rain
That falls by minutes in the summer night.
These are the voices of Earth's secret soul,
Uttering the mystery from which she came.
To him who hears them grief beyond control,
Or joy inscrutable without a name,
Wakes in his heart thoughts bedded there, impearled,

Before the birth and making of the world.[12]

Earth is our chosen physical home while we are incarnated here and is so much more than the bodily senses can perceive. It is a place of great diversity and miracles, an expression of astounding beauty and creativity.

Many believe the Earth is a living, breathing entity with an expansive consciousness and a deep spiritual connection with all its inhabitants and Creator Source. While the ancients and many indigenous cultures have revered the Earth and taken their stewardship of and belonging to it with great seriousness and as a sacred commitment, modern society has become more utilitarian and self-absorbed.

Modern attitudes have been more in keeping with the idea of Earth as being here for humanity to dominate and exploit to its own ends. This has led to mass destruction of habitats, resulting in endangerment and even extinction of many species. Contamination of land, air, water and now space, continue to poison Earth's inhabitants in many ways. Although Earth is resilient, regenerative, and generous in providing for her children in phenomenal ways, she has her limits.

Some who feel a deep connection and reverence for Earth feel visceral, psychological, and spiritual pain for how Earth is mistreated. Mined for ore and gems, drilled for oil and gas, and polluted by many manufactured components because of the production of items such as plastics, our planet is becoming more challenging for humans and other species to inhabit. Burning fossil fuels and the existence of confined farming operations (CFO) are contributing to global warming and wreaking havoc on our planet by

12 *Voices of Earth,* a Poem by Archibald Lampman

contributing to the formation of superstorms. Consider the damage from war that rains down and destroys layers of soil, trees, plant life, and animals in its wake, not to mention manufactured structures of cement and steel. Humankind's egoic self-absorption, carelessness, and aggression have led to multidimensional catastrophes and woundings of our planet.

Since everything has a form of consciousness, including every blade of grass, animal and rock, albeit unique to a particular species and element, there are vast modes of communication on Earth, oftentimes too subtle to notice with humanity's chronic busyness and obsessive nature. Humans worry about not having enough of this or that and tend to lead a fear-based existence, striving for more and more, with a fear of scarcity and greed prevailing, steering the planet toward potential destruction. Earth, and even the sun, feel humanity's disruptive and careless energies, emotions and acts, and respond violently with hurricanes, tornadoes, droughts, floods, Earthquakes, volcanic eruptions, wildfires, and tsunamis. Humanity has overpopulated the Earth, leading to more pollution, increased creation of inhospitable environments, and increased diseases and pestilences. Humanity's overpopulation has contributed to a grave imbalance on Earth in many ways.

There are many souls here in human bodies and other forms whose purpose for being here is to aid Earth during these difficult times. These souls have chosen to strive to teach, protect and heal our beautiful planet as their life's purpose. Protection and healing can be offered in many ways, some of which are obvious, like efforts toward recycling and cleaning up ocean litter. Decreasing air pollution by reducing carbon emissions from burning fossil fuels is another. Other interventions are more subtle and energetic, such as worldwide group meditations to manifest peace. Many contribute in small ways by taking simple actions such as turning off lights when not in use and composting organic matter. As souls in human form, an LBL can shed light upon what our purposes are here on Earth and can reveal much about our planet and our relationships to it.

There are many types of beings, including discarnate beings, who watch over Earth and care deeply about what happens to it and its inhabitants. Some clients refer to these beings as the "Earth Watchers" during a Life Between Lives session, although other names are used. Indigenous people are familiar with this concept. Souls from different star systems also help to guide humanity through its blindness and into the light of awareness and connection. Each one of us can contribute to Earth's healing by cultivating peace, reverence, and gratitude within, which then radiates outward to All That Is. The purpose or intention of many souls and collectively is to assist in Earth's healing through connection, understanding, appreciation and love, and to use their unique gifts, talents, abilities, knowledge, and wisdom to that end.

Elizabeth Lockhart
Editor

# IT ALL STARTS WITH ME

## Diana Paque

**D**orothy is a 67-year-old woman at a transition point in her life. For years, she has been the director of a small rural non-profit that serves people with disabilities. It has been incredibly stressful this past year, causing her to have increased health issues, including hand pain and seizures. Dorothy is now at the point of retiring, and so she is seeking support for her transition and for being productive for the rest of her life. She has been happily married for 35 years, although about 20 years ago, her husband acquired a traumatic brain injury.

Dorothy herself experienced such an injury earlier in her life as the result of a drowning accident. She had a near-death experience, leaving her body, going into the light, and sensing unending love, light, and peace. As we discussed this experience, she revealed that she wanted to see if it was real– could we replicate it in our session or find something completely different? In addition, she tried to understand this life and her lessons to learn and find out if there is anyone she is here to help or work that she has missed. Her relationship with her mother and younger brother is also concerning to her. This brother is set to receive the entirety of the mother's estate and has never left home; he is now in his early 60s.

In our first session, we decided to bypass going into past lives and go Home. We moved across the rainbow bridge to go Home, calling on her guides to support her on this journey and with her intentions. As she struggled to go home, a horse joined her to help with her travels. She expressed her sadness as she traveled yet continued to push on.

> C: I just sense loss. I've asked the horse and the guide to lead me to a place with flowers.
>
> F: And are you there? You're there. Okay. And how is the sadness outside of you now?
>
> C: Still feeling sadness, but a little more removed from it. Yeah, I just felt like I needed to break free of something, so I galloped with the horse through the meadow to get that rush, that sense of freedom. And now we're both done with galloping and kind of resting and waiting.

Dorothy attempts to engage her guide to release or explain the sadness with no results. However, her guide leads her through a forest, walking through tall redwood trees. She explains that she knows something is on the other side of the forest with a shiver, and realizes it is her Council.

> F: How many are you picking up on?
>
> C: Oh. Gosh, there could be five or six, easily five or six, not more than that, okay.
>
> F: And are they kind of in a semicircle in front

of you, or?

C: No, there's a great big Redwood slab table, very rustic. Okay. And they're sitting on the far side of this slab table. They're ensconced, yeah. But it's all very simple. Yeah, it's not elaborate, and it's very Earthy. And as I was going through the forest. I got the message that I'm just way too disconnected from nature. I have it right around me. I have total access to nature, and I have to get in it again. And maybe that's why the Council is so, so simple and just sort of ... I don't know.

F: Let's start with what you need to know right now. What would be most helpful right now?

C: They're having a conversation and they're light energy. Sparkles at different rates. But I don't know what they're saying.

F: So, realize that you are picking up the energy, and you're not hearing it with your human ears, and so they may, in fact, be downloading or giving you that in an energetic form.

C: (with another shiver) They're very busy. There's a lot going on. Uh, I don't understand this, but you don't have to hear it; you will feel it. There's nothing I have to hear right now. They're communicating. It's a feeling. My right hand is hurting. Right. It's like my feelings are blocked. I'm not feeling the sadness anymore, but it's there to stop feeling the sadness. I've blocked all feelings. I am not feeling the love. That joy was very brief.

F: I'm wondering if they can explain this process that you're going through—this intense feeling and then no feeling, so intense pain, intense sadness.

Intense joy. And then nothing. Can they support you in greater understanding now? So, what are you getting?

C: Their lights have melded they're not pulsing or sparking. Or vibrating. It's like they've melded into this essence that has pastel colors kind of going through it, and they're expanding it over and around the table towards me, trying to reach me and envelope me in that light. But it only gets so far. I'm closer to the Council table now. I've moved closer to them. And there, the melded light essences are much larger. It's really big. But it's close to me. But I'm still so separated from it. I'm a speck of light now. It's like now I'm in the same form. And just very slowly letting someone engage with my light. Trying hard not to try hard. Wow. Just so tiny, and so little light coming out. Compared to this vast, beautiful melded flowing pastel essence. I want to be part of it. A little better. It's slow, but I'm progressing. It's slow, but I'm progressing. Okay.

F: So just let that opening happen. It's like they're entering you and reworking you. Giving you this energy that you need.

C: Now I'm getting it. I'm starting to calm down. I'm getting that I'm trying too hard. Too high of expectations of yourself. Enjoy it, they're telling me. It's not a marathon. You have lots of time. The Council's melded pastels engulfed me, and then it became like a funnel. Uh-huh. With me going down in circles down into the funnel, and it's darker, not pitch dark, but just darker versions of some of their colors, and I don't know where I'm going.

Now it's like a flower like a hummingbird would go to, and the tunnel narrows and narrows and narrows and it goes down and it winds around. Then it just opens out into this really open space. And I'm out in this open place. I see this giant flower that I just went through. It's like a flower, not like a tunnel, actually. Like I was inside the flower, and it's like an abandoned medieval parade ground. You know, it's not like a meadow; it's trampled. What the heck? It's not like it's permanently deserted. It's just not in use right now, okay?

F: Does it have a feel of familiarity to you at all?

C: Well, yeah, there's like a lot of souls have been here. Uh-huh. It's just like being at a fair after everything's been taken down. Okay. Where there's still the feeling and the sense of a lot of people and excitement, and movement and interaction. But they're gone. It's just empty. But it doesn't feel lonely. It's empty, but it's full: their energetic imprint is still there. I can walk around this place, and it's almost like I can visualize that there was this, you know, seller of copper wire here and this, you know, rope maker over here, but they're not there.

F: Is this a capacity that Dorothy has in this life that she is awakening, or is this something that you have on a soul level?

C: I can feel it. But my eyes don't see anything. I'm starting to see some of the people. I'm just wandering around, taking it in. There's so much activity.

F: Is your guide with you? No. Okay, so this is just you at this point. And I'm wondering if there is anyone among the energies who are surrounding you who you were meant to meet. And we can call out to them those who are here to support you, or to teach you, or to be here so that they can come into your range of vision or knowing.

C: Well, there's a guy in green. He's just kind of hanging apart from all the activity. I just noticed him because he is just hanging out. Rather than doing anything, he doesn't seem to have a purpose like everybody else does.

F: Are you able to talk to him?

C: Let's see. No, no, I can't talk to anybody. No, nobody's reacting to me. They don't want me to see the people. They want me to feel their souls. Ah, that's what it is. Feel their energies. Contact with the souls. Not with what they look like.

F: Is that part of your purpose in this life also to feel the energy and connect with the soul?

C: I had to feel the soul energy first. And it all felt good. It was exciting. It was interesting. It was, you know, happy people were having a good time, and I could feel all that. I'm going to go back and see if there's something with that guy, OK? No, I don't get the sense that I have anything to do with him. Wrong there. It's my guide. He was just hanging out, waiting for me to go through all of this. He just doesn't look the same. Yeah, he's smiling at me. I seem to be done here, but I don't know what's next. He says follow me, and we're going through a vegetable garden, okay? He actually communicated with me! Very vibrant vegetable garden that's a well-tended, well-loved garden. Very vibrant and healthy. Very bountiful.

F: Is the garden important?

C: Well, I just saw a rabbit. The message here again seems to be to connect to the Earth. And there's just so much bounty. The message is really about vibrancy and bounty and how life just gives that. Sort of, you know, just overflowing with vibrant life energy in this garden. Yeah, this vegetable garden is important to me. I'm not here to harvest anything. I'm just here to feel it. To connect with it. Okay, now we're leaving the garden. Now we're in a ... we've moved to a hut with a thatched roof. And we're inside. There's a dirt floor. It's very simple. Very sparse. Nobody's there, but it's well cared for. It's just like their way. I'm inside, and I'm looking around. It's just one room. But it's loved. It's simple. It's very Earthy and simple. And uncomplicated. I would say unencumbered. It's just simple wooden benches and a stool and simple table.

F: Is it about this place and how it looks as opposed to the people who might own it?

C: Yes, it's not about the people. Keep it simple, stupid.

F: So, this seems to be a big lesson about simplifying, getting back to the Earth, engaging yourself with the abundance that exists without complicating it. Yeah, so far slowing down. Being one with nature allows you to engage with other souls in a different way to feel them.

C: I'm really getting a strong message that that's the main thing I need to do. And the rest will come.

F: It's like you had to slow down in order to let the Council in. It's not about doing; it's about being.

C: Thank you. I'm outside the hut, taking deep breaths and enjoying the clean, crisp air. There's a freshness and a purity. I can see the garden from where I am. Here comes the horse again. The horse has come up to me, and it's nuzzling me. Okay, we're headed off to a forest again. Maybe the horse is my guide, seems to be doing different things so.

Uh, we've gone to a place in the Redwood Forest; it's a place where the mother tree has been burned out or died out, and there's the ring of all the babies. And I'm standing in the middle of that circle. Really powerful. Again, it's just power and energy from nature and being in nature; it's there for me. And then just waiting for me to come and be a part of it. Get out from behind the desk.

Oh, here's my guide. He has the light again. And he's communicating and getting it. It's not what I expected. That's what I need. Don't worry about the pain in your side. This is really nice being in this circle with him. This is the most relaxed I've felt this whole time. It's so peaceful here. So quiet. This is the place I go to. Redwood Circle is my place. And I can go there in my mind.

It's a sanctuary. It's a safe place. It's a place to recharge to connect to access this solar energy. I've gone up as an energy light. Not really a ball, but essence up through that middle between the trees all the way up through the trees and out. Into the sky. And I'm like a mist. There's no me to see. There's so much freedom here. There's no queries. So lovely. And absorbing energy from above and from the trees below.

My guide is with me now and taking me up higher, somewhere higher. I don't understand this, but I'm expressing that I would like to meet my soul group or, you know, connect with some other souls, and I'm strongly being told that's not what I need right now.

F: So, what do you need right now? Your ego wants these things, but you're being told that isn't what you're here for today.

C: I just need to replenish my energy. I just don't have the energy to do the people thing. Yeah, that's a pretty strong message that I have to make these connections to be able to restore my energy or access my energy. No, they're not going to let me connect with anybody, that's clear. Now, what I'm getting is that it's very peaceful, but also getting that it's very personal. That this place that they've brought me to is for me only for me to just do something for me. It's not about anybody else.

F: That's a good point because a lot of what you've done in life is about other people. And this is about you and your soul.

C: I just thought that the pain in my side may be about healing myself. And trying to draw my attention to me, to focus on me and what I need. Kind of like a big neon flashing neon sign. Pay attention.

F: Is there anything that your guide needs you to know about this place, or is there anything beyond what you're currently experiencing that he is guiding you towards?

C: Just that I'm resisting something. There's something I'm resisting mightily that I need to release to be able to move forward, yeah.

F: So, it's all about the release.

C: Yeah. And that's connected to the sadness. Uh-huh. There's still a somberness. It's like I'm looking at myself from afar, and there's a deep sadness, very deep sadness, that seems to be driving a lot.

F: I'm wondering if since you are in this place of infinite connection, as you look at yourself, if you are able to go into it, and go back to the source, and clear it with compassion, and love, and all of the energy that you have in connection. Just to open that up with the light.

C: And I'm disconnecting myself from the ultimate Source. And I'm hooked on my sadness over the choices that humanity is making right now.

F: And at this point you're able to see that it's humanity's choices as opposed to your personal engagement? And so, when we are ultimately sympathetic, we receive all of that energy in addition to understanding, so we get the pain and the suffering in addition to our knowing. That's the pain.

C: It's the pain, and you are able to shift it, so you don't have to feel as much and so that you are more empowered because you're not disempowered by the pain. You're able to use the energy that you have to replenish yourself, which makes you more available to others. And to lift the vibration out of pain. And that's my dilemma right now. The world needs people who can bring high vibration into the energy field because it shifts the energy upward out of the pain. And right now, I can't do that because I don't have the energy.

F: And that's why you need to replenish. Because you can feel this, and they're drawn into it as opposed to supporting healing it. And that's a big task.

C: Depleting my energy so much, I can't just connect, and pain can't rise above it.

F: So, that is part of your healing, so that you have more within you, more energy within you, that will support you raising your own vibration which then helps you add higher vibration into the world.

C: And that's why all my other questions and inquiry are just not relevant. Helping others is not for today. This is the big inquiry. That's why the first thing I felt was the sadness. I'm not accepting that the choices, that free will is leading people to do what they need to do. Sort of rebelling against that, I don't want to accept that. I want it fixed.

I think the garden is about that. It's going to be okay, and I don't need to worry about that. I don't need to be sad about it. That life has its own rhythms, its own abundance, its own paths.

I can go to the garden for faith that life will continue. Life will. And I go to the Redwood Grove with the spiritual connection and the energy, okay? Two very different places and purposes. The garden is a reminder. The Grove is my connection. And they are just not going to let me connect with anybody today at all. Or any other soul. Even at the fair, the market, they wouldn't let me connect with any souls. You've connected enough for now.

F: This isn't about others but about you replenishing you. You don't need to connect with others too. That isn't why you're here right now. Yeah. You can't help others if you aren't full yourself.

F: Okay, I'm asking. I'm asking if there's anything

about or regarding my husband that I should know now. He has his own course, and I have mine. And we can and should be together, but I have to go my course within that. And it's not even going to let me get any more than that because it's not about that, no. It just keeps coming back. Yep, Yep. We're not going to involve anybody else. This is just about you and your energy. All it will give me about others is to feel for the soul. Respond to the soul and not the visual, which I've known I've needed to.

F: So, when our soul is in full connection, we feel others? The pain of others, because we don't have any buffers. When we don't have the stamina within ourselves to raise the vibration, we sink into it.

C: That's what feels exactly like what's happened. I need to keep the horse with me. I don't know what that means.

F: So it may be that when you go on your journeys, your spiritual journeys, that you call on the horse to support you on your journeys.

C: I'm going to go back to the Council, okay? Yeah, now I don't feel isolated from them. They're just sending out their energy to envelope me again, just saying that that's what I need from them. That's all I need from them right now. And I'm checking in with my guide to see if there's anything else. He just handed me the reins of the horse.

F: So, they're giving you the horse to take with you?

C: The horse is to remind me of where I can experience unconditional love when I'm on Earth. Because we don't have any animals right now, and we've always had cats. And I got unconditional love from them, and I don't have that now. So that's what the horse is to remind me. It may have other purposes, but you know, love that you just get freely. Just because it's a horse and not a cat because I need a lot of it to remind me.

I'm checking in to see if there's anything else from the Council. I know they're not going to let me go anywhere else or see anybody else. I asked again.

F: And you know how to check back in with them when you're back in your body. Right. Okay, that's the most important thing, that you can check in with them on the fly.

C: That's the Redwood Grove answer I got for that. The other thing I'm getting is that the closeness, the resistance to trance, the protectiveness. It's all because I've got so much sadness. So much sadness from humanity that if I'm not careful, I won't even be able to function.

Yeah. Then I'm on the right track by having left my job and having things be open-ended right now. That was absolutely the right path. Not to worry about what's next. I'm getting that the sadness may not go away. But when I connect with my spiritual energy, I can access it, and it will help me be able to hold that sadness in a way that won't tear me down or make me throw up protective walls. Hmm, yeah, it's not promising to make it go away. Just make it so I can function. I'm surprised; I thought I would be able to not have the sadness, but it's all part of having embodied it in this lifetime. Right. It's that I have that feeling I can feel bad. And then just keep saying that's what I have to do.

They just clarified the horse is not my guide. The horse is a reminder of the infinite love that exists, unconditional love.

As Dorothy returned from the journey, she had many things to consider. She had wanted answers about her career choices and felt she received reinforcement that now is the time to step back and renew herself. She was reminded of beautiful, peaceful places where she connects to the Earth in the circle of redwood trees, where life emerges naturally, and where she can find spiritual connection. She felt the energy of the garden of faith where she can intentionally grow, and she was given the horse to remind her of the unconditional love that is always hers.

She was feeling slightly frustrated as questions that she came to explore remained untouched, and her Council had explicitly told her that today was about replenishing her before approaching work with others.

Dorothy was also left with a very uncomfortable feeling that she expressed at the end of her session: When she had drowned, she had a near-death experience where she was welcomed home into an environment of infinite love and support. Yet, in her journey today, she went home but felt none of the cozy warmth she had anticipated. We discussed the session and what had happened, recognizing that she received unequivocal and relevant messages, yet that feeling she hoped to recreate didn't emerge.

After she left, I continued to think about her session to understand why she didn't get what she had anticipated, even as she got the communication and support, she needed and appreciated. I realized that we simply went home without any connections to love on the human plane and without any intention to connect with the infinite, unconditioned love of home. I contacted her about this a few days later and suggested that I would be willing to do another session to see if we could accomplish the connection she hoped to feel. Even though it was a 5-hour drive, she returned a few days later, and we took another journey.

This second journey took her into a past life where she was married to a wonderful man, her true soulmate, and she had been raised by loving parents in an environment of care and gentility. Her husband died very early in their marriage, so she was left to live on her own. This was a great loss for her, and she suffered as a result, becoming a recluse by the time of her death. As she left her body, she was surrounded by light, and her face illuminated.

As she saw her soulmate's face, she melted into him, feeling the joy of pure love. The beautiful cloud of love that she anticipated was now here, and she was able to open into the fullness of the experience that she had desired. This was not a journey of working with her guides and Council, but rather, it was to reinforce that her NDE experience of Home was real and that she truly knew and remembered the feelings of her soul connections.

My takeaway following this session was that my guides supported me in figuring out what was missing. In the first session, we went to work without implied or engaged love connection. In the second session, we established love relationally so that as she returned home, she experienced relational love with her soulmate and the unconditioned love of Home. Details matter, and the debrief we did at the end of the first session gave me the information to support her in finding the connections that truly mattered to her. In her first session, she was given reminders and resources to create peace and renew her soul. The second session gave her the peace of Home, the love she craved. Both experiences were needed for Dorothy to feel complete.

# Lacey's Journey with Her Spirit Guides

## Gayle Barklie

Lacey, a 41-year-old lawyer, was going through a difficult time in her life. She was navigating the end of her marriage to a partner with narcissistic tendencies while raising her two young children. This challenging period also sparked a spiritual awakening for Lacey, a desire for a perceptual shift, and a newfound sense of purpose.

Lacey's journey towards discovering her true self and unlocking her potential began when she lost her job. She turned to the book *Journey of Souls* for guidance and inspiration in a time of uncertainty and change. Her experiences while reading the book sparked a desire within her to connect with her spirit guides and gain a deeper understanding of herself.

Seeking guidance and inspired by the book *Journey of Souls*, Lacey sought counseling through the Michael Newton Institute and found me. She asked me to assist her in connecting with her guides and seeking answers to her burning questions.

Lacey felt a deep sense of excitement and awe as she lay in a trance during her first hypnosis session. She could sense that she was undergoing a profound transformation, moving from a 3D state of awareness to a higher, more expansive 5D state of consciousness. She felt her DNA activating, and her awareness of being an empath and concepts of astral projection growing stronger.

As an old soul just now waking up, Lacey saw this time as a precious opportunity to connect with her spirit guides and embark on a journey of personal growth and spiritual evolution. She felt a deep sense of purpose and connection to the greater universe and a deep desire to contribute to the upcoming period of change for the human race.

In that moment, Lacey felt truly alive and awakened, and she knew that she was destined for great things. She felt a sense of belonging and connection to the divine, and a sense of power and possibility that filled her with excitement and wonder. She was ready to embrace her new path and fully awaken to her true potential.

Despite Lacey's initial fear and resistance, her higher self was eager to dive in and explore. She came to the session with questions about her purpose and direction in life and sought guidance and clarity. Despite having a strong sense of intuition, she struggled with a lack of confidence due to her family's fear of individuals with "the Sight" (Seers).

Growing up as a fifth-born black child in Texas, Lacey often felt out of place in her family and faced discrimination due to her darker skin. These challenges left her feeling inadequate and unsure of her place in the world. Contrary to her family's lack of support and acceptance, Lacey refused to let their narrow-minded views define her. Instead, she used that rejection as motivation to work harder and prove herself.

She remained determined to overcome these barriers and forge her path in life. Through her sessions, she was able to tap into her inner strength and unlock her full potential.

During Lacey's fourth remote session, the focus was initially supposed to be on Past Life Regression in preparation for her Life Between Lives session. However, the session ended up covering a past life and several key stages of between lives work. As a practitioner with over 30 years of experience, I have learned to trust Spirit and go with the flow of the session. Spirit always guides us to the work that is needed. Sometimes, it doesn't always fit the mold that we have intended.

During this fourth session, Lacey entered hypnosis and was guided through a 4x4x4x4 breath exercise to help her relax from an anxious state. As she slipped into a state of relaxation, she described feeling cold and traveling through dimensions.

She saw a silhouette of a figure in the fetal position and identified it as her aunt, who had died in a house fire before her birth. The aunt said," Hi, I'm here with you." She offered Lacey her energy and strength. She reminded her that all spirits are interconnected, and that separation is destructive. Lacey's Uncle Willy appeared as a spirit guide to assist. It became apparent that this spirit guide was also her grandfather, Willy. Grandpa Willy, who had passed before Lacey's birth, used to come to play with her when she felt ostracized by her family members as a child.

Lacey then described disassociating and floating away. She found herself in a barn surrounded by animals and engulfed in smoke and fire. She could control the fire and use it as a powerful element, and she felt a sense of relief and contentment as she emerged from the other side.

Throughout the regression, Lacey's guides offered insight and encouragement, reminding her to trust and not be afraid. This experience provided Lacey with a greater understanding of her past and the support available as she continues her journey.

As the session concluded, Lacey's guides emphasized the importance of gathering the wisdom from her past life experiences and sharing it with others so they can benefit from her story. They reminded her she was a light worker, here to assist others and heal the Earth. They emphasized the interconnectedness of all beings and the need for humans to ascend from 3D to 5D consciousness in order to heal and come together as one. Lacey's guides also encouraged her to stop running from her identity and embrace her past to step into her greatness.

Lacey also had visions of ancient Egypt and Mesopotamia, and she was told that each soul has an identity and comes to Earth with a purpose. She saw herself as a public speaker and household name but feared embracing this role. However, her guides reassured her that she was meant to help usher in a paradigm shift and trust her truth.

Just shy of two hours in, Lacey asked, "Can we stop now? That was a lot!" To which her guides replied, "Trust, trust, know your truth." This final message seemed to provide Lacey with a sense of clarity and direction as she continued on her journey.

Following her sessions, I received a message from Lacey encapsulating her learning, which follows.

*The average human mind lacks the capacity to conceive of this higher understanding. They are stuck in a limited 3D perspective, trapped by their own fear and ignorance. It is my mission to help them ascend to a higher dimension of consciousness, to see the world through a 5D lens, and understand the true purpose of their existence.*

*To do this, I must first heal myself. I must let go of my own fear and embrace my past, stepping into my greatness and using my unique talents to bring light to the world. I see myself as a public speaker, sharing my knowledge and wisdom with others through platforms like Ted Talks. I will be a household name known for my androgynous energy and my message of oneness.*

*I am not alone in this mission. There are others like me who are also traveling through time and space, working to bring about the necessary changes for our planet. We are connected by spirit energy that supports and guides us. We are here to help the Earth and the people, to bring them out of the darkness and into the light.*

*But it will not be easy. The Earth is on the verge of disaster, and the people must wake up to the reality of their situation. They must stop fighting and stop engaging in destructive behaviors like greed, envy, and murder. They must come together as one and work towards a common goal of healing and ascension.*

*It is all part of the process; this is how we heal. And it is up to each and every one of us to do our part, to provide light and love to save this Earth. We are light beings, and it is our duty to bring others to the light as well.*

# RETURN OF THE DIVINE
# FEMININE

## Janna Aidarkhanova

In recent years, there has been talk in the spiritual community that the next step in humanity's Spiritual Growth and evolution will come from the return and embracing of the Divine Feminine energy in all of us. It has been missing for a good part of recorded human history, and the imbalance is still reflected in deep patriarchal structures through cultural traditions, religion, education, politics, professional career life, family roles, and social stereotypes.

Sheree, a reiki healer, teacher, and the founder of the popular Women's group in the south of France area, came for her first Life Between Lives (LBL) session in search of some answers to her personal questions on life purpose, the next direction of her professional life, and deeper understanding of the family circumstances she was born into. Her LBL session answered these questions and gave her a much broader perspective on what is happening on Earth with the current shift in consciousness and the role of women and solidarity in this evolutionary growth and transition.

Regressing to her past life, Sheree saw herself as Eloisa, a mother to a big family on the farm, very much in touch with land, animals, and family: husband, children, and grandchildren. On her last day, Eloisa met her death with much peace, surrounded by all of her family and husband, Harrold.

> C: I am drifting in and out of sleep. The village doctor is there, everyone is there. The minister from the village church has been. Sad to leave my husband, he is very old now too. He is sitting next to the bed, holding my hand; we are saying our last farewells. I am promising to wait for him. He says: I won't be far behind; I will be with you soon. I feel sad and happy at the same time. He will be joining me soon. I know all the family will be rejoined at the beautiful place...
>
> F: What do you feel about the life you just lived?
>
> C: I feel satisfied that I have accomplished things that I wanted to do. I led a very honest, happy life.

After the client's energy left the body and after quite a prolonged period of saying goodbye to the family members, animals, and the land in an out-of-body state, Sheree started to describe her ascent into the spirit realm.

> C: I am moving upwards, looking back and smiling, allowing myself just to float up ... I just feel like I am in the mist, going through different energy layers, which are familiar to me. Feels like cleansing

and letting go of what happened on Earth and then it is a happy welcoming feeling or 'welcome back'. It's like every lifetime in one in me. I am like the mist, and the mist is part of everything and everyone. No separation.

Other energies are around me, and we know each other… It's like a homecoming, but at the same time feels like I haven't left or gone anywhere. Feels like something special has happened and they are bringing me back.

Then Sheree meets Alla.

C: One big light with beautiful rays is coming to meet me… very comforting and… incredible… I feel embraced by it. It's spectacular to see; like my heart is full of joy and happiness, everything is beautiful and happy. The accompanying lights are also enjoying this. It's a big embrace from Alla, very reassuring, and he says, "I am glad you are back; everything will be fine, and I am glad you had a joyful experience."

She couldn't pinpoint Alla's predominant gender. "Its energy is androgynous, switching between male and female energy. Alla is calling me Araknikaba, my spiritual name. I feel androgynous as an energy, too.

C: Araknikaba then finds themself in a hut. A beautiful statue of Alla above radiating into different male and female energies… The significance of this symbol is that we all have both female and male, don't have to be called one or the other; we are all One.

There, she meets her Spirit Guide.

C: Kalutha is the name of my Mentor, who has been mentoring me for a while.

Kalutha reminded Araknikaba about the objectives of the most recent past life: To feel happy in your body, to experience the emotions, to be okay whatever the outcome, and to find peace with Mother Earth. He praised Araknikaba on the life as Eloisa.

He also reminded Araknikaba about the objectives in this current life as Sheree: to know that you can remain in your power even if you are on your own and feel love and support all the time; to listen to your Godspace and follow your passions; to learn how to conquer the ego and truly connect to Mother Earth; to listen to messages from Mother Earth; and to help other people find their pathway.

F: How would Sheree do that? Help other people find their pathway?

C: By being myself the peace that I would like the World to be.

The client switched here to the 1st person, but it felt that Araknikaba's and Sheree's soul objectives are one and the same. This would happen many times in the session, but it felt organic energetically. The client continued to explain the differences in circumstances and objectives of the past and current life.

C: The previous life was different in a sense that there were not many external factors and internal expectations. This one will be different because everyone in the family is so different, and Sheree would need to learn different things from each of the siblings and be okay with that. This life is also to bring understanding of different levels of journeys and that she can't be the rescuer and savior for everyone unless they want to be helped. The challenges of this and the past life are different…

F: How does Kalutha think Sheree's doing relative to these goals in this current life?

C: Kalutha thinks that I, as Sheree, am progressing.

It is then time to meet the Council.

C: Kalutha said I can go to another place of Higher Wisdom for answers to other questions. And he will come with me. Both the energy of the place and of the beings, about ten, is familiar. You can feel their presence more than see them. It is a place for any doubts or questions and just for being. Another coming home. They are happy I am back and that I did well.

Here, the Council has addressed Sheree's prepared questions. If all the previous energies that the client met on the way had an androgynous feel about them, communicating the message that we are both male and female, the answers that followed from the Council were very gender specific.

F: Why has Sheree's family been attracting jealousy and possessiveness into their lives?

C: It's part of the old Celtic culture that women

were seen but not heard. And men have the voice. These times, it's an opportunity for the females to stand as One in their power and to bring the peace about. We have to teach the men how to see, feel, and be Love, so that they can feel and trust the Oneness and learn to harness their power in a positive way and that control and jealousy are not needed.

F: How can women find the opportunity to stand in their power and bring peace?

C: We have to meet as ladies in sacred circles, have meditations and reconnect with the love inside us and shower men with love at the distance. Women were true leaders, had always had the power, and wanted to empower the men. But 2000 years ago, and 200 years ago, a new cycle of intense jealousy and a lot of vulnerability started ... We all had to experience that destiny as souls – male and female. Women now have to stand and regain their power, so that men can feel that strength in love and change their ways.

F: Does this relate to the Celtic culture or the whole of humanity?

C: The whole of humanity. Women need to bring Divine Love to the Planet and reconnect us to Mother Earth by spending more time in nature, meet and live in nature, talk to the trees and plants, regain that connection with the Universal Power. Baby steps by physically going to nature and by meeting with women in nature, having fresh plants at home, and sit outside, and let the sun shine on you, or visualize the sun shining and pouring through your body, connecting with this love and giving this love to the

plants and feel this love coming back to you and
have more women around you and trust them, let go
of competitions, help women find love inside their
heart, make them remember that they are Divine
Beings and that they are powerful.

F: Can you ask Kalutha, the Elders or yourself if
you have you reincarnated as a man before?

C: Many times before, and I know what it is to
abuse women, and now this lifetime is to be there for
the women and lead the women, and as a big number
of women together, we can make a change.

F: What's holding women back?

C: Living in fear, forgetting their purpose. To get
out of living in fear, women need to take baby steps:
having a bath and reconnecting with the comforts of
being in their mother's womb, light a candle, bring
their angel in the bath with them to remind them they
are not alone, using essential oils and reconnecting
with Mother Earth through the oils, in the safety of
the bath. These are first steps...

F: What should Sheree focus her energies on, the
podcasts or on gathering and helping women?

C: Again, it doesn't matter what you do. They
tell me I have to get the chatter out of my head, get
out of my head, and go into my heart, and when I
am there, I will do everything that I am meant to do.
Both things can and will happen in divine timing.
My main focus is to remain in my heart, be happy in
my body, and be in the Light.

F: What does 'being in one's heart' mean?

C: It is to trust that you are a divine being and
connect with the soul inside and be divinely guided.

Ask the questions to the Soul inside and listen for the answers. Not listening and caring about what people think, say, suggest, or what they want me to do.

I am here for a specific reason which is to help people on their spiritual pathway, and I will do that by being present in people's lives and helping them to find peace in their heart.

F: How does it feel to be in your heart and being present?

C: It's pure joy and bliss. Light and expansive. Like I am just Light. Feeling calm. The Council want to reassure me that I am doing a good job and making good impacts, helping many people. My help is expanding and radiating within the community. I can see that.

After selecting her body and life and before reincarnating, Araknikaba receives the last words of advice and wisdom from her spiritual family and the spirit guide.

F: Can you reiterate the purpose for this life?

C: To connect with the love inside my heart, to remember I am the divine being, let my light shine, and help with the women. The Elders are supposed to remind you of your purpose, and they do. But it's easy to block them out in our human experience; it's important to reconnect and listen so that we can complete our purpose. The spiritual family is saying to me: the more I am in my power and courageous, the easier it is to learn my lessons. And I have to use my voice.

C: (Just before awakening, she expressed the

following) The whole world needs to be awakened to Respect. Respect for Oneself will lead to Respect for All. I would like to call on my Soul energy now to connect the right people to help make these changes on our planet for Respect. I can't believe I was born at these times when there are still wars and abuse of the Earth … I thought I was reluctant to be born into a big family, but now I realize it's because of the decision to be born into these challenging and conflicting times…

After the session, Sheree shared more.

C: I felt in the womb my anxiety and doubts about being born, and I thought I didn't want to be born into a big family, but now I understand it is because of the uncertain times that I decided to be born."

Sheree was conflicted before the session about the professional direction of her life, but now she knew it didn't matter what she did. What mattered was 'how'. By disregarding other people's opinions, she could pursue any direction as long as it was within her life purpose of helping with women's empowerment, healing humanity, and our relationship with each other and the Earth. The Divine Feminine energy is there to be recalled, embraced, and used by all of us for the next stage of the spiritual growth of humanity.

# REVERENCE AND
# GRATITUDE

## Elizabeth Lockhart

**B**rian is a 57-year-old computer programmer, Reiki master, and shamanic practitioner. His son and young granddaughter, Fiona, live with him. Previously, I had facilitated two past life regression sessions for him. Brian embraces a Native American heritage and is spiritually connected with the Earth. Going into this session, Brian has questions about a stroke he recently suffered and why he prefers solitude and avoids romantic relationships. He is curious about his purposes and lessons in this lifetime, a "distant energy" he feels approaching and wonders why he doesn't "play much." The insight, support, and encouragement he receives during his LBL from his guide and his Council of Elders prove very helpful.

He experienced a past life in Lorraine, France, in the mid-1800s as a 26-year-old man named Mark. The opening scene involved Mark being run over by a carriage and unable to breathe. This would be the last day of his lifetime. In this scene, Mark tells the story of his life. He was hired for a job in the city to make enough money to take a wife. He had to impress the bride's father by attending church, becoming part of the congregation, and getting married in the church. His dress is "very dapper" because it's his wedding day. As he stood on the side of the street and bent down to pick up his fiancé's handkerchief, he heard a horse and carriage coming. The horse bumped into him, knocking him over, and the carriage ran over him.

> C: That was a stupid move that didn't work so well. I don't die right away, but as I drift towards the soul realm, I think … at least now I don't have to breathe.

Mark hovers over his body, studying it. People flock around, including his fiancé, Julianne, with her mother and sister. There is much crying. Mark thinks he looks stupid lying in the street with a good suit on, all muddied up. He is frustrated with this ending but says:

> C: I have a new job now, and I'm free to go … all that stuff is gone."

Mark's journey onward finds him in a space of light. He notices points of light as he drifts in a beautiful purple vapor that feels "delicious like the aurora". He feels good and free. He then experiences a beautiful clear dark, with many points of light everywhere. He needs to curve to the left to connect with a larger light that starts as white, then yellow, then violet, red, and then white again, with colors merging.

C: This is all light. The shape is round like a ball, not a tunnel, and engulfs me so that I go inside the light, and it gives me everything. There are spaces like caves that look like seeds, which provide a type of cleansing; they are all over the place.

His guide, Alhew, then appears and calls him by his soul's name, Vincent. Alhew directs him to enter a tunnel, which he whacks on with his stick, so he does not have to worry about anything because he is totally in control. Alhew resembles a wizard with blue eyes, long whitish-gray hair, a beard, and a black robe. Alhew's light is navy blue, with some yellow and white. More tunnels appear that lead to different dimensions and different lifetimes. Alhew feels that Vincent's achievements in this past life were neither positive nor negative. His greatest accomplishment was learning kindness in the face of adversity and disappointment. Coping with disappointment is a large part of what needs to be learned from this short lifetime. Alhew whacks at the entrances to other tunnels with his stick and leads Vincent through, first to his soul group and then to his Council of Elders.

Vincent and Alhew then fly up to the top of a cliff where two "Grandfather" Elders are waiting: Anzi, who emanates soft red and blue colors, and Michu, who emanates darker red and blue colors. Alhew says there are 12 members in Vincent's Council, but only three are coming to this meeting. The proceedings occur at a small rectangular table with Alhew standing in a corner. Mace is a third "grandmother" Elder and is a solid sky-blue color. They dismiss the past life and want to know why Vincent has called them there now. He asks how he is progressing as a soul and watches them chattering.

They tease him, saying he is "trying to cheat." Regarding his current life, Grandmother Mace talks about the Red Oak tribe and how this has gifted him with art, color, and beer-making talents. The beer-making, she mentions, relates to my client's former alcoholism and current sobriety through AA. Vincent laughs and says,

> C: I've learned the lesson of the beer. More importantly, I need to learn the right relationship between all things. That's what Michu says to me. Family and nature. The lessons overlap … and that's some of what I'm working on right now.
>
> F: Would the Elders be willing to answer a few questions you have going into this session?
>
> C: (After a long pause) Sure.
>
> F: Why did you have a stroke?
>
> C: I needed to slow down and focus on more important things than I was focusing on, and I wasn't getting the message.
>
> F: I see. And what other things did this stroke intend for you to focus on?
>
> C: Well, the whole thing with the trees is very … not only were the trees offended at the way it was going on, chopping for firewood, but just the relationship with fire, the relationship with heat, the stress that this focus on survival can cause, and the amount of time you can spend on a problem that really isn't a problem. The stroke forced me to look at other areas of my life. I had to change, and I have to change.
>
> F: Can you describe for me in what ways you

have to change?

C: Right now, the Elders know I am just trying to get back to where I was before the stroke. I was riding bikes; now I can barely walk. I have a different set of cards to play with, and the tree that fell on my head, I've revisited many times. There's a lot that came out of that. The stroke came out of the tree. That's why I bring the stroke up with the tree.

F: You mean because of that bump on the head from the tree limb?

C: Yes, even though the stroke happened months later, that is what led to the stroke. After that first hit, every time I was in the woods, I would have branches hit me in the same spot on my head, in the third eye, and I wondered what that was all about. That's a wake-up call and just enough signage, so needs to be looked into.

F: Can you ask your Elders what that was all about?

C: Well, they're saying it will help me see more clearly and have more dreams. And when I went to shaman camp that was one of my goals. I have been getting my dreams back. Now, they're saying that's a payoff for following the guidance instead of fighting it.

F: Can your Elders help us to understand why you prefer solitude and avoid romantic relationships?

C: Because I ran around too much anyway, in a previous lifetime.

F: What do you mean?

C: That's what I'm looking at right now. (long pause) I just didn't have good relationships, so I need to spend some time to get that act together.

F: So, in this lifetime you're learning more about relationships in general?

C: Learning more about me, my relationship with myself. Once I can do that, then I can move out, you know.

F: And what about relationships with family?

C: Yeah. Really anything but romantic. Everything is a relationship. I don't know where those words get so mixed up. When you mention relationships, everyone seems to go right to romance, and that's not what I'm talking about.

F: Yes. You told me your Elder, Michu, emphasized this.

C: All things. Your relationship with yourself, with everything that you touch, the way you walk in this world, everything. Anything you come into contact with is a relationship. Everything. The air you breathe is a relationship. You live with everything else.

F: Tell me more about the right relationship. What kind of place would you be coming from, what attitude?

C: Well, to live in right relationship is to have everything that you want without taking it from anything else – reverence … and … gratitude.

F: Beautiful. Coming from a place of gratitude, reverence.

C: There's definitely not enough reverence. I mean this world is an amazing place.

People just don't seem too impressed. I'm still impressed.

We then moved on to another subject my client had brought up, that of a distant energy approaching the planet.

F: Can the Elders help us to understand that sense that you have about a distant energy approaching?

C: Well, they're saying that the world is changing. Change is coming. Things are changing, and everything's going to change. There's going to be a new way of doing things. The way we're living our lives is going to change. That's the period of this current lifetime – turning around in turmoil and change. Adaptation. Can you do it?

F: Does this group of Elders have any further messages or words of wisdom?

C: Ah, Grandmother says to be kind to myself. Play more … music, art, coloring, and painting with Fiona. The Grandfathers say, "You're doing good. Keep going!"

When asked why Brian doesn't play much in this lifetime, Vincent says that it's because Brian places too much stress on himself and pressure to get things done, when taking things slower and spreading tasks out over time would be healthier. Grandmother Mace shows him coloring books and painting with his granddaughter, Fiona, which will be fun and helpful.

The theme of "right relationships" offers Brian much insight and understanding. These Elders support Vincent as a soul and what he is learning in this lifetime as Brian. Since I facilitated this session a couple of years ago, Brian's sense of significant changes coming for humanity and Earth has proven prophetic, especially amid the pandemic, climate changes, and other dramatic upheavals and disasters. As we completed the session, Vincent thanked the Elders for us and said he looked forward to visiting them when embarking on a shamanic journey as his current self, Brian. Support from the soul realm is ever-present; we only need to reach out and connect.

# Bringing Light

## Petra Brzović

Unlike other stories, this one is written from a client's perspective following an LBL regression that revealed some important insights into our world's destiny and the number of souls involved in renewing Earth's energy.

For this story, I will focus solely on the time in the spirit realm. After spending a short time in my most recent past life, my hypnotherapist takes me through the death scene.

F: So, you are slowly moving up. And what's going on now?

C: I am like stardust! A light stardust... I am slowly moving up ... it's like I am moving in a slow dance. I can see the light ... I had to go through some dark tube ... and now I am up. I can sense the presence of my guide.

I speak slowly and quietly. My guide is taking me somewhere.

C: My guide is taking me to a place to do the adjustment, adjustment of brain or head ... something like that. I am in kind of room that looks like a space with stars. I am floating there. It feels strange. I feel strong pain in the middle of my forehead, and I feel like I am in some kind of blender. My guide tells me I need to be here for the adjustment. I can see stars and shapes and electricity ... it is unexpected ... I can see millions of stars. They are just turning me around in this Universe. It's like I am being upgraded, or ... they are making some kind of antenna for receiving. I can just see Universes and Universes and Universes ... everything is just swirling ... I am just letting them do whatever is needed. The Universe is just endless. They want me to be aware of that. That the Universe is endless, they are saying, "You need to know." When I ask "why?" they say it has something to do with consciousness, information, communication, like communication with distant intelligence, distant knowledge that I can now receive what I need to receive from that distant intelligence. They are upgrading me now so I can have the sense of vastness of space, and they are showing me there is great intelligence but not near Earth. We need to be high enough to be able to receive that information. It is too dirty around the Earth.

F: Can you receive that information now with your antenna?

C: Yes, it will keep on coming. It is so endless, unbelievable. I can see life in distant galaxies ... so much wiser than us. And we think we are clever!

F: And what is happening now?

C: I am just being aware of these intelligent places ... like galaxies. They are waiting for us to grow. We are like little kids to them. Yes, we are like little kids not knowing what we are doing. We are doing so much damage to the planet. I can so see it now. (it feels so sad) Oh, we need some order! We are like kids without anybody to take care of us and put us in order. I can see people like kids in kindergarten throwing food, throwing broccoli on each other. We need somebody to take care of us!

F: Is there a guidance? Someone watching over the Earth?

C: Yes, there are many, but they are still watching. It feels like they don't know where to start. It is a mess! Looking at Earth from this perspective it is such a mess.

F: I wonder what is your role in this mess?

C: To wake them up. To bring light. I can see little reflectors being put around the Earth, bringing light. It is not just me. There are more of us. We are working all at the same time, putting lights around the Earth. The lights are so interesting that people stop doing what they are doing and turn to look at the lights. They are still making the mess, but eventually, they stop and turn towards the lights one by one. I just got an image of mosquitos and flies going to the light; they become mesmerized.

F: And how do you do it when you are on Earth?

C: Talk. I need to do talks. I can see myself talking. That's why I have to be a woman. That's why they listen. Research is important. So I can show them. They need facts. Then they will believe. And then they will start to change. But it is not just me. It is happening at the same time on the Earth. And we are communicating with those far away galaxies, getting the information.

F: Is this a time to ask some questions that Petra prepared?

C: Yes.

F: So, Petra wants to know why does she feel so alone and want to go Home?

C: (smiling) Because this is Home. Now, it will be easier for her as she knows what Home truly is.

My therapist then directed me to ask my guide to take me to a place where I could meet the souls of my children. I expected to go to my soul group, but then I understood I didn't have one. That also explains the deep feeling of being alone.

C: I had to leave my group. That's why I feel alone. I am with others that are putting lights on Earth. My children are there, too. They are being prepared to put the lights on Earth.

F: Who else is there?

C: Teachers. They look like lights. They are brighter in the head area, with lots of colors – orange, yellow, red, and purple – like little rainbows. They are teachers of the ones that bring light. They teach how to integrate on Earth and at the same time stay connected to the higher intelligence.

F: Tell me more about what you are doing.

C: We are so busy, so busy on Earth, we didn't leave much energy here. The Earth is in such bad state we had to take almost all energy down. They are preparing more souls. Everything is so busy, focused on healing; there is no time for relaxation and having fun; they are not losing a second of time. That's why I am fast and busy. I wouldn't mind if we could do it slower ...

The teachers finally slowed down to answer my questions.

C: I have to do this research. That's the way information will come. They are saying, "Brain ... Energy ... Waves ... Colors." It's hard to understand.

F: Ask them to explain it to you. Use your antenna to understand.

C: I have to connect to that galaxy and then the information will just pour. This area is more like a station, a working place where we are closer to Earth. From here, we connect to our Homeplace, and then the information comes as energy to us, into our brains. I see I have to talk, and do research and show the results, but I don't see what kind of research. They don't want to tell me more. They say it won't be fun if they tell me. They just say that I have to stay connected, and that information will continue coming. In my meditations, I need to be aware of my antenna and connect. Not just be in space. I need to use the antenna because light carries the information. They want me to learn. They still treat me as a student. They are saying: "Keep on connecting from one side and working from the other side."

After this experience at the "working station," I am taken Home. It is the most profound moment I will never forget. I am taken to this amazing golden galaxy.

Aaah ...

F: How does it feel to be here?

C: Like Home. We are so intelligent, so loving. Everything is full of love. Everything is in order. Although there are millions of us – millions of lights – everything is in order and full of love. And there are places like this all over the Universe. Everything is made of lights, little golden lights. When I get closer to the source, it gets brighter.

One of the lights approached me and said: "I told you that you are not alone." I recognized him from this life.

Others have the same mission as us – putting lights around Earth.

They are telling me we need to form a network to put the lights on. We need to connect; it will be stronger and more efficient that way. Through meetings, conferences, meeting each other, supporting each other, remembering where we are from. Love, it will come. We need to meet and share information, be coherent, in tune, not being separate like a wave. If we work together, we create a stronger wave; if we don't, we create a mess.

We need to create a network of those waves.

Then my guide took me to a big place with books where I got answers to my other questions that were important for me as Petra. After we went through all the questions and got answers it was time to return to this life ... to this time and place ... to this body. There is a lot of work waiting for me to do.

After the session, it took some time for all the information to sink in. I felt like I had wind under my wings, and soon, my life took an amazing turn.

People have started coming into my life and supporting my mission in such a beautiful way that I feel blessed and humbled. I started researching the connection between brain, body, and soul with some of the world's top experts. I am living my life's purpose every second of the day.

This LBL session changed my life and renewed my passion for work on this planet. I am more than grateful for all the insights I got. I trust that Earth will be healed, and my heart is filled with joy because of it. The work that we do is truly sacred, and I will dedicate the rest of my time here to make it more accessible and known to every being on Earth, making sure there will be only love and peace … as it should be.

# CONCLUDING INSIGHTS
## on Healing the Earth

The Earth, our home, is facing unprecedented challenges due to human activity—climate change, deforestation, pollution, and habitat destruction threaten the delicate balance of ecosystems and jeopardizes the wellbeing of all life forms. There is an urgent need for collective action and commitment to heal the Earth and safeguard it for future generations.

All living beings and ecosystems are connected, and every organism plays a vital role in maintaining the health and resilience of our beautiful planet. This delicate balance has been disrupted, leading to biodiversity loss, habitat degradation, and ecological imbalances that threaten the stability of global ecosystems.

Recognizing the interconnectedness of life calls us to embrace a paradigm of stewardship and cooperation, where we acknowledge our responsibility to protect and preserve the Earth for the wellbeing of all beings, present and future.

Many souls are involved in renewing Earth's energy, protecting it, and healing it. Witnessing the process of healing the planet Earth in a session is beautiful beyond words.

Sanela Čović
Editor

# AFTERWORD

It was around 2007 that Michael Newton started to hand his work over to those he had been teaching and encouraging for many years. At that time, he knew that he was moving to an age where he was slowing down, and the world desperately needed what LBL offered, even more than when he started.

I mention 2007, as that was the year we trained a group in Chicago and held one of our first LBL Teacher Trainings the day before the students arrived. Around fifteen of us sat around a conference table in the basement of that hotel. The group included Michael and, of course, Peggy Newton, who was always there with us. I made mention of the future of 'his work,' and he corrected me in front of everyone: "...it's *our* work, Pete."

In one sentence, he had made life's work for one man, the purpose of many who would follow him. What you have just read is the result of his legacy in handing this incredible gift to the people who make up the Michael Newton Institute collective.

The rest of that handover continued rapidly. At the board

meeting following that same training, he announced he would no longer be attending training, and it was our turn. We cried that day, not just for ourselves but for the world. How could we replace such a powerful ambassador for the spiritual realm?

We were saved by the power of the work itself, knowing that our souls had chosen this path, and we were now to lead the Life Between Lives work. It had become our role to take his gift to humanity forward in new ways.

Michael retired from the board, though he stayed online in our discussion group, offering advice and support to our growing global network of LBL Facilitators. I would talk to him every few weeks to discuss organizational issues, then monthly… and finally, that final phone call came when I knew he was fading and was being called home. Like many years before, he encapsulated so much into one sentence as he summarized his life's work: "We have something to offer people in terms of personal meaning they can't get elsewhere."

I read this from an aging sticky note on my computer and captured the moment he spoke those words. The best way to honor Michael is to continue what he started, and at the Michael Newton Institute, we are doing just that.

The stories you have read are a tiny yet powerful snapshot into what we bring to the world, and it has taken well over 200 people for us to continue what one man started. You will find us in over 40 countries and 20 languages. You will find us on social media and speaking at conferences. It is time to shout from the rooftops the power of the human spirit, the courage of souls who choose to incarnate here, and how we are amid a global awakening of consciousness that will change this world as we know it.

We invite you to join what Michael loved to call "The

LBL Movement," a wave of energy helping people understand who they really are. We are seeing this work speed up at a rapid rate, evidence of the acceleration of the evolution of consciousness on our planet.

Many now don't need the structure that Michael trained us in and soar into spirit, lighting their path under our guidance. We see a more significant influence of cosmic frequencies coming into our sessions as souls with universal heritage come here to diversify the individuals that comprise the collective of human consciousness. Most of all, though, we are seeing a move from 'me to we.'

Twenty years ago, people would come to us wanting to know 'my purpose.' An increasing number are telling us they are here to be 'part of something amazing,' and we are all contributing uniquely. As I write, we are relaunching our training and support systems, opening new research areas, and planning how to tell the world about what we offer in ever-expanding ways.

By reading this book, you are already part of The LBL Movement.

All who have been involved in this book project have donated their time and energy to something that will be life-changing for them.

All proceeds from this book go to the Michael Newton Institute, a registered 501(c) not-for-profit organization in the USA, which furthers the work of Dr. Michael Newton. By buying this book, you are part of his legacy to humanity.

For that, we send you much gratitude.

We receive many questions on social media from those who wonder what we do and if it is real. I'll offer to anyone who doubts the work what Michael said to me many years ago...

I asked Michael, "What do we say to people who doubt what we do?" He replied, "That's okay. Encourage them to have a session when they are ready. After that, they won't have any of those questions."

Thank you for being here in these times, courageous soul.

Peter Smith
MNI Advisory Council Member & Adviser – The Newton Legacy
(Past President of MNI 2009-2019)

# Meet the
# Contributors

Janna Aidarkhanova
jaidarkh@gmail.com
www.transcendence-coach.com

Gayle Barklie
soulpurposemaui@gmail.com
www.soulpurposemaui.com

Nino Borsari
ninoborsari@icloud.com
www.newtoninstitute.org/profile/ninoborsari/

Tatjana Braun
tatbra68@web.de
www.hypnose-alpenregion-allgaeu.de

Petra Brzović
info@petrabrzovic.com
www.petrabrzovic.com

Eric J. Christopher
eric@ericjchristopher.com
www.ericjchristopher.com

Ann J Clark
hypnoannclark@gmail.com
www.birmnghamhypnosis.com

Sanela Čović
sanela@sanelacovic.com
www.sanelacovic.com

Veronika Elias
info@veronikaelias.com
www.veronikaelias.com

Toby Evans
toby@sagebrushexchange.com
www.sagebrushexchange.com

Patricia Fares O' Malley (in loving memory)

Hila Kedem-Ferguson
hila@door2change.com
www.door2change.com

Ricardo Mones Gonzalez
rmonesg@gmail.com
www.vidaentrevidas.mx

Jerry Joseph
jerjoseph@aol.com
www.drjerryjoseph.com

Sophia Kramer
sophia@sophiakramer.com
www.sophiakramer.com

Elizabeth Lockhart
elizabeth@mariposahypnotherapy.com
www.mariposahypnotherapy.com

Lisbeth Lysdal
lisbeth@lisbethlysdal.dk
www.lisbethlysdal.dk

Joy Nicholson
joynicholson@aapt.net.au
www.reikihobart.com

Tahmineh Nikookar
dr.t.nikookar@gmail.com
www.lionsgateacupuncture.ca

Diana Paque
diana@dpconsulting.biz
www.sfbayregressions.com

## Elisabeth Iwona Roepcke (Kupisz)
kontakt@trance-forming.pl
www.trance-forming.pl

## Tianna Roser
tianna@awakeningtransformation.com
www.awakeningtransformation.com

## Indrani Sinha Seth
mittzpvt@gmail.com
www.newtoninstitute.org/profile/indranisinha

## Elisa Shine
elisa@elisashine.com
www.elisashine.com

## Sally Stone
sally@drsallystone.com
www.drsallystone.com

## Teoh Hooi-Meng
unseratoz@gmail.com
www.hypnosismalaysia.com

# FIND LBL FACILITATOR

Life Between Lives° (LBL) sessions offer opportunities for people to reconnect with their immortal identity. They are offered by over 200 facilitators in 40 countries around the word, with sessions available in over 25 languages, both in person and online.

All LBL facilitators run their own independent practices (separate from MNI).

Only LBL Facilitators currently listed on the Michael Newton Institute's website under www.newtoninstitute.org/find-lbl-facilitator/ are currently certified and endorsed by the Michael Newton Institute.

# ACKNOWLEDGEMENTS

**M**any remarkable people have come together to create *MNI Publishing*, a new division of the Michael Newton Institute.

Our inaugural publication is the book you have before you: *Finding Purpose: Stories of the Afterlife that Inspire* and we thank you for your support.

*MNI Publishing* is our new voice to the people of this planet, sharing what we at the Michael Newton Institute continue to offer each and every day in all corners of our world.

We have already acknowledged the 26 authors in this book, though they are part of a much greater number of well over 200 MNI Certified Members who continue what Michael has started and are the custodians of his legacy. Their dedication to our collective purpose, ensures our LBL movement continues to prosper and grow.

Our quarterly journal *Stories of the Afterlife* – our original voice, has been collecting the journeys that are contained in this book for many years. A vote of thanks to all whose contributing energy has made SOTA our platform to create

*MNI Publishing.* Much gratitude is offered to Dr Diana Paque, SOTA's Editor-in-chief and Judith Huffman our MNI Manager. (For SOTA subscriptions: https://www.newtoninstitute. org/stories-of-the-afterlife/) We are grateful for the contributions of Jeff Bennett who brought additional editing skills at the time we needed them most, Angela Cotza who brought to life our *MNI Publishing* logo designs and Rose Newland of K.Rose Kreative for our book design.

A heartfelt thanks to Pete Smith for his unwavering support, strategic vision, and invaluable assistance in bringing this book to life.

And finally…

Gratitude to Indrani and Soumitra Sinha for their donation towards this book's publication, made in memory of their late parents Nomita and Suresh Sinha and godfather Suven Mukherjee.

# GLOSSARY

**All there is** – A phrase that represents the full realm of the multiverse in all its dimensions and permeations. It simply contains everything in existence.

**Alternate Realities** – Other realms of existence where another version of the client exists who took a different path. This is a concept created by the Many Worlds Interpretation theory in Quantum Physics, originating from Hugh Everett's PhD Thesis in 1957.

**Androgenous Beings** – A state of being that has transcended gender, usually a sign of advancement, though still with the ability to return to a gender-based incarnation for learning purposes.

**Brain Waves in Hypnotherapy** – A model that usually includes Beta (Waking State), Alpha (Subconscious), Theta (Superconscious) and Delta (Sleep state). An LBL experience is characterized by brain wave patterns in the Theta range.

**Consciousness** – A term that denotes awareness that goes beyond the human senses or refers to a collective awareness shared by a group, or even single unique awareness of an individual.

**Council/Spiritual Council/Council of Elders/High Council** – A group of advanced beings that steer souls from lifetime to lifetime, providing wisdom, guidance, insight and support.

**Divine Guidance** – Wisdom usually obtained from sources beyond us in human form and come from the spiritual or metaphysical realms. It can take the form of intuition, contact with advanced beings, messages in dreams or psychic phenomenon.

**Earthbound Souls** – Used as a term to describe souls that are still in a stage of transition back to spirit. They may remain for a short while to complete unfinished business, support loved ones, heal or reflect on the life just passed. Guides usually hover around these beings providing comfort and support.

**Gateway** – A place of transition, where a soul leaves the physical world and enters the spiritual realm. Sometimes a form of healing takes place here before full transition is possible and a Guide will occasionally meet a soul here to assist.

**Guides** – An advanced being who supports a soul through their physical incarnations with love and wisdom. Whilst they usually remain invisible to the human eye, they never leave our side.

**Free Will** – is the currency of the multiverse. We have choice in this realm and in all others that echo the divine nature of our immortal essence. Whilst we may be offered advice and support, our free will remains the determining factor, even though it may be in use unconsciously in human form.

**Healing Chamber** – A place where a client's soul may need to go to raise their vibration before continuing their journey back to the Spiritual Realm. Often occurs after a difficult incarnation.

**Hypnotherapy** – the art of working therapeutically with the subconscious mind through a process that accesses Alpha brain wave patterns and beyond.

**Karmic Lessons** – The concept of balance is modified in the experience of LBL work to be more conceptually; a planned lesson that draws on the experiences of other lifetimes. Often a client will bring an issue into this lifetime so that when it comes into their line of sight, they have an opportunity to clear a pattern from the soul lineage.

**Life Between Lives (LBL)** – The phrase coined by Dr. Michael Newton to describe his work with the Spiritual Realm.

**Life Between Lives Facilitator** – A practitioner who conducts sessions into the Spiritual Realm, who has been trained and accredited by the Michael Newton Institute.

**Life Selection** (a.k.a. Ring of Destiny) – The place where we go to plan our next incarnation often in the loving support of advanced beings.

**Modalities** – General term used to describe any or a number of the healing arts and techniques available.

**Michael Newton Institute** – The only organization founded and authorized by Dr. Michael Newton to continue his life's work.

**Multidimensional Beings** – The ability to exist in various realms of existence simultaneously. Human beings are an example once we realize time is a construct for the physical realm to enable learning development. We are both our human identity, our other lifetimes outside time and space as we know it and we continue to reside in the spiritual realm.

**Oneness** – A term that describes the connection between all things that shows us to be a single fabric of the greater reality in which we find ourselves.

**Parallel Lives** – When a soul splits into two incarnations in linear time and co-exists in the physical realm, often in different parts of the world to accelerate learning.

**Past Life Therapy (PLR***)* – The use of other incarnations to explore or heal certain aspects of this life.

**Psychic Surgery** – the ability to bring physical change in the human body through energy waves, intention or powers of the mind. It is non-invasive physically.

**Past Life Trauma** – Echoes from other incarnations that call to us with learning opportunities. These often-deliberate echoes are simply opportunities to heal and clear patters from the soul lineage. (See Karmic Lessons)

**Reincarnation** – The name for the cycle of birth and rebirth that makes up the lineage of the soul. It carries the view of linear time for the sake of human understanding. LBL work has shown that time doesn't exist as we know it in human form and this concept can then be viewed with greater flexibility.

**Reiki** – A form of energy healing with Japanese origins, based on the concept that we all have access to universal life force energy and that it can be shared with others.

**Soul Group** – a group of souls that incarnate regularly together. Often, they play different roles for each other to round out learning experiences.

**Soul Name** – Every soul has a unique name, often able to be translated into human language though can also exist as a sound, symbol or vibration. Knowledge of a soul name brings us closer to our immortal identity.

**Spiritual Hypnotherapy** – The art of Hypnotherapy that embraces transpersonal and metaphysical models and is often conducted in Theta brain wave patterns.

**Spirit World** – The environment that Michael Newton mapped through his Life Between Lives research, conducted originally over 35 years and 7000 clients.

**Superconscious** – a state of being where a client is in touch with their immortal memory that includes knowledge of the soul lineage and the spiritual realm.

**The Wise Ones** – see Council

**Traveler Souls (a.k.a. Hybrid Souls)** – souls that have started their incarnations in other dimensions or on other worlds. Usually incarnating on earth to bring change.

Printed in the USA
CPSIA information can be obtained
at www.ICGtesting.com
LVHW091543101124
796163LV00001B/13